# THE INDUSTRIAL REVOLUTION IN EUROPE

## GERMANY, FRANCE, RUSSIA, 1815-1914

# THE INDUSTRIAL REVOLUTION IN EUROPE

## GERMANY, FRANCE, RUSSIA, 1815-1914

*by*

W. O. Henderson

**Q**

QUADRANGLE PAPERBACKS

QUADRANGLE BOOKS / CHICAGO

# CONTENTS

## CONTENTS

## MAPS

*following page 260*

# INTRODUCTION

IN this book I have attempted to survey in broad outline the history of the Industrial Revolution on the Continent in the nineteenth century. The fact that my inquiry has been restricted to France, Germany and Russia is not intended to belittle the contributions made by other countries such as Italy, Switzerland, Sweden and Austria-Hungary to the industrialization of Europe. The studies of Heckscher,[1] Rappard,[2] Morandi,[3] Luzzatto,[4] Slokar,[5] and many others have shown the significance of the growth of great modern industries in countries other than those which are examined. My account of the Industrial Revolution in Germany is somewhat briefer than that of France since I have already discussed various aspects of Germany's economic history in my books on the *Zollverein*, the *State and the Industrial Revolution in Prussia*, and *Britain and Industrial Europe*.

My thanks are due to Mr. A. E. Musson who has read my typescript and has made many valuable suggestions; to Professor Costello who has read the chapter on Russia; to Dr. R. Frei for permission to reprint the substance of an article on the "Origins of the Industrial Revolution in France and Germany", which appeared in *Kyklos*; and to Mr. J. G. O'Kane, Secretary of the Liverpool University Press, for permission to reproduce two maps from my book on *Britain and Industrial Europe*. I am grateful to my colleague, Dr. W. H. Chaloner, for the help he has given me in the correction of proofs.

---

[1] E. F. Heckscher, *An Economic History of Sweden* (1954).
[2] W. Rappard, *La révolution industrielle et les origines de la protection légale du travail en Suisse* (1914).
[3] R. Morandi, *Storia della Grande Industria in Italia* (1931).
[4] G. Luzzatto, *Storia economica dell'eta moderna e contemporanea*, Vol. II (1952).
[5] J. Slokar, *Geschichte der österreichischen Industrie und ihrer Förderung unter Kaiser Franz I* (1914).

# CHAPTER I

# CHARACTERISTICS OF INDUSTRIAL GROWTH

THE nineteenth century witnessed many striking changes in Europe. Nationalism brought about the unification of Germany and Italy and the independence of several peoples who were formerly under alien rule. Liberalism reshaped numerous constitutions and gave political power to once submerged social classes. Even more important perhaps was the rise of industrial capitalism which fundamentally changed the economies of Britain, Belgium, Germany and many other countries.

The older type of economy gradually disappeared. In the country-side enclosed farms or small holdings, run as individual enterprises, replaced communal methods of cultivation. When the serfs were emancipated some became independent farmers, tenants, share-croppers or agricultural labourers, while others migrated to the growing factory towns or to newly developing territories overseas. In the towns domestic handicraft industries, controlled by guilds and municipal authorities, were replaced by manufactures carried on in large factories by the new machines.

The age of industrial capitalism was marked by great technical advances. In the second half of the eighteenth century the textile inventions of Hargreaves, Arkwright, Crompton and Cartwright and the improvements in the production of iron and steel introduced by the Darbys, Cort and Huntsman laid the foundations of the industrial expansion which by the time of the Great Exhibition of 1851 had turned Britain into the workshop of the world. The wind-mill and the water-wheel gave way to the steam engine, which was largely responsible for the establishment of factories, since this form of power could not be used in the domestic workshop. When steam power was applied to transport the new railways and steamships revolutionized commerce. It was now possible to send heavy bulky commodities such as coal, iron, wool, grain, and so forth from one end of the world to another.

There was a remarkable extension of the raw materials used by

1

industry. Metals—particularly iron and steel—replaced wood in the construction of harbours, bridges, machinery and railway tracks. Coal was used instead of wood for heating houses, offices, and industrial establishments. The steam engine, fired by coal, replaced the water-wheel for driving machinery in the factories. Railway locomotives and steamships were driven by coal. Again, coal and coke replaced charcoal in the smelting of iron and other metals. Petroleum products replaced animal and vegetable oils for lighting and lubrication. Coal-tar dyes replaced vegetable and animal dyes in the textile industries, and as far as foodstuffs were concerned beet sugar and margarine competed with cane sugar and butter.

Another characteristic of industrialization was specialization in its various forms. The craftsman who saw a job through from start to finish was replaced by the skilled factory worker who concentrated on one part of a manufacturing process. The functions of the manufacturer, the wholesaler, the retailer and the banker ceased to be carried out by a single individual but were performed by specialists. Moreover particular regions, such as the Ruhr, Upper Silesia, Alsace and the Donetz basin specialized in the manufacture of a limited range of manufactured products. At the same time the one-man business and family partnership gave way to the joint-stock company and eventually to trusts (agreements between firms) and to great undertakings formed by the amalgamation of formerly indepent businesses. Vertical combinations embraced firms interested in the successive stages of production from the raw material to the finished product while horizontal combinations included firms producing similar products.

Industrialization required capital. This came from various sources. Sometimes the savings of an individual or of a family were sufficient to start a business. Landowners, whose incomes were derived from farm-rents, sometimes invested spare capital in mines or manufacturing enterprises. Merchants who had made money in trade at home or abroad were also among the early investors in industry. The establishment of credit banks, which attracted the savings of small investors, enabled many new industrial enterprises to be started in the middle years of the nineteenth century. In a relatively poor country, where insufficient private capital was available, it was necessary for the state to assist new firms by subsidies or loans and to establish nationalized undertakings. In Prussia, for example, the state owned and operated a number of coal-mines, ironworks, textile factories, corn-mills, paper-mills, chemical works and railways.

A feature of industrialization has been the more or less regular recurrence of ebb and flow in trade. In Britain (which became industrialized first) each business cycle lasted for about ten years in the first two-thirds of the nineteenth century. The troughs of the cycles were marked by commercial crises which occurred in 1825, 1839, 1847, 1857 and 1866. From the 1870's onwards long periods of bad trade and unemployment took the place of the short sharp panics of the earlier part of the century. The great depression of 1873–96 and the world slump of 1929–33 were very different from the crises of 1847 or 1857. As both continental countries and the United States became industrialized the booms and slumps in economic activity became world wide in scope. The crisis of 1857 was the first of the world slumps since New York, Hamburg, Berlin and many other commercial centres were just as much affected as London. Much research has been done on the causes of the trade cycle. Pigou, for example, believed that the psychology of the entrepreneur was the main cause of rhythmic business fluctuations, while D. H. Robertson argued that "most of the great upward and downward swings of trade in the nineteenth century, from the great English railway boom of the forties to the great German electrical boom of the late nineties, can be explained in terms of the essential bumpiness and jerkiness of the process of investment in capital equipment". Economists have also observed regular trends in business activity other than the ten-year cycle. Kuznets and Hoffmann have examined the "long waves" of the economic activity in Britain which lasted from fifteen to twenty-three years, while Kondratyev claims to have discovered the existence of a very long trend-cycle of fifty years or so.

The change from an agrarian to a manufacturing economy began much earlier in some states than in others and the pace of industrialization has varied in different countries. Both economists and economic historians have examined the problem of the growth of industrial economies. The views of Hoffmann and Rostow are of particular interest.

Hoffmann considers that the process of industrialization always tends to follow the same general pattern. He argues that, in the process of industrialization, an economy passes through three phases:

(i) The first phase of industrialization is marked by a very high output of the products of either a textile industry (such as cotton cloth) or of a food-processing industry (such as flour milling or sugar refining) and a relatively low output of the products of heavy industry (such as pig-iron and machinery).

(ii) In the second phase of industrialization the output of goods produced by the textile or food-processing industries still predominates but the output of pig-iron and engineering products is increasing rapidly.

(iii) In the third phase of industrialization the output of consumer goods (such as textiles) and of capital goods (such as engineering products) is approximately equal.

Rostow's theory of economic growth also divides the process of industrialization into three phases:

(i) A preliminary phase of a hundred years or more during which economic, technical, social and political conditions are gradually established which make possible the transition from a predominantly agrarian to a predominantly manufacturing economy.

(ii) A brief period of thirty years or so during which the rate of investment rises from five per cent to over ten per cent and fundamental advances in production techniques take place.[1]

(iii) A long period of industrial expansion (interrupted by fluctuations in the economy) during which the new rate of saving is maintained and the potentialities of new manufacturing techniques are fully exploited.

For Rostow the second period, which he calls the "take-off", is of fundamental significance. He suggests that it occurred in Britain in 1783–1802, in France and Belgium in 1830–60 and in Germany in 1850–73. While Hoffmann argues that one of the consumer-goods industries has normally played the dominant role in the early stage of industrialization, Rostow believes that "the introduction of the railroad has been historically the most powerful single initiator of take-offs". "It was decisive in the United States, Germany and Russia; it played an extremely important part in the Swedish, Japanese and other cases."

Rostow points out that it might appear to be difficult to reconcile his theory with evidence assembled by such scholars as Colin Clark and Kuznets which tends to show that industrial growth is a steady process and is not promoted by a sudden burst of abnormal expansion. Rostow explains the apparent discrepancy by arguing that the statistics used by Colin Clark and Kuznets relate to the third phase

[1] W. Arthur Lewis has expressed the view that "the central problem in the theory of economic development is to understand the process by which a community which was previously saving and investing 4 or 5 per cent of its national income or less, converts itself into an economy where voluntary saving is running at about 12–15 per cent of national income or more. This is the central problem because the central fact of economic development is rapid capital accumulation (including knowledge and skills with capital)".

4

of economic expansion (i.e. the period of "self-sustained growth") and not to the vital period of "take-off".

Britain was the first country to become industrialized. Her geographical location and good ports had enabled her to develop the fishing industry and a flourishing overseas trade. Her colonies in India, North America and the West Indies—rich in raw materials and tropical foods—fostered shipping and overseas commerce. After 1745 Britain enjoyed freedom from both civil strife and foreign invasion. Supplies of coal and iron-ore were available and were situated close to good ports. Wool and flax for the textile industry and hides for the leather industry were produced at home. Landowners, merchants and the early manufacturers themselves provided the capital needed to start new industrial enterprises. The Bank of England, the country banks and the commodity exchanges provided the financial framework within which a new industrial economy could expand. Long-established craft industries provided the skilled labour for the new factories. The inventions in the textile and metal industries, the provision of improved transport (by turnpike roads and canals) and the agrarian changes associated with enclosures and scientific farming were all factors favourable to the extension of industrial enterprise.

It might appear surprising that large-scale modern industries were not developed on the Continent at about the same time as in Britain. France, with a larger population than Britain in the eighteenth century, had a potentially larger labour force and a potentially larger home market than her rival across the Channel. France was a wealthy country and had a flourishing overseas trade, particularly with the Levant and with her colonies in the West Indies. In many of her domestic industries—as also in the State factories which made tapestries and porcelain—high standards of craftsmanship were attained. French scientists, such as Réaumur and Lavoisier, applied scientific knowledge to solve industrial problems. The State actively promoted the expansion of manufactures. Germany, too, had high standards of industrial skill and the technique of her miners enjoyed a world-wide reputation. Very large resources of coal were available in the Ruhr, the Saar and Upper Silesia. The fairs of Leipzig and Frankfurt am Main were of international importance and large quantities of goods were carried on the Rhine and other German rivers.

Nevertheless various factors delayed the industrialization of France and Germany. In both countries the long wars of the eighteenth century seriously drained the national resources. In both countries internal customs barriers and vexatious road and river tolls checked industrial and commercial expansion. In France wealth was very unevenly distributed at the time of the *ancien régime* while inadequate coal resources hampered the growth of heavy industry. In Germany the division of the country into a large number of separate states and the failure to establish possessions overseas were factors which adversely affected industrial growth. Despite these difficulties some progress towards industrialization was made both in France and in Germany in the second half of the eighteenth century.

# CHAPTER II

# THE GENESIS OF THE INDUSTRIAL REVOLUTION IN FRANCE AND GERMANY

So rapid was the growth of British industry in George III's reign that the significance of parallel, though more modest, developments in France and Germany may be overlooked. If the pace of British industrial expansion be taken as a yardstick of economic development, then the progress made by continental countries between 1740 and 1815 was relatively slow. But if the extension of manufactures in France and Germany be studied without reference to so exceptional a standard, it will be seen that important economic advances were being made.

One factor which influenced British industrialization was the increase in population. It has been estimated that England's population rose from about six millions in 1720 to nearly nine millions in 1801. On the Continent too the population was increasing. Between 1700 and 1789 France's population rose from about eighteen millions to twenty-four millions. In Germany the population of Prussia is estimated to have grown from 2,380,000 to 5,750,000 (1740–83), while that of Saxony rose from 1,600,000 to 2,000,000 (1722–1802). There was a tendency for people to move from the countryside to the towns and for the number of large cities to increase. In the eighteenth century London grew from 675,000 to 865,000 inhabitants, Paris from 500,000 to 670,000, and Berlin from 29,000 to 141,000.

Population growth and urbanization foster an increase in agricultural output. New mouths have to be fed, while expanding industry needs more raw materials such as wool, flax, hides and madder. In Britain scientific farming, enclosures and the extension of the area under cultivation led to a substantial increase in agricultural output in the eighteenth century. In France and Germany too the level of agricultural output increased. Arthur Young, who travelled in France between 1787 and 1789, praised the progress that was being made on many farms in Flanders, Alsace and Languedoc,

7

while the rise in the value of agricultural land suggested that farming was becoming more profitable. In various parts of Germany clover, lucerne, potatoes, beet, hops and tobacco were introduced in the eighteenth century; the amount of fallow was reduced; indoor winter feeding of cattle was extended; the quality of livestock was greatly improved; and marshes and heathlands were reclaimed.

One major factor which fostered British industry in the eighteenth century was the invention of many new machines and processes, particularly in the manufacture of textiles and in the iron'and steel industry. The invention of the steam engine greatly increased the pace of industrialization. But improvements in industrial technique were not confined to Britain. In France Réaumur popularized new methods of producing iron and of turning wrought iron into steel; Clouet made cast steel; Jacquard invented a silk loom; Berthollet invented chlorine-bleaching; Oberkampf and Widmer made a cloth-printing cylinder; Leblanc produced artificial soda. The training of engineers was fostered by the establishment of the College of Highways and Bridges (1747), the College of Mines (1793) and the Polytechnic (1794). In Germany Winterschmidt constructed a water-pressure engine; Diesbach and Barth invented new dyes; Achard set up the world's first beet-sugar refinery; and technical education was fostered by the establishment of the *Carolina Wilhelmina* college at Brunswick (1745), a commercial college at Hamburg (1767), mining academies at Freiberg (1765) and Clausthal (1765), and the Royal Academy of Sciences at Berlin.

Details concerning English inventions were soon available on the Continent despite the efforts of the British authorities to keep such information secret. A number of foreigners—Jars, Marchant de la Houlière, Reden, Stein, Eversmann, Baader and Reichenbach for example—visited English factories. Some of them smuggled machines, models and blueprints across the Channel. By these means some Newcomen and Watt pumps were erected in mines on the Continent; a few coke furnaces were introduced into ironworks; fly shuttles, water frames and mule jennies appeared in some of the textile factories while rotative steam engines were set up to work corn-mills and textile machines. Moreover English experts crossed the Channel to introduce machines to the Continent and to show local workers how to use them. John Holker, an exiled Lancashire Jacobite, fostered the development of the Normandy textile industries and (as an Inspector General of Factories) travelled widely in France to promote the adoption of new textile machinery. Michael Alcock established metalworks at La Charité, Saint-Etienne and Roanne. William Wilkinson supervised the erection of a royal cannon foundry at Indret and set up at the Le Creusot ironworks the first furnace on the Continent to use coke successfully. Later he smelted lead ore with coke in a Prussian State mine at Tarnowitz (Silesia). John Baildon erected coke furnaces in Silesia at State ironworks at Gleiwitz and Zabrze and at the privately owned Hohenlohe Foundry.

Improvements in communications promoted the progress of manufactures in Britain in the eighteenth century. On the Continent, too, the construction of roads, bridges, canals and harbour-works increased industrial efficiency by improving the transport of raw materials to the workshops and of finished goods to the consumers. In France D. C. Trudaine reorganized the administrative arrangements for maintaining the highways (1743–69) while Pierre Tresaguet invented a new method of road building which was particularly successful in the Limousin district in the days when Turgot was in charge of the local government of this region. Turgot substituted a tax for forced labour on the roads and he engaged contractors to repair bridges and highways. Stein's highways in the County of Mark may serve as an example of road improvements in Germany at this time. Stein came to the County of Mark—which included part of the Ruhr coal-field—in 1784 as a Prussian mining official. But he soon accepted new responsibilities in the wider field of local government. Stein, like Turgot, dispensed with forced labour in the building of roads and he laid the foundations of the modern system of highways in the Ruhr. Some progress, too, was made in the improvement of inland waterways. A network of canals was constructed in the industrial district of north-east France (Hainault) in the eighteenth century while in Prussia the Finow, Plauen, Templin, Fehrbellin, Bromberg and Klodnitz canals were opened to traffic.

Industrial expansion requires capital to build machinery and communications. In Britain this was provided by landowners whose wealth came from rents; by merchants who had made money in home or overseas trade; and by entrepreneurs who ploughed profits back into industrial undertakings. Similar developments occurred on the Continent on a more modest scale. Thus in Upper Silesia some of the great feudal lords financed collieries and foundries on their estates, while in Saxony the Lauchhammer ironworks owed their existence to aristocratic landowners. The investment mania associated with John Law's Mississippi scheme suggested that ample funds were available in France, but they were attracted to public loans, chartered trading companies and tax-farming rather than to industrial enterprises. Comparatively little wealth from overseas trade appears to have found its way into industrial enterprises on the Continent in the eighteenth century. France's colonial trade received a setback when

Canada and India fell into English hands, while Germany's exports to Latin America—over ten million pesos a year at the beginning of the nineteenth century—financed the purchase of tropical products rather than the establishment of new manufactures. In the last quarter of the eighteenth century, however, some of the leading French and German ports were in a flourishing condition. Marseilles had a profitable trade with the Levant; Bordeaux and Nantes traded with the rich sugar island of San Domingo; while Hamburg handled large quantities of grain in transit from the Baltic to English ports and opened up a new trade with the United States when the American colonies gained their independence.

The leading continental banks in the eighteenth century were to be found in Switzerland and Holland rather than in France or Germany. The Bank of Hamburg grew in importance in this period while the activities of the Berlin merchant David Splitgerber (who was one of Frederick the Great's financial agents) showed how in Prussia the function of private banker was beginning to be differentiated from that of merchant.

Since continental manufacturers frequently found it difficult to raise sufficient funds for their needs, governments themselves invested money in industry and also tried to tempt private investors by granting various privileges to manufacturers. In Britain in the age of *laissez faire* there was no nationalized sector of the economy and there were virtually no State industrial undertakings. In France and Germany, on the other hand, the climate of public opinion was entirely different. In those countries governments were expected to promote the expansion of manufactures in many different ways. The establishment of nationalized coal-mines, ironworks, textile mills and other factories and the granting of State aid to private firms were regarded as normal methods of fostering economic prosperity.

Many factors influenced the attitude of continental governments towards economic affairs in the eighteenth century. The years 1740–1815 marked the initial phase of a transition in the structure of the economy. The force of tradition was strong and it was natural that the policy of the State towards agriculture and industry should follow well-established precedents. But in the second half of the eighteenth century there were manufacturers, merchants, civil servants and ministers of State on the Continent who realized the importance of changes that were taking place in Britain. They saw that a new industrial economy based upon coal, iron, machinery, steam-power and factories was making Britain both wealthy and powerful. They believed that similar opportunities lay within their grasp but that what was being accomplished in Britain by private enterprise alone could hardly be achieved on the Continent unless the State gave effective assistance and encouragement to private manufacturers. The industrial policy of continental governments in the eighteenth century was thus partly the continuation of a traditional policy which aimed at strengthening an old-established economy and partly an attempt to adapt well-tried methods to the needs of a changing age.

Werner Sombart has discussed the significance of the armaments industry and of certain luxury industries in the history of the evolution of modern capitalism. All countries were obviously bound to make adequate defence preparations. It was common for states to establish foundries and forges; factories for the manufacture of small arms, gunpowder and ammunition; and dockyards for building naval vessels. The motive for fostering the production of luxuries was different. Silks, porcelain, glassware, carpets, tapestries and curtains were articles of high value in relation to their weight and bulk which could be sent long distances without incurring high transport costs. Their export secured foreign currency with which to pay for essential imports. Sometimes a branch of manufacture originally founded as a luxury industry expanded so that it produced cheaper articles for a wider market. The development of the glass industry in France illustrates this. In the seventeenth century the output of this industry, which grew up under the shelter of State patronage, consisted largely of high quality glassware. In the eighteenth century, however, French glassmakers were turning out not only luxury articles but also bottles and other types of glassware in common use. Relatively large factories using coal for fuel were now taking the place of the old-fashioned small wood-burning workshops.

During Colbert's administration the French Government spent some 7,500,000 livres in promoting the cloth, silk, lace and carpet industries. Colbert established State workshops and granted subsidies to privileged "royal manufactories". After his death less money was available for subsidies and several establishments founded by Colbert closed down. Later his policy was revived and between 1740 and 1780 the Government gave or lent 6,800,000 livres to manufacturers and merchants while the King invested heavily in chartered overseas trading companies in the early stages of their development. Frederick the Great of Prussia—like Colbert—made great efforts to promote the growth of industry and trade. Here again some of the branches of manufacture fostered by the State did not long survive the death of their founder. But the silk industry of Crefeld and the collieries of Silesia were among several Prussian industries which continued to flourish in the nineteenth century.

In the light of the available evidence it may be suggested that the genesis of the industrial revolution in France and Germany may be sought in the second half of the eighteenth century rather than in the years following the Napoleonic wars. De Tocqueville has pointed out that in France a new spirit began to influence the *ancien régime* after about 1740. The same might be said of the Prussia of Frederick the Great and other enlightened rulers. In both France and Germany a new vigour animated both the central governments and the provincial authorities. Men like Trudaine, Turgot and Necker in France and Hagen, Heinitz and Reden in Prussia pressed forward with schemes for expanding industry and commerce. In both countries private enterprise responded to this stimulus. In both countries the growth of population encouraged farmers to produce more food and manufacturers to produce more consumer goods. For both countries the industrial revolution in Britain was an example to be followed. Eighteenth-century statistics are far from reliable but there is evidence to suggest that in France in the closing years of the *ancien régime* the total output of both iron and textiles was greater than the contemporary British output.

Of course the economic progress made in France and Germany between 1740 and 1815 should not be exaggerated. Throughout this period there were many regions and industries which were as yet hardly affected at all by the new machines and the new methods of production. There was, however, a sufficient move towards industrialization to justify the view that it is in the eighteenth century that the origins of the industrial revolution on the Continent are to be found.

# CHAPTER III

# THE INDUSTRIAL REVOLUTION IN GERMANY

## (i) 1815–1848

### THE GERMAN ECONOMY IN 1815

MANY adverse factors hampered the economic growth of Germany after the Napoleonic wars. Germany was divided into thirty-nine states. The powers of the German Federation (*Bund*) were very limited and, as far as economic affairs were concerned, the states enjoyed complete independence. They controlled their own tariffs, currencies, communications, agriculture, mining, manufactures and banking. But the position was better than it had been in the eighteenth century since Church territories had been secularized and many formerly independent states (including the lands of the Imperial Knights and all but four of the Imperial Cities) had been absorbed by neighbouring states. Progress towards industrialization was hampered by the absence of economic unity. It was in central Germany and in the Rhine valley that the existence of many small states had serious economic and political drawbacks. The map of the Anhalt duchies and the Thuringian states resembled a patchwork quilt. Treitschke has observed that since Frankfurt am Main was surrounded by the territories of five states the city was an asylum "for all the rascals of central Germany; anyone who was ejected over the Hesse-Darmstadt frontier entered by another gate after a short walk through Homburg or Nassau".

The political geography of both north and south Germany, however, had been simplified by recent territorial changes. Two states—Prussia and Hanover—dominated Germany north of the River Main. But there was a gap between the eastern and western provinces of Prussia. There were only three states in south Germany—Bavaria, Baden and Württemberg. But the Bavarian Palatinate (on the left bank of the Rhine) was separated by Baden territory from the main part of Bavaria.

Certain adverse geographical factors may be mentioned. First,

13

there were several districts where poor soil—sandy heaths and marsh-land—made farming difficult. These regions could hardly be expected to provide food for growing industrial towns. Secondly, Germany's mineral wealth—the coal of the Ruhr, the Saar, Silesia and Saxony—lay on the periphery of the country and could not be properly exploited until a network of railways had been built. In 1815 the coal output of the Ruhr was only 380,000 tons and of the Saar only 113,000 tons. Thirdly, the expansion of the Baltic ports was hampered because Denmark controlled the Sound, while Germany's North Sea ports were less favourably situated than British or French harbours for trading on the North Atlantic route. It was not until the coming of the steamship that Hamburg and Bremen were able to compete on more equal terms with Antwerp and Liverpool.

The Napoleonic wars had seriously disorganized the German economy. The depredations of the invaders had left a legacy of heavy national, provincial and municipal debts, only a small proportion of which was recovered from the French indemnity. Overseas trade had been drastically curtailed, while internal commerce had been forced into unaccustomed channels. Various industries—particularly ironworks and the manufacture of arms—had been stimulated during the war and now had to be reorganized to meet peace time require-ments. The high tariffs of Germany's neighbours impeded the revival of former export trades such as cereals, timber, wool and linens. Rapid recovery was also hampered by the survival of medieval institutions in the towns (such as the craft gilds) and of feudal obligations in industry, farming and commerce. The flood of imports of manufactured goods (particularly textiles and hardware) from England when the German ports were opened on the collapse of the Continental System seriously hampered the efforts of German industrialists and merchants to increase their sales in the home market. The depression of industry and trade at this time reached its climax in 1817 when the failure of the harvest led to a serious shortage of food supplies.

## THE ESTABLISHMENT OF THE ZOLLVEREIN

In Prussia, which eventually became the most highly industrialized German state, strenuous efforts were made both by the Government and by the business community to revive industry and trade after 1815. Two loans, raised through the Rothschilds in London in 1818 and 1822, enabled the Government to meet its most pressing obligations, and then a policy of strict economy and austerity eventually balanced the budget and reduced the national debt. Motz, Minister of Finance between 1825 and 1830, sold some Crown lands, introduced tax reforms and encouraged road building. Beuth, head of the Department of Trade and Industry (Ministry of Finance) between 1815 and 1845, fostered the modernization of Prussian industries. He reorganized the Technical Commission, founded the Berlin Technical Institute and played a leading part in the establishment of the Association for the Promotion of Industrial Knowledge in Prussia. Rother, who was in charge of the Overseas Trading Corporation (1820–48), controlled numerous nationalized enterprises such as textile factories, flour-mills, ironworks and chemical works which were valued at 10,500,000 Thalers in 1848. He also reorganized the Bank of Prussia—formerly the Royal Bank of Berlin—which had been nursed back to solvency by Friese. In the provinces able officials such as Vincke in Westphalia and Schön in East Prussia actively promoted economic recovery and expansion.

Prussia's greatest contribution towards Germany's economic recovery after the Napoleonic wars was the founding of the Customs Union (*Zollverein*) in 1834. In the 1820's and 1830's the economic leadership of Germany lay within Prussia's grasp if she had the courage to seize it. The extension of her territory in 1815 gave her control of the main German coalfields as well as many important industries in the Rhineland and Westphalia. Moreover she commanded the most important German commercial routes running from north to south (the valleys of the Rhine, Elbe, Oder and Vistula) and from west to east across the north German plain (e.g. Cologne–Minden and Magdeburg–Berlin–Königsberg). But before Prussia could aspire to the economic leadership of Germany she had to put her own house in order. The tariff of 1818, for which Maassen was largely responsible, was one of the most important steps taken by the Prussian Government to foster the economic expansion of the country. Clapham has described it as "immeasurably the wisest and most scientific tariff then existing among the great powers". A medley of customs duties and other tolls levied at provincial boundaries and town gates was replaced by a single tariff levied at the frontiers of the State. In an age of prohibitions and high tariffs Maassen adopted a system of very moderate tariffs—a free list of raw materials, duties of ten per cent on manufactured goods and twenty to thirty per cent on "colonial goods" (e.g. sugar and coffee), and a transit duty of 1*s*. 6*d*. per cwt on goods crossing Prussian territory. Critics complained that the duties on manufactured products were far too low to give Prussian industrialists adequate protection from English competition. But Prussian manufacturers learned how to stand on their own feet and meet the challenge of foreign rivals in the home market.

Soon afterwards a number of enclaves in Prussian territory were absorbed into the Prussian customs system. The first was the Lower Lordship of Schwarzburg-Sondershausen which joined Prussia in 1819. Several other enclaves were admitted to the Prussian customs system in 1822 and 1823. Considerable pressure had to be brought to bear on the Duchies of Anhalt-Köthen and Anhalt-Dessau (notorious centres for smuggling goods into Prussia) before they too joined the Prussian customs system in 1828. The enclaves accepted the Maassen tariff and received a customs revenue in proportion to their populations.

Meanwhile the problem of abolishing tariff barriers in Germany as a whole had not been neglected. In 1819 Friedrich List drew up a petition to the Federal Diet in which he declared that only "the erection of a general tariff for the whole Federation can restore national trade and industry". The Federal Diet failed to take any action with regard to the establishment of a customs union and nothing came of ministerial discussions at Vienna in 1819–20 on the subject. In the circumstances several states in south Germany and the Rhineland discussed at Darmstadt (1820–23) and then at Stuttgart (1825) the possibility of forming a regional union. In the end all that came of these negotiations was an agreement of January 18, 1828, between Bavaria and Württemberg to establish a customs union between those two states.

A fortnight later (February 14, 1828) a second treaty for the setting up of a regional customs union was signed. This was an agreement between Prussia and Hesse-Darmstadt. Motz had hoped to link the economies of the eastern and western provinces of Prussia by persuading Hanover, Brunswick or Hesse-Cassel to enter the Prussian customs system. In this he was not successful. He welcomed a suggestion from the government of Hesse-Darmstadt that negotiations for closer economic co-operation should be opened even although the adhesion of this state to the Prussian tariff system would not solve the problem of the division of Prussia into two parts. Motz realized that the adhesion of Hesse-Darmstadt would increase Prussia's prestige in north Germany and that Hesse-Darmstadt's example might one day be followed by other German states.

The establishment of these two regional unions greatly alarmed the other German states. They wished to prevent the extension of these unions and to maintain the free transit of goods from Hamburg and Bremen to great inland commercial centres such as Leipzig and Frankfurt am Main. With these objects in view, Saxony, Hanover, Oldenburg, Brunswick, Hesse-Cassel, Nassau, Frankfurt am Main and the Thuringian states formed the Middle German Commercial Union in December 1828. They agreed to remain independent of any other customs union and to improve their network of highways. A treaty of October 1829 prolonged the life of the Union from 1834 to 1840. But the Union did not adopt a common tariff. The policy of the Union was simply to maintain the *status quo* and to prevent the expansion of either of the customs unions recently established in Germany.

The mutual jealousies of the members of the Middle German Commercial Union proved to be an insuperable obstacle to the building of the new roads that were required if it were to attain its main objective. Then Motz defeated the plans of the Union by the very method which the Union had hoped would embarrass the Prussian Government. Motz planned to construct two highways joining the territories of the Hesse-Darmstadt and the Bavaria-Württemberg customs unions. These unions had signed a commercial treaty in 1829 and if Motz's proposed roads were under Prussian control the economic links between the customs unions in north and south Germany would be greatly strengthened. Motz's projected highways crossed territory controlled by the Middle German Commercial Union and if the members of this Union kept their word the roads could not have been built. In 1829, however, several small Thuringian states (Saxe-Meiningen, Saxe-Coburg and the Reuss principalities) virtually deserted the Middle German Commercial Union since they allowed Prussia to build a road through their territories. In the same year Motz also succeeded in improving trading facilities between north and south Germany by bringing pressure to bear on the Dutch to relax their restrictions on shipping at the mouth of the Rhine.[1]

The Middle German Commercial Union, already rent by internal jealousies and dissensions, collapsed soon after Motz linked the northern and southern customs unions by constructing roads which were under the control of Prussia. Hesse-Cassel joined the customs system of Prussia and Hesse-Darmstadt in 1831 and so at last a route was opened for unrestricted trade between the eastern and western provinces of Prussia. Saxony and the Thuringian states soon followed Hesse-Cassel's example and the way was now clear for

---

[1] It was in the spring of 1829 that the Dutch gave way. But owing to delays caused by the July revolutions the Rhine Navigation Act was not signed until March 1831.

Bavaria and Württemberg to join the other states which had accepted the Prussian customs system. The German customs union (*Zollverein*) came into operation in 1834. It covered an area of over one hundred and sixty thousand square miles and had a population of nearly twenty-three and a half millions. It was soon joined by Baden, Nassau, Luxemburg and Frankfurt am Main. But Hanover, Brunswick and Oldenburg formed their own union (the Tax Union), while Hamburg, Bremen, Lübeck, Schleswig-Holstein, Lauenburg, Mecklenberg-Strelitz and Mecklenburg-Schwerin retained their economic independence.

It was agreed that the Prussian tariff should be adopted by the Zollverein and that the Prussian Government should conduct negotiations with foreign countries on behalf of the Zollverein. Member states were responsible for levying customs duties on their own frontiers and the revenue was distributed in proportion to population. The customs union was not a permanent organization. The first Zollverein treaties ran for only eight years but they were subsequently renewed for two periods of twelve years. Changes in the tariff could be made either at one of the periodic Zollverein Congresses or in the renewal treaties. Since unanimity was required for decisions taken by the Zollverein Congress many changes in the tariff had to be deferred to the next occasion on which the Zollverein treaties were renewed.

The establishment of the customs union greatly facilitated the expansion of the German economy and was a factor of major importance in promoting the industrialization of the country. Hostile tariffs no longer hindered the movement of raw materials, manufactured articles and foodstuffs over a large part of Germany. Increased competition between various manufacturing regions was a spur to technical improvements and to efficiency. Moreover, Prussia was able to secure favourable concessions from foreign countries when negotiations for commercial and shipping treaties were undertaken since she now spoke not for herself alone but for all her partners in the customs union. In 1841, for example, Britain agreed to modify her Navigation Code by treating all ports between the estuaries of the Elbe and Meuse as "natural outlets" for Zollverein trade. In 1844 Belgium agreed to levy no transit dues on freight conveyed by the Antwerp–Cologne railway and received preferential treatment for her iron exports to Germany. The vast majority of the member states were satisfied with the commercial and financial results of the customs union in its early years. The revenue from customs duties increased from 14,500,000 Thalers in 1834 to 27,400,000 Thalers in 1845. Prussia had no difficulty in securing a renewal of the Zollverein treaties when the original agreements expired in 1842.

A lively controversy developed in the 1830's over the Zollverein's fiscal policy. The Maassen Tariff had been the most liberal in Europe in 1818 but in time import duties rose owing to circumstances which were not foreseen when the tariff was drawn up. Since duties were levied by weight or quantity the decline in prices since 1818 had considerably increased the duties when calculated by value. The Free Traders (led by Prince Smith) wished to abolish these fortuitous increases in the tariff while the Protectionists (led by Friedrich List) demanded substantially higher import duties to shield German manufacturers from the competition of more advanced industrial countries. The Protectionists were supported by many (though by no means all) manufacturers. The Free Traders were supported by the Prussian and Hanoverian landowners and the merchants of the great ports and commercial cities. In Britain—where the agricultural interest clung to the traditional policy of Protection while the manufacturers supported a liberal commercial policy—the Free Traders triumphed in 1846 when the Corn Laws were repealed. In Germany, however, the first phase of the fiscal controversy ended in a stalemate. The raising of import duties on pig-iron and textiles fell far short of the establishment of the high tariff demanded by List's followers, while the failure to follow Britain's example and establish Free Trade was vigorously criticized by the followers of Prince Smith.

## THE ESTABLISHMENT OF RAILWAYS

In the 1830's and 1840's a great impetus was given to the expansion of the German economy by the construction of the first railways which were opened within a few years of the establishment of the customs union. The Zollverein treaties came into force on January 1, 1834, while Germany's first railway—the short line from Nürnberg to Fürth in Bavaria—was opened in December 1835. Germany's first important line was the Dresden–Leipzig railway in Saxony which was opened in 1839. List's advice was ignored and no attempt was made by the German states to agree upon a plan for a national network of lines or to adopt a uniform railway policy. Each state went its own way and the railway network was constructed in a piecemeal fashion so that the advantages which would have been gained by co-operation were lost. Nevertheless railways were built more quickly in Germany than anywhere else on the Continent except Belgium. In 1850 Germany already had 5,856 km. of railways in operation while France had only 2,996 km.

As early as 1842 lines had been opened between Leipzig and Magdeburg, Munich and Augsburg, Frankfurt am Main and Mainz, Mannheim and Heidelberg, Berlin and Anhalt, Düsseldorf and Elberfeld, Cologne and Aachen. By the middle of the nineteenth century three through routes running across the country from east to west and three from north to south had been completed.[1]

East of the Elbe the main railway centre was Berlin. Lines were quickly built to Anhalt–Köthen (1841), Stettin (1843), Breslau (1846), Magdeburg (1846) and Hamburg (1846) so that the Prussian capital was linked with the Baltic, the North Sea and the industrial regions of Silesia and Saxony. In the west Cologne developed as a railway centre of major importance. The Rhenish Railway to Aachen, opened in 1843, linked Cologne with a Belgian line running to Antwerp while the Cologne (Deutz)–Minden railway (1847) served the Ruhr industrial region.

The construction of a network of railways enabled Germany's natural resources to be fully used. New industries were called into being and established branches of manufacture were expanded. Ironworks increased their output to provide rails for the new lines, while firms such as Borsig (Berlin) were established to build locomotives and rolling stock. The production of collieries was expanded to provide coal to drive the new trains. Raw materials, foodstuffs and manufactured articles could now reach markets at home and abroad that had once been inaccessible. No longer could Friedrich Harkort complain that the ironworks of Westphalia were hopelessly handicapped because coal and iron ore lay nearly fifty miles apart in that part of Germany. A great impetus was given to the expansion of those industrial regions—such as the Saar and Upper Silesia—which lay on the periphery of the country. The rapid growth of Berlin and some other towns was fostered by the construction of the railways.

Some railways were built by joint-stock companies while others were nationalized lines constructed and operated by the governments of various states. In Prussia—as in Hesse-Darmstadt and Mecklenburg-Schwerin—all the early lines were private undertakings. But the difficulty of raising capital soon made it necessary for the Prussian State to give some assistance to railway companies

---

[1] The lines running from west to east were:
  i. Aachen–Cologne–Minden–Anhalt–Berlin–Breslau-Cracow.
  ii. Essen–Dresden–Beuthen.
  iii. Mannheim–Munich–Vienna.
The lines running from north to south were:
  i. Stettin–Berlin–Prague.
  ii. Hamburg–Cassel–Munich.
  iii. Cologne–Basel.

A Railway Fund was set up in 1842 and was used to purchase railway shares (e.g. the Cologne–Minden line), to guarantee the interest on shares and to advance loans to certain companies. In 1847 Prussia decided to construct its first state railway. This was the line running through the Saar coal-field. It ran from Bexbach (Bavarian Palatinate) to Forbach (Lorraine). In the southern states and also in Saxony, Brunswick and Oldenburg the construction of several nationalized railways was authorized in the 1840's.

## INDUSTRIAL PROGRESS

Improved machines—some driven by steam—were introduced into Germany in the 1830's and 1840's and this led to the establishment of a certain number of factories instead of workshops of the traditional type. By the middle of the nineteenth century perhaps one-third of the working population (outside farming) was employed in factories. In Prussia the number of steam engines increased from 419 in 1837 to 1,444 in 1849, while in the Kingdom of Saxony there were 197 steam engines in 1846. Most of these engines drove either pumps in the mines or spinning machines and power looms in the textile factories. In the iron industry several coke blast furnaces were in operation in Upper Silesia. On the other hand in the Ruhr the charcoal method of smelting survived for some time after 1849 when the coke-smelting process was introduced in the *Friedrich Wilhelm* ironworks at Mülheim. Puddling was introduced into western Germany by Friedrich Harkort and Dietrich Piepenstock and by the Remy and Hoesch families. Alfred Krupp, Jacob Meyer and Jacobi produced cast steel at this time.

The growth of the coal industry, too, was fostered by the use of improved methods of production. Steam pumps, steam-driven winding gear and new tramways led to the expansion of coal output. In the 1840's the great coal-field lying to the north of the valley of the Ruhr began to be exploited. In the *Grat Beusf* mine (Essen) and the *President* mine (Bochum) shafts were sunk to a much greater depth than had previously been attempted in the Ruhr.

The application of steam power to inland navigation was also important at this time. Steamships plied on the Rhine, Weser, Elbe and other German rivers. Matthias Stinnes introduced steam tugs to haul coal barges on the Rhine. Ruhrort quickly developed as a great river port handling coal shipments and building steam vessels and steam tugs for use on the inland waterways.

These changes were not brought about without some assistance from Britain which, at that time, was a much more advanced industrial country than Germany. Skilled English artisans operated mule-jennies in Bernhard's cotton mill at Harthau (Saxony) in the 1790's; built machinery for Friedrich Harkort at Wetter (Ruhr) in the 1820's; and introduced power-loom weaving to the *Maschinen Wollen-Weberei* at Wüste Giersdorf (Lower Silesia) in the 1840's. Textile machines constructed by the Cockerill brothers were installed in various woollen mills in Brandenburg. The first steamships to sail up the Rhine to Cologne—the *Defiance* (1816) and the *Caledonia* (1817)—were of British construction and the first trains on the Nürnberg–Fürth and Leipzig–Dresden railways were drawn by British locomotives.

The establishment of the Zollverein, the building of railways and the introduction of technical improvements all contributed to the expansion of the German economy. Despite large-scale emigration to the United States the population of Germany rose from twenty-five millions in 1815 to thirty-five and a half millions in 1850. The population expanded with exceptional rapidity between 1816 and 1830 owing to a very high marriage rate after the Napoleonic wars. Germany now had a larger population than any country on the Continent except Russia. The output of Germany's major coal-fields—the Ruhr, the Saar and Upper Silesia—rose from a little over a million tons in 1820 to about six million tons in 1850. The production of pig-iron rose from 46,000 tons in 1810 to 529,000 tons in 1850. The progress of the textile industries may be seen from the growth of the annual consumption of the raw materials between 1821–30 and 1841–50. The amount of raw cotton consumed in Germany rose from 7,000 tons to 41,000 tons and of wool from 330,000 tons to 490,000 tons. German shipping tonnage rose from 291,000 tons in 1816 to 534,000 tons in 1850. Germany's overseas trade expanded in the era of the Zollverein and the railways. In the 1820's the Overseas Trading Corporation (*Seehandlung*)—a state institution—had sent the *Mentor* on two voyages round the world to find new markets for Prussian goods. At the same time Hamburg and Bremen merchants took advantage of the new opportunities for expanding their trade when Spain's colonies in South America secured their independence. German ships traded regularly with the La Plata region and with Brazil. By 1848 Carl Woermann, William O'Swald and other Hamburg merchants had begun to establish themselves in both the West Africa and the East Africa (Zanzibar) trades.

The growth of modern industries in Germany led to social evils similar to those which had occurred in Britain. In the summer of 1824 reports from the provincial authorities showed that in the manufacturing districts of Prussia the labour of children was being exploited in a disgraceful manner. In 1828 General von Horn warned the Prussian Government that these districts could not supply their quota of army recruits since the health of young factory workers was being undermined. In 1839 the first Prussian Factory Law prohibited the employment of children under the age of nine and fixed the hours to be worked by young persons under the age of sixteen. The decline of the handicraft system—owing to competition from machine-made products—caused great hardships among the domestic workers. The discontent of impoverished craftsmen led to machine breaking and bread riots. In 1832—shortly after Hesse-Cassel joined the Zollverein —customs houses were attacked by craftsmen who feared the competition of factory goods made in Prussia. In 1840 Ludolf Camphausen of Cologne observed that the Rhine boatmen were "in a truly pitiable state" because their livelihood was threatened by the new steamships. In the following year the Barmen chamber of commerce declared that the linen trade "was gradually dying a natural death from old age". During the summer of 1844 some five thousand poverty-stricken linen handloom weavers in Silesia attempted to sack both the factories and the mansions of the manufacturers. This unrest among the craftsmen was one of the factors which contributed to bring the revolutionary movement to a head in 1848.

## (ii) 1848–1870

ECONOMIC ASPECTS OF THE REVOLUTION OF 1848

The political causes of the revolution of 1848 in Germany are well known. First, there were demands for the unification of the country and the establishment of a far stronger central government than that provided by the existing Federation. But the anomalous position of Austria—a German Power with a predominantly non-German population—and the traditional rivalry between Austria and Prussia proved to be insurmountable obstacles to unity in 1848. Secondly, there was strong opposition to the repressive policy of Metternich and demands for the reforms of the constitutions of the various German states to include the establishment of parliamentary institutions and liberal reforms such as trial by jury, freedom of the press, freedom of speech and the right of public assembly.

While middle-class liberals—mainly professional men and businessmen—advocated reforms of this kind, the craftsmen, factory workers and peasants had other grievances. Some domestic workers could not make ends meet owing to the production of cheap manufactured goods by the factories, while the urban proletariat complained of long hours, low wages and bad housing conditions. In the 1840's there were poor grain harvests and potato-crop failures which raised food prices paid by townsmen and reduced the earnings of farmers and peasants.

In south-west Germany the agrarian economy was breaking down. The traditional system of farming had been undermined by the division of the common lands and the reduction in the area of forest and woodland. Small peasant proprietors were losing rights of pasture and sources of fuel supply which they had enjoyed for generations. Meanwhile on the great estates east of the Elbe the serfs were discontented because the freedom promised to them in 1811 was so long in materializing. In Prussia only 240,000 peasants had been freed from manorial dues and obligations since the promulgation of the emancipation edict.

There was serious social unrest in Germany in the 1840's. The rising of the Silesian weavers in 1844 was on a sufficiently large scale to secure wide publicity.[1] Thousands of spinners and weavers perished of hunger-typhus in the 1840's. Moreover there were numerous strikes and riots in the towns which showed that urban domestic workers and factory hands were no less discontented with their lot than rural craftsmen, peasants and small holders. The commercial crisis and harvest failures of 1847 led to bankruptcies, unemployment and starvation. In Berlin the high cost of living and lack of work led to serious disorders in 1847 and 1848. There was an outbreak of rioting in April 1847 which began with the plundering of a baker's shop. Early in 1848 troops were called out to disperse an unruly meeting of workers in the Tiergarten. The revolution broke out in the Prussian capital on March 18 and 19 when there was fierce street fighting and 183 civilians—nearly all young craftsmen and factory workers—were killed. Next came unrest among the clothing workers and the printers. In October rioting broke out again—this time in Koepenick where labourers building a canal went on strike because of the introduction of a steam pump. Again the troops had to be called out. In November Berlin was placed under martial law. Similar disturbances took place at this time in several other German cities such as Cologne, Breslau, Elberfeld and Solingen.

The revolution in France in February 1848 was followed in March and April by popular risings throughout Germany. In many states reactionary ministries were set aside and constitutional reforms were introduced. A National Parliament of representatives elected in all the German states met at Frankfurt am Main in May. The vast

[1] Gerhard Hauptman's well-known play *Die Weber* (1892) gives a dramatic portrayal of the sufferings of the Silesian spinners and weavers and of their revolt.

majority of its 564 members were professional men and the consideration of political and constitutional problems took up most of their time. Economic and social questions, however, were not neglected. The Economic Committee of the Frankfurt Parliament drafted some clauses of the constitution of 1849. This constitution provided for the economic unification of the country. Germany was to have a single tariff and the Federal Authority alone was to legislate on the tariff, on the customs administration, and on common taxes and excises. River tolls were not to exceed the cost of the services rendered to shippers. Although this constitution never came into force the work of the Frankfurt Parliament and of its Economic Committee had not been entirely in vain. For the first time popularly elected representatives from all over Germany and Austria had discussed vital economic and social problems. And some of the reforms proposed by the Frankfurt Parliament were put into effect by various states at a later date.

## The Austro-Prussian Struggle for Economic Supremacy

It was not only the members of the Frankfurt Parliament who considered the possibility of securing for Germany a greater measure of economic unity than that already achieved by the Zollverein. In 1849 Ludwig Bruck, the Austrian Minister of Commerce, proposed that all Germany and Austria should be united in a single customs union which should levy substantially higher import duties than those charged by the existing Zollverein tariff. Bruck claimed that a union of the Habsburg dominions, the Zollverein, the Tax Union and the states which still retained their economic independence would establish a vast free trade area of seventy million inhabitants in which foodstuffs, raw materials and manufactured goods could circulate with complete freedom. This, he argued, would be of immense benefit to both German and Austrian manufacturers and farmers. Bruck tried to prepare the way for Austria's entry into such a customs union by introducing a series of economic reforms—the abolition of the Austro-Hungarian customs frontier, the ending of prohibitions and differential duties, the improvement of postal arrangements and the building of the Semmering Pass section of the Vienna–Trieste railway. The Austrian historian Friedjung has described these reforms as achievements "almost equal to the founding of the German Zollverein".

Bruck's scheme for a central European customs union secured some support both in Austria and in Germany. In Austria the new Chancellor, Schwarzenberg, favoured a plan which would deprive

Prussia of the economic leadership of Germany. The Magyar land-owners and the Bohemian industrialists hoped to benefit from the wider markets open to them if the plan came into operation. In Germany some states supported a scheme which would curb Prussia's economic influence and the Protectionists saw in Bruck a valuable ally. On the other hand the more backward manufacturers and craftsmen in Austria and Germany disliked the plan. So did the Free Traders who opposed a scheme which involved the introduction of a protectionist tariff.

Above all Bruck's plan met with implacable hostility from the Prussian Government which was determined that the Zollverein should not be absorbed in a larger union dominated by Austria. Delbrück, one of the Prussian officials responsible for Zollverein affairs, dealt a fatal blow to Bruck's plan when he persuaded Hanover and her associates in the Tax Union to join the Zollverein in 1854. Prussia and Hanover together could dominate the economy of Germany north of the River Main. If some of the small states were to desert the Zollverein and join a new customs union with Austria, the north German states, under Prussian leadership, would still control the major industrial regions in the country. Austria's negotiations with some of the Zollverein states eventually broke down because the Austrian Government was unable to give a firm guarantee that any state which joined her proposed union would receive an annual payment at least equal to that which it already enjoyed as a member of the Zollverein. Eventually all the Zollverein states renewed their treaties with Prussia and the life of the Zollverein—now united with the Tax Union—was extended to 1866.

Although Bruck failed to set up a central European customs union he did succeed in establishing a special economic relationship between Austria and Germany. By a commercial treaty of February 1853 Austria and the Zollverein, by agreeing to a system of mutual trade preferences, placed the commerce of the two regions on a different footing from that of any other countries. It was decided that negotiations for an Austro-German monetary convention should be undertaken in 1853 and that negotiations for a customs union should be resumed in 1860.

Bruck hoped that this treaty would be a first step towards the realization of his plans for the economic unification of Germany and Austria. Delbrück, however, was determined that Prussia should pursue a policy which would ensure the failure of any future Austrian attempt to gain the economic leadership of Germany.

Events favoured Delbrück. The economy of the Zollverein flourished during the boom period of 1852–7 when the output of

26

Germany's major industries increased rapidly while the overseas trade of Hamburg and Bremen was also expanding. Neither the commercial crisis of 1857 nor the depression in the cotton industry during the American civil war checked the advance of the German economy. Austria, on the other hand, remained relatively backward and her economic development was checked by the Crimean war and by the Italian war of 1859. Her finances were in a state of chronic disorder. In Prussia the tide of public opinion was now running in favour of Free Trade, but in Austria there was general agreement that high tariffs were still needed to protect manufacturers from foreign competition. Thus while the German economy was expanding in the 1850's the Austrian economy was making much slower progress and at a time when the Zollverein was moving towards a more liberal fiscal policy Austria remained faithful to Protection. Bruck had died in 1856. His successors faced a formidable task since the economies of Germany and Austria were developing on very different lines.

In 1860—the very year in which negotiations for the establishment of an Austro-German customs union would have been resumed—Britain and France signed the Cobden Commercial Treaty. The French Government abandoned its prohibitions and high protective tariff in favour of quite moderate import duties. While the British tariff concessions were made to all foreign countries, the reductions of French import duties were made only in favour of Britain. The Prussian Government was anxious to secure for Zollverein exporters the same opportunities in the French market as those now enjoyed by British exporters.

Negotiations between France and Prussia concerning a Franco-Zollverein commercial treaty were completed in March 1862. The new French import duties on German goods were, in general, similar to those levied on British products under the Cobden Treaty. The most significant reductions were on iron goods and textiles. In return Zollverein duties on French wines and textiles were reduced. The agreement included a most-favoured-nation clause. One of the demands of the French negotiators—the abolition of transit dues—had been met before the commercial agreement was signed. The treaty was due to come into force on January 1, 1866, at the same time as the treaties between Prussia and other German states for the renewal of the Zollverein.

The Austrian Government protested against the conclusion of the Franco-Prussian commercial treaty. Rechberg pointed out that the existing mutual preferences on Austro-German trade were obviously incompatible with the most-favoured-nation treatment granted to France after January 1, 1866. The Austrians tried to stiffen the

27

opposition of the south German Protectionist states to the French treaty. At first several Zollverein states refused to ratify the new agreement with France.

The Prussian Government remained firm. Bismarck had taken office as Minister President of Prussia a few months after the conclusion of the commercial agreement with France. He made it clear that all the Zollverein states must accept the Franco-Prussian treaty —and therefore the Free Trade tariff—if they were to rejoin the customs union on the expiry of the existing Zollverein treaties. The recalcitrant states gave way and the Zollverein treaties were renewed on the conditions laid down by Prussia. The Austrian Government had to accept the new situation and signed a fresh commercial agreement to replace the treaty of February 1853. The new Austro-Prussian trade treaty included a most-favoured-nation clause but the Austrians had lost their former preferences in the German market. The long struggle for the economic leadership of Germany had ended in 1865 with a decisive victory for Prussia.

Within six months of their renewal the Zollverein treaties came to an end owing to the outbreak of civil war in Germany. The economic ties which had linked so many German states since 1834 did not prevent most members of the Zollverein from siding with Austria against Prussia in June 1866. Although from a legal point of view the customs union was automatically dissolved when war was declared, the belligerents allowed commerce between its members to continue with as little interruption as possible. Customs duties were still collected and the revenue was shared between the members of the Zollverein in the usual way.

Prussia quickly defeated Austria at Königgrätz and annexed Hanover, Hesse-Cassel, Nassau, Schleswig-Holstein and Frankfurt am Main. The Federation of 1815 came to an end and a smaller union of German states north of the Main was established under Prussian leadership. The Zollverein now consisted of the North German Federation (itself a customs union), Bavaria, Württemberg, and Baden. The Zollverein treaty of 1865 was renewed but a new provision was introduced by which six months' notice could be given by any member to withdraw from the union. This placed a powerful weapon in Bismarck's hands since he could at any time threaten to exclude the south German states from the Zollverein.

Bismarck was now able to reform the constitution of the Zollverein on lines which some of its members had successfully resisted in the past. The south German states agreed to the substitution of a Customs Council and a Customs Parliament in place of the former Zollverein Congress. In these new organs of administration decisions were taken by majority vote. The south German states accepted these arrangements with some misgivings. Indeed they had no choice in the matter if they wished to remain members of the Zollverein. In the circumstances it is hardly surprising that they firmly resisted a new change which Bismarck now proposed. Bismarck hoped that the new Zollverein organs of administration could be used to tighten the political links between north and south Germany. He wanted to extend the powers of the Customs Parliament beyond its traditional limits. But when elections were held in south Germany to choose representatives to sit in the Customs Parliament the opponents of Bismarck's plan gained a decisive victory. Bismarck gave way and made no attempt to turn the Customs Parliament by stages into a German Reichstag. Between 1867 and 1870 the Customs Parliament confined its attention to tariffs and commercial treaties.

After the Franco-Prussian war of 1870–71 a united Germany was established. The Zollverein was now superfluous as an independent organization since the new Reich was itself a customs union. Hamburg and Bremen, however, retained their economic independence until the 1880's.

## Industrial Expansion in the 1850's and 1860's

The 1850's and 1860's were years of vital significance in the development of the modern German economy. This is the period that Rostow calls the "take-off" when industrialization gets under weigh. It was in these years that Germany's main branches of manufacture expanded to such an extent that the whole character of the economy was changed. From being a predominantly agrarian country with industries organized on the basis of domestic crafts Germany became a great manufacturing centre with large units of production. The German economy became strong enough to withstand shocks which formerly might have seriously checked its continuous advance. The great commercial crisis of 1857, the shortage of raw cotton during the American civil war, and Prussia's wars against Denmark, Austria and France did not hinder the progress of Germany's industrial revolution.

Some of the factors which promoted the early expansion of German industry in the 1830's and 1840's continued to be of significance in later years. The Zollverein (strengthened by the adhesion of Hanover) and the construction of railways (soon resumed after the setback of 1848) were of major importance in promoting the circulation of goods between various German economic regions. The railway policy of August von der Heydt (the Prussian Minister of Commerce) was of particular significance at this time. He worked hard to increase the length of the railway network and to secure for the State the control of as many lines as possible.

Various new factors, however, influenced the development of the economy between 1850 and 1870. There were important changes in the banking system. Central banks, such as the Bank of Prussia (reorganized by Rother in 1846) and note-issue banks provided the German business community with new financial facilities. Joint-stock credit banks fostered industrial expansion in various ways. They acted as intermediaries between investors and industry by placing the shares of new companies on the market. They held blocks of shares and made loans to firms. The Schaafhausen Bank of Cologne—a private bank reorganized by Gustav von Mevissen as a joint-stock bank in 1858—has been described by Benaerts as "the first large credit bank established in Prussia as a joint-stock company and its policy served as a model for most other European credit banks". The Darmstadt Bank, the Discount Bank and the Berlin Commercial Company played an important role in fostering the rise of German industry. A French consul, writing from Leipzig in 1856, declared that "as much energy is being put into covering Germany with a network of credit-banks as has been put into creating a railway network".

A new form of industrial organization was developed well suited to the needs of Germany's expanding economy. This was the joint-stock company which enabled relatively small investors to contribute to industrial development. It was the railway companies which first used the joint-stock principle on a large scale. By 1845 some twenty lines had been built with a capital of nearly sixty million thalers. In Germany, as in Britain, there was a "railway mania" in the 1840's and the Prussian Government tried to check speculation by insisting that no new railway stock should be issued without the consent of the Minister of Finance. Once confidence had been restored after the business depression of 1847 numerous joint-stock companies were set up in Germany—particularly coal-mines, ironworks, engineering establishments and textile mills. Some of the famous Ruhr firms— such as the Phönix and Hörde companies—were founded at this time. The movement gained momentum in the 1850's and reached its climax in 1856–7 with "a veritable torrent of speculation". The commercial crisis of 1857 checked the establishment of new firms for a time but in the 1860's many new joint-stock companies were established. In 1860 there were about 320 joint-stock companies in Germany.

Industrial progress was also fostered by changes in the climate of public opinion. An end was made of many laws and practices originally designed to safeguard the interests of producers and consumers in the age of craftsmen working for a local market. The authority of gilds and the privileges of particular groups were abolished. It was now possible to set up a workshop or factory without a licence and people were free to move about the country or to emigrate. The supporters of the policy of *laissez-faire* were gaining ground. In Prussia, for example, protests from businessmen in the late 1840's had led to a reduction in the State enterprises controlled by the Overseas Trading Corporation (*Seehandlung*). In the 1860's von Itzenplitz (Minister of Commerce) left railway construction to private enterprise whereas his predecessor had pursued a policy of nationalization and State control. The Free Traders were gaining the ear of the public and the Franco-Prussian commercial treaty of 1862 heralded a brief era of low tariffs. The "industrial freedom" achieved in the 1860's gave an impetus to the progress of manufactures. This phase of Germany's economic development was, however, not quite the same as the era of *laissez-faire* in Britain. The State in Germany continued to play a more decisive role than the State in Britain in fostering the development of the economy. The governments of the various German states not only ran nationalized railways, ironworks, coal-mines and so forth but actively fostered industrial progress in many ways such as the provision of improved facilities for technical education.

Between 1848 and 1870 the production of textiles was the most important industry in Germany. Over three-quarters of a million full-time workers found employment in these industries and in addition there were still some thousands of handloom weavers. No other economic activity (except farming) provided work for so many people. In no other industry were there so many large units of production. The value of the net exports of the textile industries was estimated at nearly seventy million thalers in 1860 and this was a significant item on the credit side of Germany's balance of international payments. The different branches of the industry, however, made very unequal progress towards technical efficiency and large-scale factory production. The modernization of the old-established linen industry was a slow and difficult process. The woollen and worsted industry and the manufacture of silk made more rapid and more substantial progress though there were small isolated centres of production in which antiquated methods survived into the 1860's. The cotton industry, on the other hand, advanced rapidly towards large-scale capitalist production.

In 1860 the cotton industry was larger than the other textile industries, the number of cotton machines being twenty per cent greater than the total of the machines in the woollen and linen industries combined. At this time the German cotton industry had 2,250,000 spindles (in 310 mills), 142,000 handlooms, and 23,000 power looms. The labour force included nearly 38,000 spinners and 193,000 weavers. The consumption of raw cotton had risen from a mere 15,000 tons in 1836 to 67,000 tons in 1861. The main centres of production were the Rhineland (Elberfeld, Barmen, Crefeld, Rheydt and München-Gladbach), south Germany (Augsburg and Göppingen) and Saxony (Erzgebirge and Voigtland districts). In Berlin certain finishing processes, such as calico-printing, were carried out. In Silesia the cotton industry, still run in small workshops, was declining.

There was a considerable expansion in the cotton industry in the 1850's and some large spinning mills were established such as the *Baumwollspinnerei am Stadtbach* in Augsburg and the *Aktienspinnerei Chemnitz*. The American civil war led to a serious shortage of raw cotton in Germany. Many operatives were unemployed or on short time. The crisis had important effects on the industry. Cotton manufacturers used more Indian cotton than before. A number of smaller firms disappeared while the more modern larger mills survived. The use of steam power increased. An official Prussian report stated that the Cotton Famine had "considerably fostered technical improvements, particularly in spinning". By 1870 the industry had recovered from the crisis of the early 1860's and its annual consumption of raw cotton was over 100,000 tons. This was about one-sixth of the consumption of the British cotton industry at that time.

The woollen industry was more widely scattered than the manufacture of cotton yarn and cloth. There were woollen centres on both sides of the lower Rhine, in Brandenburg, in Silesia and in Saxony. In 1860 the German woollen industry had over a million spindles, nearly 2,600 power looms and 11,800 handlooms. Most of them were in the carded-wool branch of the industry. At one time the home clip not only provided all the raw material that the industry needed but there was also a surplus for export. Wool from Saxony found a ready market abroad. By the middle of the nineteenth century, however, Germany was importing considerable quantities of wool from Australia, Cape Colony, Russia and Austria, although some German wool of high quality was still being exported. Clapham remarks that as late as 1870 the home clip still provided the woollen mills with three-fifths of their requirements—"a very creditable proportion in the then conditions of international trade". In

1864 the value of net exports of woollen goods exceeded that of the net imports of raw wool and yarns by nearly thirteen million thalers. German woollen cloth was of high quality. A report on the Paris industrial exhibition of 1855 stated that the Zollverein woollens displayed were superior to those of other countries though the design of the cloths showed little originality.

The manufacture of linens had once been a very important industry in Germany and had dominated the markets of the world. Various types of cloth—such as Osnaburgs and Tecklenburgs— were known by German names. At the end of the eighteenth century about a quarter of Prussia's exports were linen cloths. But in the first half of the nineteenth century the German linen industry declined. Less flax was produced at home and the industry depended more and more upon flax imported from Russia. Markets abroad were lost to more efficient Irish and Belgian manufacturers. While rival industries were being rapidly mechanized the German industry remained mainly a domestic manufacture. Many German linen spinners and weavers were part-time workers whose main employment was on the land. They were reluctant to give up their farm work to become factory hands. In 1850 there were still 100,000 linen hand-loom spinners and weavers in Silesia. Eleven years later the Zollverein had only 38 linen-spinning mills and 300 weaving sheds.

The silk industry was located in the Prussian provinces of Brandenburg and the Rhineland and also in Baden and Württemberg. The Crefeld factories made pure silk for export to western Europe; the Berlin and south German works produced silks for the Russian and Balkan markets; while the Elberfeld manufacturers made rather cheaper goods for the home market. In the middle of the nineteenth century the industry was dominated by wealthy silk merchants who purchased the raw material and passed it on to the owners of small factories to whom they gave credit.

Although the textile industries were the most important branch of manufacture in this period, it was the rapid expansion of the coal, iron and engineering industries which was of the greatest significance from the point of view of Germany's future economic development. The largest coal-fields—the Ruhr, the Saar and Upper Silesia—lay in Prussia and two mining laws of May 12, 1851, gave an impetus to the expansion of coal-mining in that State.

The first law ended the special status of private collieries in Prussia. Hitherto the State had exercised a much greater control over mining than over any other industry. Government officials had controlled mining exploitation, colliery finance, the sale of coal, and the fixing of wages. The day to day running of every privately owned colliery had been subject to strict supervision. Now all this was swept away and coal-owners and colliery managers were given the same freedom as other industrialists to manage their own affairs. The second law reduced from ten per cent to five per cent the tax on the gross output of mines. This rate was already in force on the left bank of the Rhine where a French mining law of 1810 was still in force. A Prussian law of 1860 abolished the last privileges of the miners' gilds. A miner could now move freely from one part of Prussia to another and could seek employment in any colliery. This made it possible for the labour force of the Ruhr to be rapidly expanded since farm workers from eastern Germany and Poland could now migrate to the Rhineland and Westphalia.

The output of coal in Germany expanded rapidly in the 1850's and 1860's. New coal-fields were opened up. Thus the deep seams north of the Ruhr valley between the *Hellweg* and the Emscher were exploited for the first time. Technical improvements were introduced. Deeper shafts were sunk; steam engines were used to drive pumps and to haul coal to the surface; tramways were laid both underground and at the surface; and improved safety precautions were introduced. All this required capital. In the nationalized mines of the Saar and Upper Silesia the Prussian Government found the necessary money. In the privately owned mines of Upper Silesia the landed gentry who exploited coal on their own property invested in mining some of the money that they received as rent from their tenants. In the Ruhr foreign entrepreneurs brought new capital to the region while the development of joint-stock mining companies—supported by credit banks—enabled German investors to play a part in developing the country's greatest coal-field. The efficiency of the industry was increased by closing small pits and by colliery amalgamations. In Upper Silesia six mines produced two-thirds of the coal in the district. In the Eschweiler coal-field a single company dominated the region. In the Saar the governments of Prussia and Bavaria owned practically all the mines.

In 1864 there were 670 coal-mines in Germany employing 99,000 men. Between 1860 and 1871 the output of bituminous coal increased from 12·3 million tons to 29·4 million tons and the output of lignite rose from 4·4 million tons to 8·5 million tons. By 1871 Germany had become the second coal-producing country in the world. Her output was still far behind that of the United Kingdom but it was greater than that of the United States, or France, or Belgium. This increased output coupled with the completion of the railway network, the building of the Saar Coal Canal, the reduction of freight charges on railways, and the introduction of powerful steam tugs on the

Rhine enabled German coal to capture more and more of the home market. Coal imports declined from a million tons in 1855 to three-quarters of a million tons in 1864. Germany was even exporting a little coal at this time. Ruhr coal, for example, was sent to Holland while Saar coal was exported to France.

The career of W. T. Mulvany may serve to illustrate the expansion of the German coal industry in the 1850's and 1860's. Mulvany was an engineer who had been a Commissioner of Public Works in Ireland. He first visited the Ruhr in 1854 on behalf of some Irish capitalists and he was greatly impressed by the potentialities of the district. In 1856 a group of Irish business men opened the Hibernia mine near Gelsenkirchen. Mulvany was both a shareholder and the salaried manager of the colliery. William Coulson, a mining engineer from the Durham coalfield, used the "tubbing" method of lining the shafts of the mine with iron casings. In 1860 the partners established the Shamrock mine near Herne. By 1872 the output of the two mines was 338,000 tons of coal. Mulvany also had an interest in the Erin (Castrop), the Hansa (Hucharde) and the Zollern (Kirchlinde) collieries. These three mines together with the Vulkan ironworks at Duisburg were subsequently amalgamated and were controlled by the Prussian Mining and Ironworks Company.

Mulvany's services to his adopted country were not confined to the successful management of a group of important collieries. In 1858 he took a leading part in bringing the coal-owners of the Ruhr together in the Ruhr Mineowners Association and in 1871 he was equally successful in promoting the establishment of a wider association open not only to coalowners but to ironmasters and other industrialists as well. Mulvany took the initiative in agitating for a substantial reduction in the freight charged by railways for the carriage of Ruhr coal. He advocated the extension of the Ruhr's markets for coal and was chairman of the Westphalian Coal Export Association of 1877.

Iron, like coal, was of fundamental significance in the development of Germany's modern industrial economy. Iron-ore had long been mined in various parts of the country. There were deposits in the Erzgebirge and in the Harz mountains as well as in south Germany and Upper Silesia. East of the lower Rhine iron-ore was quarried and mined in the valleys of the Ruhr, Sieg, Dill and Lahn. West of the lower Rhine iron-ore was obtained in the valleys of the Moselle and the Saar as well as in Luxemburg and the Eifel district. In the middle years of the nineteenth century the demand for iron-ore increased. In 1850 Germany's output of iron-ore (838,000 tons) was less than half that of France and was only one-sixth that of Britain. Twenty years later Germany's output of iron-ore amounted to 4,300,000 tons. This was achieved partly by the exploitation of new deposits— blackband in the Ruhr and *minette* in Luxemburg—and partly by the use of more efficient methods of working older deposits. There was at this time an important regional change in the production of iron-ore. Between 1851 and 1861 Silesia's output dropped from fifty-two per cent to twenty-five per cent of Prussia's total production while the output of the Rhineland and Westphalia rose from twenty-nine per cent to forty per cent.

When the Zollverein was established in 1834 Germany's output of pig-iron amounted to only 130,000 tons. Most of the furnaces were quite small and were generally situated in well-wooded districts near deposits of iron-ore. The traditional charcoal method of smelting was normally employed. Only in Upper Silesia was iron smelted by coke on a fairly large scale. The first coke-smelting furnaces in that district had been erected by State ironworks at Gleiwitz (1796) and Königshütte (1802). By the middle of the nineteenth century nearly thirty such furnaces were in operation in Upper Silesia. Western Germany had only a handful of coke furnaces before 1849. In that year the first coke furnace was set up in the Ruhr at the *Friedrich Wilhelm* foundry. On the other hand the manufacture of wrought iron by the puddling process had made more rapid progress in the Rhineland and Westphalia than in Germany east of the Elbe.

The 1850's and 1860's saw a great expansion in the production of pig-iron and steel by modern methods particularly in the Ruhr and the Saar. Great ironmasters such as Krupp of Essen and Stumm of Neunkirchen played their part but it was new joint-stock companies which largely contributed to the increase in production. Between 1852 and 1861 seventy-five companies with a capital of 80,000,000 thalers were established to make pig-iron and other iron products. In the Ruhr alone twenty-seven coke blast furnaces were erected between 1851 and 1857 and Germany as a whole had about sixty such furnaces in 1857. By 1870 Germany, with an output of 1,400,000 tons, had overtaken both France and Belgium as producers of pig-iron. Changes in the location of the industry were taking place at this time. Iron smelting was moving from the ironfields to the coal-fields. Small charcoal furnaces in districts like the Sieg valley and the Eifel hills declined while the large new coke furnaces of the Ruhr and the Saar expanded.

Steel output in Germany was also expanding. In 1864 steel valued at 11,900,000 thalers was produced as compared with only 1,600,000 thalers in 1848. Bessemer converters were installed in the Ruhr by the Hörde Company and by Krupp. In Berlin the firm of Borsig introduced the Siemens-Martin open hearth process. These new methods were, however, introduced more slowly in Germany than might have been expected. It appears that at this time the quality of German puddled iron was superior to that of either Bessemer or Siemens-Martin steels except for rails and boilers.

The numerous industries which used iron and steel made considerable progress. Large firms were engaged in the manufacture of locomotives, rails and railway equipment at Berlin, Cassel, Augsburg and Munich. Several important establishments for the making of machinery had developed. This branch of the engineering industry employed 51,000 men in 1861. On the other hand the manufacture of iron smallwares such as chains, scythes, locks, needles, cutlery and small arms was still very largely a craft industry.

The development of the iron and steel industry in Germany in the middle of the nineteenth century may be illustrated from the expansion of the Krupp works at Essen. Friedrich Krupp, the founder of the firm, had been ruined as a result of his search for the "secret of cast steel". In 1826 his widow and fourteen-year-old son Alfred inherited a bankrupt little foundry employing only seven men. Alfred Krupp had a long uphill struggle for over twenty years before he at last achieved success as a manufacturer of railway springs, axles, and cast steel tyres. His first steel gun, made in 1857, was a three-pounder muzzle-loader. At the Great Exhibition in London (1851) he showed a six-pounder. In 1859 he at last secured from the Russian Government his first really big contract for 120 steel guns and this started him on his new career as one of the leading manufacturers of armaments on the Continent. A large steam hammer had been installed in Krupp's works in 1858 and this was soon followed by the erection of a Bessemer steel converter. The Sayn ironworks were purchased from the Prussian State. The size of Krupp's works increased with astonishing rapidity. In 1864 he was employing six thousand men as compared with two thousand in 1861. In 1865 his output was valued at eight million thalers. At the Paris exhibition of 1867 Krupp showed a cast-steel ingot weighing 80,000 lb. as well as "a monster such as the world has never seen"—a steel cannon with a barrel weighing 50 tons.

In the 1850's and 1860's some large concerns developed in Germany which controlled their own supplies of coal and iron-ore, manufactured iron and steel, and operated engineering works as well. In the Ruhr Jacobi, Haniel and Huyssen owned the *Gutehoffnung* ironworks (four blast furnaces), the *Antonhütte* foundry, rolling mills at Oberhausen, works for making machinery at Sterkrade and a shipbuilding yard at Ruhrort. The firm also controlled several iron-ore mines. The firm of *Phönix* operated eleven blast furnaces at Berge-Borgbeck, Ruhrort and Kupferdreh; owned a number of iron-ore mines; and leased two large collieries. The Berlin locomotive firm of Borsig acquired both coal-mines and ironworks in Upper Silesia.

## THE SOCIAL QUESTION, 1815–70

The progress of manufactures in Germany brought with it the same social problems as those with which England had long been familiar. Industrial workers complained of long hours, low wages, harsh factory discipline, and the truck system. Their work was often exhausting and detrimental to health. The factory workers frequently had to live in overcrowded "rent barracks" which soon degenerated into slums. The labour of women and children was exploited. Workers suffered from periods of short time and unemployment when trade was depressed.

The following memorial addressed to the Cologne factory owners in April 1848 vividly summarizes both the grievances of the workers and their demands for reform:

'The time for hypocrisy is over and done with. When you wanted to overcome the competition of foreign rivals you cut down our wages and you made no personal sacrifices. When you wanted to drive the goods of other German manufacturers from the home market it was the factory hands who had to work harder for longer hours. When you aimed at artificially raising the prices of manufactured goods you closed your works without turning a hair even although hundreds of workers were ruined.

Do you want proof? Your own enormous wealth and our extreme poverty—these facts speak louder than words. Our labour—the sweat of our brows and the ruin of our health—has made you rich. So it is to you that we look for redress. It is to you that we make the following demands:

(i) All factory workers dismissed since April 8 shall be reinstated at once unless it can be proved that they have violated the law.

(ii) The hours of work shall be from 6 a.m. to 6 p.m. Workers shall have half an hour for breakfast in the morning, half an hour for lunch at midday, and half an hour for coffee in the afternoon.

(iii) All overtime shall be paid for. The rate of pay shall be proportionate to normal day-rates.

(iv) If a workers clocks in late he shall either make up for lost time by working overtime or he shall forfeit a proportion of his day's pay—the money forfeited to be paid to the workers' association.

(v) The wives and children of workers absent from the factory owing to sickness shall receive half-pay for three months.

(vi) The minimum day wage of an adult worker shall be 20 silver groschens.

(vii) The authorities shall establish a board of arbitration composed of an equal number of masters and men. This board shall deal with all arbitrary actions for which either party is responsible.

We expect you to accept these demands in your own interests. Our distress is so serious that some desperate act of violence may occur. The responsibility is yours. The factory owners are asked to insert a notice in the *Cologne Gazette* within three days to fix the time and place of a meeting between the representatives of masters and men to discuss these demands.'

There were many German critics of the new factory system. Social reformers like Buss, industrialists such as Harkort, revolutionaries like Marx and Engels, and churchmen like Bishop Ketteler agreed in condemning the evils of industrialization though the remedies which they proposed were very different. As early as 1837 Franz Josef Buss, in a speech to the upper house of the Baden legislature, declared that industrial capitalism had turned the factory worker into the slave of his employer and of the machine. Factory owners had to put up with unskilled and unreliable workers. The economy suffered from periodic slumps. For society as a whole industrialization had grave drawbacks. The national income was very unevenly distributed since the new factory owners constituted "an oligarchy of wealth". The class of formerly independent craftsmen was becoming a wage-earning proletariat. There was always a danger that industrial expansion would degenerate into senseless speculation.

The Westphalian manufacturer Friedrich Harkort, writing in 1844, condemned the exploitation of child labour in factories. Parents should not have the power "to sell their children into industrial slavery". Child labour was not only immoral but had the effect of depressing the wages of adult workers. Harkort argued that the length of the working day should be fixed by law and that employers should help their workers by subsidizing friendly societies and co-operative stores. He also advocated the introduction of profit-sharing schemes so that workers could receive an annual bonus if a factory prospered.

The following year saw the appearance of a powerful indictment of the factory system. This was Friedrich Engels's book on *The Condition of the Working Class in England*.[1] Engels confined his survey to England but he warned his readers that when Germany became industrialized the German factory workers would suffer the same fate as the Lancashire operatives. Engels believed that the wretched state of the English workers would lead to an outbreak of violence against the manufacturers. The same views were expressed by Marx and Engels in the Communist Manifesto which appeared in London in February 1848. The manifesto confidently asserted that the fall of the bourgeoisie and the triumph of the proletariat were inevitable.

The governments of various German states made some attempt to improve the lot of the industrial workers. In Prussia, for example, the first Factory Law of 1839 forbade the employment of children under the age of nine. Young persons under the age of sixteen were not to work longer than ten hours a day. They were not to work at night or on Sundays or public holidays. Illiterate and semi-literate children might be employed only in works in which there was a factory school. The law applied to all factories, ironworks and mines—in contrast to the English Factory Act of 1833 which regulated work only in textile mills. A Prussian Law of 1849 provided for the payment of wages in cash and the truck system was brought to an end. A second Prussian Factory Law of 1853 provided that the minimum age of employment in factories and mines should be raised to ten in 1853, to eleven in 1854 and to twelve in 1855. Young persons under the age of fourteen were not to work for more than seven hours a day. Factory inspectors were appointed to enforce the Law of 1853.

Quite apart from State intervention something was done for the workers by more fortunately situated social classes. There were, for example, some enlightened employers who provided houses, canteens and welfare services for their workpeople. In the Ruhr W. T. Mulvany built cottages for his miners while Krupp erected houses for his steelworkers and established a large co-operative store at Essen.

---

[1] The first German edition appeared in 1845. An English translation appeared in the United States in 1887 and in Britain in 1892. A new English translation by W. O. Henderson and W. H. Chaloner was published by Basil Blackwell (Oxford) in 1958.

By 1872 Krupp had provided over a thousand dwellings for his workpeople. Reference may be made to the Elberfeld system of poor relief which was devised by the banker Daniel von der Heydt in the early 1850's. The city was divided into some three hundred and sixty districts each under the supervision of an unpaid almoner. These voluntary social workers paid regular visits to distressed families and reported on their needs to the municipal authorities. This system by which social workers co-operated with the poor law authorities was widely adopted in other German towns.

The condition of the factory workers was only one aspect—and it was by no means the most important aspect—of the "social question" in Germany between 1815 and 1870. Contemporary writers on pauperism, unemployment, housing and other social problems were concerned with distress among craftsmen, peasants and domestic servants rather than with the grievances of factory operatives. They discussed ways and means of alleviating temporary poverty caused by bad harvests, severe winters and epidemics of cholera and smallpox. The plight of handloom weavers who could not face factory competition and of small holders who could not survive the loss of common pastures and woodlands raised social problems which many contemporaries regarded as being more urgent that the evils of the factory system. The workers of Lower Silesia, whose poor living standards in the 1850's and 1860's were described by L. Jacobs in an article in the journal of the Prussian Statistical Bureau (1868) were craftsmen rather than factory hands. Prince Smith, the leader of the Free Traders in Germany, wrote an article in 1864 in which he drew attention to the fact that the most distressed workers were those least affected by industrial capitalism. He argued that it was men and women who worked with tools or primitive hand-machines in small workshops who suffered from chronic under-employment and low wages. The operatives in large factories, where efficient modern machinery had been installed, were in a much more favourable situation. And indeed the work of many of the leading social reformers in Germany in the 1850's and 1860's was directed towards improving the condition of craftsmen and peasants, small shopkeepers and domestic servants. The co-operative savings banks founded by Raiffeisen and Schulze-Delitzsch, for example, helped these classes rather than the factory workers.

Working-class distress in the middle years of the nineteenth century fostered the rise of revolutionary movements. In 1842 the *Rhenish Gazette*, edited by Karl Marx for a short time, became the focus of discontent in the Rhineland where modern industries were rapidly developing. Marx's views were far too radical for the

Prussia of that day and the young revolutionary had to leave the country. He continued his agitation in France, Belgium and England. In London Marx and his friend Engels played a leading part in founding the International Communist League and they collaborated in drawing up the Communist Manifesto. When revolutions broke out all over Germany in 1848 the committee of the Communist League went to Cologne where Marx revived his paper which was now called the *New Rhenish Gazette*. When the revolution failed the leaders of the Communist League were scattered. Marx and Engels settled in England while a number of their associates fled to America. Those who stayed behind in Cologne were brought to trial in 1852. Although the advocates for the defence were able to show that the Prussian police had gone so far as to forge documents to bolster up their accusations the jury found the prisoners guilty and they were sent to prison.

There followed a decade of reaction in Germany. It was impossible for workers to hold political meetings or to form trade unions. In the early 1860's however the constitutional conflict in Prussia was indirectly responsible for bringing about a revival of working-class agitation. The struggle between Bismarck and the lower house of the Prussian parliament (which had refused to sanction increased expenditure on defence) was widely discussed by workers in clubs and associations which had originally been formed for social or educational purposes.

Ferdinand Lassalle seized this opportunity to foster the growth of a new working-class movement in Germany. He was elected President of the General German Workers Union which was established in 1863. At that time its delegates probably represented no more than six hundred members. He introduced into Germany the technique of mass meetings of workers to foster a political cause. Lassalle's association demanded manhood suffrage. Lassalle believed that once this reform had been achieved the representatives of the workers would secure majorities in the parliaments of the various German states and then Socialist measures would easily be passed.

Lassalle's views differed from those of Marx in certain important respects. Marx believed that in a capitalist society the state was bound to wither away and that only a revolution would bring the workers into power. Lassalle saw no likelihood of the Prussian State disappearing in the 1860's. He believed that if manhood suffrage were secured the workers would dominate parliament and seize control of the administration of the State in that way. Moreover Marx held that Socialism must be a world-wide movement—he was largely concerned with the establishment in London of the International Working Men's Association (the First International of 1864)—while Lassalle considered that Socialism should begin at home. Lassalle was a patriotic German who wanted to see a united Reich as well as a Socialist Reich. Lassalle also differed from Marx in advocating the establishment of producers' co-operative societies. He held that workers should own the factories in which they were employed. He scoffed at Schulze-Delitzsch who was trying to persuade the workers to save their own money for this purpose. Lassalle argued that factory workers were far too poor to raise the capital necessary to finance a modern factory. So Lassalle demanded that the State should raise a huge loan to defray the initial cost of setting up factories to be run on the co-operative profit-sharing principle.

As a demagogue Lassalle was increasingly successful and Marx himself admitted that he "reawakened the workers' movement in Germany after fifteen years of slumber". Even Bismarck was impressed by Lassalle's agitation. At Bismarck's request Lassalle came to see him and the two strangely assorted politicians had several conversations. In 1864 at the height of his fame Lassalle was killed in a duel. The Socialist and radical groups in Germany quarrelled among themselves for a time and then in 1869 August Bebel and Wilhelm Liebknecht established the German Social Democratic Workers Party at Eisenach. The programme of the new party was based upon principles advocated by Karl Marx and the First International but included also demands for universal suffrage and State credit for co-operative factories which were policies inherited from Lassalle.

Social distress in Germany would have been much worse had it not been possible for people to emigrate. Statistics of emigration are far from reliable but it appears that about 2,500,000 Germans left their homeland between 1815 and 1870. Immediately after the Napoleonic wars (in 1816 and 1817) when there was serious distress some 200,000 emigrants left south-west Germany for the United States. In the 1820's however there were only about 8,500 emigrants. Then the number of Germans leaving the country increased rapidly. In the 1830's there were 167,000 emigrants—30,000 in the year 1830 alone—while in the 1840's the number leaped to 470,000. In the three years 1847-9, a period of economic distress and political upheavals, about 300,000 Germans migrated. Most of the migrants went to the United States and settled either in the region north of the Ohio and east of the Mississippi or in Texas. Some went to British colonies or to South America.

Between 1815 and 1850 the peak periods of migration followed bad harvest or industrial depressions. Most emigrants braved the hardships of the long Atlantic crossing to escape from dire poverty. The 1850's, on the other hand, were years of industrial expansion and economic progress—except for the commercial crisis of 1857. Nevertheless more than twice as many Germans emigrated in the ten years 1851–60 (above 1,000,000) as compared with the ten years between 1841 and 1850 (about 470,000). In the 1850's the character of the movement of population overseas was changing. It was no longer a case of desperate families escaping from hunger. The emigrants were leaving a country in which conditions were improving. They generally left because the United States appeared to offer them a still higher standard of living. In the 1860's over 800,000 Germans emigrated. Here again it was not so much bad conditions at home as golden opportunities abroad—particularly in the United States after the American civil war—that attracted Germans overseas.

## (iii) 1870–1914

### BISMARCK'S ECONOMIC POLICY, 1871–90

As Minister President of Prussia Bismarck had been too busy with political and diplomatic problems between 1862 and 1871, to give much attention to economic affairs. These he left in the hands of his ministerial colleagues and of senior officials such as Delbrück. As a Prussian landowner he was better acquainted with the traditional agrarian economy of the great estates east of the Elbe than with the new industrial economy that had sprung up in his own lifetime in the Rhineland, Westphalia and Saxony. But his visit to Alfred Krupp at Essen in October 1864 suggests that he appreciated the significance of the industrial changes that were daily increasing the wealth and power of the country. Bismarck realized the importance of the economic aspects of the Austro-Prussian struggle for supremacy in Germany. He supported the Franco-Prussian commercial treaty of 1862 with its low tariff since its acceptance by the Zollverein states would close the door on any Austrian attempt to swallow the Zollverein in a larger Austro-German customs union. He reformed the obsolete administrative structure of the Zollverein after the Seven Weeks War by abolishing the Zollverein Congress and establishing the new Customs Parliament. Only the opposition of Bavaria and Württemberg prevented him from gradually turning the Customs Parliament into a German Reichstag. Under Bismarck's guidance the North German Federation of 1867–70 had been responsible for important economic reforms such as the establishment of the German mercantile marine and the North German Post Office and the introduction of the German Industrial Code and the metric system of weights and measures.

As Chancellor of the Reich Bismarck devoted more time to economic and social questions. He believed that the economic links between the German states should be strengthened and should be used to cement political unity. He realized the influence which the central Federal governments could exercise over industrial developments through their control over the public sector of the economy. Bismarck was far in advance of many of his contemporaries in his appreciation of the nature of the social consequences of the industrial revolution. His schemes for compulsory State insurance against accidents, sickness and old age anticipated by many years the introduction of similar arrangements in other great industrial countries.

The wars which led to the unification of the Reich secured important economic advantages for Germany. The incorporation of Schleswig and Holstein gave Germany the ports of Kiel, Altona and Flensburg. It was now possible to join the North Sea and the Baltic by a canal running through German territory. The Kiel Canal was constructed between 1887 and 1895. The annexation of Alsace and Lorraine secured for Germany the largest iron-ore deposits in western Europe as well as important ironworks, engineering establishments and textile mills. The production of iron-ore in Lorraine rose from 684,600 tons in 1872 to 1,859,000 tons in 1882. Valuable deposits of potash were discovered at Wittelsheim in Alsace in 1904.

Immediately after the Franco-Prussian war there was a trade boom accompanied by a rapid rise in prices which quickly degenerated into a speculation mania. Military success led to over-confidence and numerous schemes of economic expansion were started without counting the cost. A part of the proceeds from the French indemnity soon found its way into circulation. Some of the money was spent on the construction of fortifications and barracks. Building contractors made high profits and their workers earned good wages. Some of the money was used to repay war loans. Many investors now purchased speculative industrial shares rather than safe government stock. There was a great boom in the iron trade and in allied industries owing to an almost world-wide demand for rails, locomotives and engineering equipment. The building trades also experienced a boom since factories, houses and military establishments were being erected. The Company Law passed by the North German Reichstag in 1870 simplified the method of setting up joint-stock companies, but gave no proper protection to shareholders. Between 1871 and 1873 over 900 new companies were established in Germany.

The crash came in 1873, when numerous companies collapsed. Over 200 blast furnaces were idle in 1876. Dr. Strousberg, one of the leading promoters at that time, became the scapegoat for the follies of many people who had tried to get rich quickly by dubious methods. The slump in business and the fall in prices that followed the boom of 1871–3 turned Bismarck's attention to economic and social problems. To some extent the nationalizing of Prussia's private railways, the return to the fiscal policy of Protection, and the establishment of State welfare services were all aspects of Bismarck's efforts to bring about economic recovery after the depression.

The constitution of the new Reich gave extensive economic powers to the central authority. It had the right (formerly exercised by the Zollverein) to fix the tariff and to negotiate commercial and navigation treaties with foreign countries. The central government was also responsible for the imposition of excise duties; the appointment of consuls abroad; the regulation of the currency, banking, weights and measures and industrial relations. On the other hand the Federal States retained some powers in the economic sphere. Direct taxes, transport, technical education, and (in the southern states) the post office and telegraphs were still the concern of the federal governments and not of the central authority. Moreover the Free Cities of Hamburg and Bremen remained outside the customs area of the Reich until 1888.

The new powers to regulate important aspects of the country's economy were soon exercised by the Government of the Reich. By the Currency Law of 1873 the mark (divided into 100 pfennigs) replaced the thaler, gulden and various other coins. The gold standard was introduced at the same time. Business men and economists had urged the Government to make this change. The old silver standard had sometimes not worked well since from time to time there had been balance of payments difficulties owing to the "drain" of silver coins to the Far East. The fact that Britain, the leading industrial country at that time, had found the gold standard satisfactory was an argument in favour of its adoption in Germany. Increased supplies of gold from Australia and California—coupled with the gold available from the French indemnity—made it possible to adopt the new standard in the 1870's. In 1875 a national bank was established. This was the Reichsbank which absorbed the Bank of Prussia. It had an initial capital of 182 million marks. Immediately afterwards thirteen banks relinquished their right to issue notes. By 1914 the only banks, other than the Reichsbank, to issue notes were the State banks of Bavaria, Württemberg, Baden and Saxony. Other important economic reforms in the years immediately following the unification of Germany were the Trade Mark Law of 1874 and the Patent Law of 1877.

One of Bismarck's most ambitious projects was his plan to bring the entire German railway system under the ownership of the Reich. He believed that nationalization would greatly increase the efficiency of the railways and that the Reich would benefit both from an economic and from a military point of view. When the Reich was established there were over sixty independent railway administrations in Germany. The railway network in 1875 was 27,956 km. in length. Some lines were owned and operated by the various federal states (12,062 km.); some were private railways (12,641 km.); and some were lines which were privately owned but were operated by one of the federal railway administrations (3,253 km.). The south German states—Bavaria, Württemberg and Baden—had nationalized most of their lines. In Prussia over half the lines (9,183 km.) were in private hands. The rest were either nationalized lines (4,281 km.) or private railways under State administration (2,736 km.). The railways of Alsace–Lorraine were the property of the Reich. Among the many drawbacks caused by the multiplicity of railway administrations was the existence of no fewer than 1,400 different freight-tariffs.

The commercial crisis of 1873 led to a drop in railway receipts and a decline in the value of railway shares. Business men protested when freight rates were raised by twenty per cent. A Reich Railway Office was set up under Maybach in June 1873 to administer the Alsace–Lorraine railways, to enforce the carrying out by all railway administrations of their legal duties, and to prepare draft laws for the consideration of the Reichstag. In March 1874 and in April 1875 two memoranda on railway reform were prepared by the Railway Office which aimed at strengthening the powers of the Government of the Reich over the railway network without actually nationalizing the lines. Even these modest proposals were so severely criticized that they were never submitted to the Reichstag.

At a parliamentary reception on December 11, 1875, Bismarck discussed his plans for the establishment of a nationalized Reich railway system. The scheme received wide publicity in the press. Immediately there were vigorous protests in the parliaments of Württemberg, Bavaria and Saxony. In these circumstances Bismarck realized that it would be useless to submit his plan to the Reichstag. In 1876 the Prussian parliament passed a law authorizing the Prussian Government to negotiate with the Reich for the sale of the Prussian State Railways to the Reich. This Law, however, remained a dead letter. In 1877 the German railway administrations agreed upon the establishment of common principles in fixing freight rates.

Discussions concerning the future of the German railways were revived in 1879 when another slump made it essential to increase railway efficiency as well as reduce freight charges. Bismarck appreciated that, in view of what happened three years previously, it would not be possible for the Reich to acquire effective control over the railway network. He decided therefore to nationalize as many private lines in Prussia as possible. In October 1879 a draft Law was presented to the Prussian parliament to nationalize the Berlin–Stettin, the Berlin–Magdeburg, the Magdeburg–Halberstadt, the Hanover–Altenbeken, the Cologne–Minden, the Deutz–Giessen and the Rhenish railways. The total length of these lines was 5,000 km. At the same time Bismarck issued a memorandum in which he drew attention to the disadvantages of the existing situation. He declared that since there were so many private lines in Prussia the cost of running the railways was very high. There were a large number of directors, managers and officials who all had to be paid. There was an unnecessary duplication of lines, stations and rolling stock. There were still too many different freight tariffs and both passenger and freight suffered from excessive competition. Maybach, the Prussian Minister of Public Works between 1878 and 1891, had been responsible for carrying through the negotiations with the railways concerned and in the years that followed he was able to nationalize many more Prussian lines. In 1882 another 3,145 km. of private lines and in 1884 a further ten private railway companies (3,766 km.) were nationalized by the Prussian Government. In 1897 Prussia and Hesse-Darmstadt came to an agreement to nationalize the Ludwig Railway and to operate it jointly.

By 1914 nearly all the Prussian railways were owned by the State. There were seven State railway networks in Germany administered by the governments of Prussia, Bavaria, Saxony, Württemberg, Baden, Mecklenburg-Schwerin, and Oldenburg. Only a few lines (about 3,000 km.) were still in private hands. The various State railways in Germany were all prosperous. In 1917 they made a profit of 786 million marks. In 1919 the policy advocated by Bismarck in 1876 was at last carried out. Under the Weimar Constitution the entire railway network was acquired by the Reich.

The trade depression of the 1870's which aggravated the railway problem also had significant effects upon fiscal policy. It was one of the reasons for the return to Protection. As early as 1818 the Maassen tariff had been the most liberal in Europe. In 1862 the Franco–Prussian commercial treaty had substantially lowered the Zollverein import duties. But in the 1870's the situation was changing. It was clear that in France the Third Republic was reversing the liberal fiscal policy of the Second Empire. In the negotiations for a peace treaty in 1871 the French had declined to renew the commercial treaty of 1862. So by Article XI of the Treaty of Frankfurt Franco–German trade was simply placed permanently on a most-favoured-nation basis.[1] Russia and Austria-Hungary had highly protective tariffs. Germany was surrounded by states which levied far higher import duties than her own. Only Britain and some of the smaller continental countries remained faithful to Free Trade. In Germany the depressed condition of trade stimulated demands for the raising of import duties. The Central Union of German Industrialists was established in 1876 to agitate for a reform of the tariff to protect the home market. A petition, with 60,000 signatures, urged the Government to maintain the iron duties due to expire in 1877. Some of the great landowners, too, were changing their traditional views on fiscal policy. So long as Germany—particularly Germany east of the Elbe —was a great exporter of cereals the agrarian interest had favoured Free Trade. In the 1870's the German farmers lost their old grain markets in Britain and France to American competitors. Moreover cereals from the United States, Russia, Hungary and the Argentino were being imported into Germany. Grain prices in Germany fell after 1873. In the circumstances the great landowners—after some initial hesitation—threw in their lot with the industrialists and demanded a return to Protection.

Bismarck had for many years accepted the Free Trade views of the Prussian landowners. But changing economic circumstances led him to alter his views. He was particularly interested in the financial side of the question. The revenues of the Reich were derived partly from customs and excise and partly from annual contributions paid by the various federal governments who were responsible for direct taxation. Bismarck disliked a situation in which the Reich was to some extent financially dependent upon grants from the federal states. The expenses of the Reich were increasing. Money had to be found for additional expenditure on defence and also for the projected welfare services. In the circumstances Bismarck favoured an increase in tariff rates so that the Reich's revenues might be increased. Moreover he felt that those who paid direct taxes were having to bear too heavy a burden. He told the Reichstag at this time that only

[1] Normally a most-favoured-nation clause refers to trade with all countries. But Article XI of the Treaty of Frankfurt limited most-favoured-nation treatment to concessions made by either party to the following countries: Great Britain, Russia, Austria-Hungary, Holland, Belgium and Switzerland.

between 3,000 and 4,000 owners of estates in Prussia could be described as prosperous. The others were struggling to pay off mortgages and were finding it very difficult to pay their taxes. He thought that it was time that those who paid indirect taxes should henceforth contribute more to the finances of the Reich.

In the general election of 1878 over two hundred members were returned to the Reichstag pledged to support Protection. A new Tariff Law secured its third reading in the Reichstag in July 1879. The rates of duty levied were still relatively low and there was a free list which included raw cotton and wool, scientific instruments and ships. A number of duties were fixed at the rate in force in 1865 before the reductions made by the Franco-Prussian agreement of 1862 came into force. The new duties on cereals, too, were low— one mark per 100 kgm. on wheat, rye and oats. On the other hand fairly high revenue duties were placed upon coffee, tea, tobacco, petrol and spirits.

An amendment to the Tariff Law—proposed by Freiherr zu Frankenstein—placed a limit upon the amount of customs revenue to be retained by the Reich. If the customs revenue exceeded one hundred and eighty million marks the surplus was to be divided among the federal states in proportion to their population. This clause denied to the Reich some of the financial advantages which Bismarck had hoped to secure by increasing the level of import duties.

In 1885 and again in 1887 the tariff was revised and import duties on cereals, cattle, wool and brandy were increased. In 1890 Caprivi, Bismarck's successor as Chancellor, was responsible for negotiating new commercial treaties with Austria–Hungary, Italy and Belgium. A similar treaty of 1894 ended a tariff war with Russia. There was now an "autonomous" tariff which governed trade with countries having no commercial treaty and no most-favoured-nation agreement with Germany. There were also various tariffs having lower rates of import duties than those in the autonomous tariff. These lower rates were included in commercial treaties. Such concessions were automatically passed on to countries which had signed most-favoured-nation agreements with Germany. Farmers complained that tariff concessions had been made at their expense and in 1893 they formed a powerful association (*Bund der Landwirte*) to act as a pressure group to defend their interests.

The raising of the tariff coupled with an increase in imports enabled the Reich to raise more money from customs duties than before. Between 1878 and 1890 the revenue from import duties rose from 2·62 marks to 7·86 marks per head of the population. It is not possible to determine the extent to which the return to Protection contributed to the growth of Germany's international trade between 1880 and 1914. Many factors played their part in bringing about a great expansion of overseas commerce and the fiscal policy adopted by Bismarck in 1879 was not necessarily the most important. Free Traders argued that Germany would have been even more prosperous if she had maintained the tariff in force in 1878. They pointed out that as far as farming was concerned the new duties on cereals and meat did not save German agriculture from declining in the last quarter of the nineteenth century. Socialists complained that the new import duties pushed up the cost of living for the workers. The cost of living remained fairly steady in Germany in the last quarter of the nineteenth century. The policy of Protection appears to have acted as a stabilizing influence and Germany did not experience the same heavy fall in prices as occurred in Britain at that time. Prices in Germany rose, however, between 1900 and 1913. On the whole increases in prices were balanced by increases in wages. The average daily wages at the Krupp works in Essen, for example, rose from 3 marks in 1871 to over 4 marks 75 pfennigs in 1900.

A few years after Bismarck had carried the new tariff through the Reichstag he embarked upon another project in the hope of strengthening Germany's industrial position. This was the establishment of a colonial empire. For many years Bismarck had opposed the acquisition of overseas possessions. In 1871 he had declared that "for Germany to acquire colonies would be like a poverty-stricken Polish nobleman providing himself with silks and sables when he needed shirts". But in the early 1880's Bismarck began to appreciate the force of the arguments of those who favoured the establishment of overseas possessions. Germany was becoming a great industrial state and her manufacturers were seeking new overseas markets and new sources of supply for tropical and sub-tropical raw materials. Between 1881 and 1890 the excess of births over deaths amounted to 551,300 and 134,200 Germans emigrated. If territories suitable for white settlement could be secured some of the emigrants might continue to live under the German flag. There were also complaints that Germans who traded overseas suffered from lack of Imperial protection. The expropriation by the British of German settlers in Fiji was a case in point.

In various parts of Africa and in the Pacific the Germans had already built up substantial commercial and maritime interests. Hansing & Co. and other German firms had been established for many years in Zanzibar—the centre of commerce for all East Africa

—and in 1870 they handled rather more than one-fifth of the island's trade.

The firm of Woermann traded successfully in the Cameroons and in Gaboon and maintained a service of packet ships between Hamburg and the West African coast. Vietor Sons of Bremen traded in Togoland. In the Pacific J. C. Godeffroy & Son had secured a virtual monopoly of the Samoa copra trade, but the firm failed in 1879. Bismarck proposed that the Reich should subsidize a new company to take over Godeffroy's widespread interests in the Pacific so as to prevent them from falling into English hands. The Reichstag, however, rejected the plan. Eventually two German banks gave financial support to a company which was formed to take over Godeffroy's business.

Thus in Zanzibar, Samoa, and the Cameroons there was a firm foundation upon which colonial enterprise could be built. There were of course others—German explorers and missionaries for example—who had also done invaluable pioneer work in regions which eventually became German colonies. And had it not been for the exploits of adventurers like Carl Peters in East Africa and Adolf Lüderitz in South West Africa the German flag might never have flown over large regions in Africa. But to secure foreign recognition of Germany's colonial claims was not the work of the men on the spot. It was the achievement of Bismarck at the conference table in Europe.

In 1884 Bismarck placed under imperial protection Adolf Lüderitz's commercial undertakings in the Namaqualand harbour of Angra Pequena. In six years Germany acquired colonies in Africa (South West and East Africa, the Cameroons and Togoland) and in the Pacific (Kaiser Wilhelmsland in New Guinea and several islands in the Bismarck Archipelago). A few extensions of territory were made after Bismarck's retirement—such as a naval base in China in 1898 —and in 1914 Germany had a colonial empire over a million square miles in extent with an estimated population of some fourteen millions.

From the first Bismarck stressed the commercial significance of the new colonial territories. He desired to avoid the expense of governing colonies and wished merely to "protect" chartered companies which should themselves administer territories overseas. In June 1884 he told the Reichstag: "I would follow the example of England in granting to these merchants something like Royal Charters . . . I do not wish to found provinces, but to protect commercial establishments in their own development . . . We hope that the tree will flourish in proportion to the activity of the gardener but if it does not, the whole responsibility rests with him and not with the Reich, which will lose nothing."

Unfortunately the merchants who traded in Africa and the South Seas were not prepared to accept the role that Bismarck had designed for them. The German firms in business at Zanzibar and on the west coast of Africa refused to have anything to do with Bismarck's schemes for the establishment of chartered companies with sovereign rights. No companies enjoying such powers were ever set up in the Cameroons, Togoland or South West Africa. It was only with considerable difficulty that a company was induced to accept sovereign powers in New Guinea and that the Jaluit Company was persuaded to pay the costs of administering the Marshall Islands. In East Africa a charter was originally given not to a trading company but to a penniless private colonization society.

This was no auspicious inauguration of a policy of colonial government by chartered companies. Bismarck's plan failed completely. The chartered companies operating in East Africa and New Guinea had surrendered their administrative functions by 1890 and the Jaluit Company followed suit in 1906. The South West Africa Company never accepted a charter and soon gave up the few administrative functions which it had exercised. The responsibility and cost of conquering and ruling the colonial empire fell upon the Reich. The failure of Bismarck's plans had unfortunate results since the former chartered companies survived as commercial companies which enjoyed special privileges. They secured large grants of land and received exclusive rights to build railways and to exploit mines. They received cash payments in return for giving up administrative functions which had sometimes been exercised for only a very short time. Moreover several companies which had never enjoyed administrative powers secured substantial concessions. In South West Africa, for example, nine companies owned nearly one-third of the land in 1903.

The economic development of Germany's overseas possessions was somewhat disappointing. By 1913 deficits on colonial budgets had cost the German taxpayer over a thousand million marks and only Togoland and Samoa were self-supporting. Neither as reservoirs of raw materials nor as markets for manufactured goods did the colonies play a very significant part in Germany's economic life. In 1913 the colonial trade of the Reich amounted to a mere half of one per cent of her total trade. At this time there were only 24,000 Germans in the colonies, many of whom were officials and not permanent residents.

Bismarck hoped that the adoption of Protection and the founding of colonies would reconcile the industrialists to the financial burdens of the social services which he proposed to set up. In the 1880's Germany was confronted with a more serious "social question" than in the 1860's. Social distress had followed in the wake of industrialization. Wage increases gained in the short boom of 1871–3 were soon lost again in the depression that followed. Poor law authorities and charitable organizations fought an uphill battle against the effects of low wages, unemployment, sickness and bad housing. In many of the rapidly growing mining towns in the Ruhr, for example, conditions were very unsatisfactory. Even in 1900 about seventeen per cent of the inhabitants of Essen lived in attics. Some migrants when they reached the Ruhr looking for work could find no accommodation in the towns and had to live in barns and byres in the rural parts of the district. One writer states that in 1895 well over a hundred people were crammed into a ramshackle barn where they were disgracefully overcrowded and shared two wretched privies. The towns and industrial regions were less healthy than the countryside. The number of recruits unfit for military service was much larger in the towns than in the rural districts.

Few workers could save enough money to face the loss of wages that followed absence from work owing to an illness or an accident. Many old people did not have enough to live on and were dependent upon their children. Efforts had been made by friendly societies and by savings banks to help people to save money. In 1874 Prussia had 5,000 friendly societies with 800,000 members. Some enlightened employers were providing admirable welfare services for their workers. Bismarck realized that, owing to the magnitude of the problem, State intervention was essential.

Moreover Bismarck's policy concerning the provision of welfare services was part of his campaign to wean the workers from the Socialist party which had grown considerably since the days of Lassalle's agitation. In the first Reichstag to be elected after German unity had been achieved two seats went to the Socialists. The discontent of the workers at the time of the commercial crisis of 1873 strengthened the Socialists and in the following year they gained ten seats in the Reichstag. In 1875 the two wings of the party—those who supported the Eisenach programme of 1869 and those who accepted Lassalle's policy—came together at Gotha and a new Socialist party was established. Its programme was a compromise between the views of the two groups—a compromise which Marx vigorously attacked. In the Reichstag elections of 1877 the Socialists polled nearly half a million votes and gained twelve seats.

The Government tried to check the growing strength of the

Socialist party. Employers were warned by the Prussian Minister of Commerce against giving employment to Socialists. In 1876 the party was dissolved under the Coalition Law but the activities of individual members could not be restricted under this enactment. The civil law offence of "insulting royalty" was also used to harass the Socialists. Two attempts on the Kaiser's life in 1878 aroused public opinion against the Socialists although there was no evidence that they were responsible. The Reichstag elected in the previous year was dissolved and at the new elections the two Conservative parties gained seats at the expense of the National Liberals and the Progressives. The new Reichstag promptly passed a law similar to one recently rejected by the old Reichstag. This was the "Exceptional Law against the universally dangerous endeavours of Social Democracy" which banned the Socialist party and prohibited all its political activities. Fifty Socialist newspapers were suppressed. A state of minor siege was proclaimed in Berlin and some other large cities. The Socialist party was driven underground. Its vote had fallen at the elections of 1878 and fell again in 1881. But subsequently the votes cast for the Socialists increased at a surprising rate. It may be added that the Exceptional Law could not be used against members of the Reichstag so that the Socialist leaders Bebel and Liebknecht[1] were able to attack Bismarck with impunity in the Reichstag. Having used the stick on the Socialist donkey with little success Bismarck proceeded to try the effect of a few carrots. He presented to the Reichstag schemes for compulsory State insurance against sickness, accidents and old age—plans far in advance of any welfare schemes in other industrial countries. At first Bismarck proposed that the money to pay for these services should be raised by means of a tobacco monopoly. This scheme was rejected by the Reichstag and other methods of financing the insurance schemes had to be devised.

The Health Insurance Law of 1883 compulsorily insured factory workers, miners and the lower paid black-coated workers. Subsequent legislation extended the scheme to farm workers, craftsmen, apprentices and casual workers. By 1889 over five and a half million persons were included in the scheme.[2] Certain persons were exempted from the Law of 1883 because they were already covered by the schemes operated by the Reich, the federal states or municipalities.

[1] There were two Liebknechts, father and son, who were both Socialist leaders in Germany. Wilhelm Liebknecht was one of the first Socialist deputies to sit in the North German Reichstag of 1867–70. He was the editor of *Vorwärts*. His son Karl became a leader of the Spartakists (Communists) in 1918 and was shot during the Berlin rising of January 1919.

[2] This figure excludes members of friendly societies attached to miners' gilds.

The scheme was operated through friendly societies. A worker (liable to compulsory insurance) had to join such a society but he was not required to join any particular society. Both contributions and benefits varied from one society to another. Normally two-thirds of the contribution was paid by the worker and one-third by his employer. Self-employed persons and voluntary members paid the full contribution themselves. Benefits generally included free medical attention and a weekly payment during the period of sickness.

The Accident Insurance Law of 1884 covered over thirteen million persons (in 1889). Employers had to pay the whole cost of insuring workers against accidents. Associations of employers, established on a regional basis, were required to raise from their members the money needed to meet all claims. If a worker died after an accident—and 15·6 per cent of industrial accidents were fatal in 1888—his widow received a burial grant, a weekly pension and an allowance for each dependent child.

The scheme for old age and disability pensions, passed in 1889, covered factory workers, miners and some black-coated workers. Certain small employers and independent craftsmen could join as voluntary members. The pensions fund was made up of equal contributions from employers and workpeople to which was added a Government grant of fifty marks a year in respect of each insured person. The cost of the Reich subsidy was between five and six million marks when the scheme started. An old age pension was paid at the age of seventy while a disability pension was paid if a worker became incapacitated. In 1899 the contribution from the Reich was increased and widows and orphans were covered by the scheme.

In 1899 the Italian economist Professor Luzzatti described Bismarck's achievement as "une oeuvre gigantesque forgée au marteau d'un cyclope social" and other foreign observers echoed his sentiments. But in Germany the introduction of the welfare schemes met with considerable criticisms. Employers complained of the financial burden placed upon industry. Accident claims amounting to nearly fourteen and a half million marks were paid in 1889, a charge which fell wholly upon the employers. In the same year employers paid 300,000 marks in safety precautions to prevent accidents. Employers contributed one-third of the fund from which sickness benefits—seventy-one million marks in 1889—were paid. The Socialists, on the other hand, argued that the workers' contributions to the health and old age schemes were too high and that the benefits were too low. They suggested that the old age pension should be paid at the age of sixty-five since few "wage slaves" ever reached the age of three-score and ten after a life-time of "capitalist exploitation". And if a worker did live to celebrate his seventieth birthday his pension of about one hundred and twenty-five marks a year could only be described as a miserable pittance. Despite these criticisms Bismarck's welfare schemes eventually achieved their main aim. They gave German workers a feeling of security. If a workman had an accident or fell ill his family was no longer plunged into poverty. The health of the workers improved. They enjoyed a higher standard of living, better housing conditions, improved sanitation and more thorough medical attention. The death rate declined from 27·2 per 1,000 (excluding stillbirths) in the 1870's to 16·2 in 1910. Eventually other industrial countries adopted schemes very similar to those adopted in Germany between 1884 and 1889.

The welfare services, however, failed to wean the German workers from Socialism. At the Reichstag general elections the Socialist vote rose from half a million in 1884 to one and a half millions in 1890. The Socialists strengthened their position by controlling not only an important group of trade unions but also some of the friendly societies called into existence by Bismarck's health scheme. Soon after Bismarck's fall the Exceptional Law against the Socialists was allowed to lapse. Although the governing classes were forced to accept the fact that the Socialist party had come to stay they still treated members of the Social Democratic Party as second-class citizens. As far as possible members of the party were barred from the public service and the professions. Professor Bernard Harms remarked that "it has been truthfully said that in Germany a Social Democrat cannot even become a night watchman". The rapid growth of the Socialist party after 1890 was accompanied by sharp ideological differences between the Marxists and the Revisionists. Bernstein, the leader of the Revisionists, argued that —contrary to what Marx had said—the continued expansion of the capitalist system was not causing a reduction in the number of the capitalists and was not leading to increased social misery. In fact the number of capitalists was growing and the condition of the workers was improving. Bernstein believed that the Socialists should cease to be a revolutionary party and should promote the interests of the workers by constitutional means. His views, however, were rejected by the party congress in 1903. The Socialists suffered only a temporary setback at the Reichstag elections of 1907. Three years later they achieved their greatest triumph when they gained 110 seats and became the largest party in the Reichstag. But they remained a party in permanent opposition. Unlike the French Socialists they never held ministerial office at this time. Meanwhile the Socialist—or "free"—trade unions were growing stronger every day. Their membership rose from 250,000 in 1895 to 2,000,000 in 1910 and they embraced over four-fifths of all organized labour.

## CARTELS

In the middle of the nineteenth century industrialization had been fostered in Germany by the development of joint-stock companies. After 1870 industrial undertakings continually expanded. Sometimes a big firm such as Krupp grew still bigger. Sometimes expansion was brought about by amalgamation of firms which had formerly competed with each other. As early as 1836 for example several coal-mining enterprises had joined together to form the United Wurm Collieries. The growth of large-scale industry may be seen from the fact that the number of really big concerns, with a capital of over ten million marks each, increased from 74 in 1886 to 229 in 1909. In the Ruhr in 1893 the ten largest colliery companies produced 14·3 million tons of coal which was 36·6 per cent of the total production of the coal-field. In 1910 the ten largest colliery companies had an output of 49 million tons and this represented 59·3 per cent of the entire production of the Ruhr.

The great industrial companies not only grew bigger but they drew more closely together by forming associations called "cartels". Cut-throat competition began to give way to a measure of co-operation. Cartels sometimes developed from earlier unions of employers which had been formed to safeguard common interests by agitating for tariffs, lower freight rates and so forth.

There were four main types of cartels. First, there were agreements to share the market. Certain regions or customers were allocated to particular cartel members. Secondly, there were agreements which fixed prices for sales at home and abroad. Thirdly, there were agreements which fixed the total volume of production of the cartel firms. Each member of the cartel was allocated a quota of this output. Finally, there were profit-sharing agreements known as "interest groups" or—in the shipping industry—as "pools".

There were also differences between horizontal and vertical cartels. The former were associations of companies producing the same type of raw materials or manufactured goods, while the latter united firms engaged in different stages of production from the raw material to the finished articles. Cartels sometimes developed into trusts (a holding company linking the firms concerned) or even into complete mergers. Thus the profit-sharing cartel formed in 1904 between the Gelsenkirchen Mining Company, the *Rote Erde* ironworks at Aachen, and the Schalk Mining & Smelting Company was followed in 1907 by the amalgamation of the three companies.

The earliest German cartel was the Neckar Salt Union of 1828. It included the nationalized saltworks of Württemberg and Baden and a private salt mine at Ludwigshalle. In 1836 the Prussian Overseas Trading Corporation (*Seehandlung*) came to an agreement with all the alum works in Prussia—the State works at Freienwalde and Schwemsal and the private works at Muskau and Gleissen—to purchase the whole of their output. This agreement lasted until 1844. In the 1840's the Oberlahnstein Association was established to control the sale of pig-iron produced in Nassau.

A number of cartels were established during the slump that began in 1873. Cartel agreements offered hard-pressed firms the possibility of improving their chances of survival at this highly critical time. Some economists have argued that cartels are always the offspring of trade depressions. This is not so. Many different factors influenced the formation of cartels and a considerable number were established when trade was booming. Sometimes the raising of import duties encouraged the establishment of cartels since firms hoped to exploit to the full the new opportunities of expanding their sales in a protected home market. Shortly after Germany's return to Protection in 1879 a number of cartels were set up including eighteen in the iron industry alone.

Sometimes the possession of a natural monopoly—the Stassfurt and Wittelsheim potash deposits for example—led to the formation of a cartel so as to secure higher prices at home and abroad. Some cartels were formed to exploit newly patented inventions. And in certain relatively new branches of industry—such as the chemical and electrical industries—only an association of firms could meet the high cost of maintaining modern research laboratories.

One of the most serious criticisms made against cartels was that they charged the home consumer higher prices than the foreign consumer. This had already been done by some large firms even before many cartels had been formed. It appears from evidence submitted in 1878 to the official inquiry into the iron industry that the Bochum Union ironworks had sold rails abroad at 115 marks per ton although costs of production were 130 marks per ton. In May 1879 Eugen Richter, speaking in the Reichstag, criticized the builders of locomotives and the manufacturers of rails for selling more cheaply abroad than at home. It has been stated that at one time Germans were actually being charged 17 marks a ton for coal that was being sold in Austria at 8 marks a ton. In 1900 the price of wire was 185 marks a ton in Germany but only 115 marks a ton abroad.

When trade was slack between 1900 and 1902 the rail cartel sold its products at 250 marks a ton in the home market and at 140 marks a ton abroad. Nevertheless there was no public outcry against cartels in Germany as there had been in the United States against trusts. There was no anti-trust legislation in Germany where the law treated cartel agreements in the same way as any other private contracts. The Government sympathized with a development in industrial organization which increased efficiency and strengthened German manufacturers in their efforts to capture new markets abroad. It was appreciated too that if the State wished at any time to control—or even to nationalize—an industry it would be easier to do so if the industry were already dominated by a cartel. It was not until 1923 that an edict was issued against the misuse of economic power but this does not appear to have hampered the expansion of cartels.

The early cartels in the 1870's were mainly in the heavy industries but the new type of industrial organization soon began to spread to other branches of manufacture such as plate-glass, cement and certain chemicals. The Gas-Coal Association was set up in 1879, the Potash Syndicate in 1881 and the Rhenish-Westphalian Coal Syndicate in 1893. The year 1904 saw the establishment of the Steelworks Association and two great cartels in the chemical industry. The number of cartels in Germany increased from four in 1865 to eight in 1875, ninety in 1885, two hundred and ten in 1890 and nearly four hundred in 1905. By the beginning of the twentieth century German firms were already taking part in international cartels and shipping pools. In 1883, for example, German manufacturers co-operated with British and Belgian firms to set up the International Railmakers Association and in 1892 the North German Lloyd and the Hamburg-Amerika line joined the shipping pool known as the North Atlantic Steamship Lines Association.

As an illustration of the establishment and working of cartels a brief description may be given of the activities of the Rhenish-Westphalian Coal Syndicate. It has been seen that a Ruhr Mine-owners Association had been established in 1858. By working together in this association the mine-owners of the Ruhr had learned to co-operate to promote their common interests. During the great depression of the 1870's coal prices fell and profits vanished. In 1876 losses amounting to 12·8 million marks were sustained by 109 Ruhr coal companies. Colliery owners tried to meet the situation by making agreements to restrict output, to fix prices and to share markets. Various attempts between 1878 and 1886 to restrict output failed. Marketing agreements too had little success at this time either because they were too limited in scope (such as the Bochum Sales

Association and the Briquette Sales Association) or because there were too many violations of the agreement (as in the case of the Mining Union of 1890). Price agreements concerning particular types of fuel—such as the Gas-Coal Association and the Coke-Coal Association—were more successful.

After fifteen years of experiments in controlling the Ruhr coal-mining industry the colliery owners made two agreements in 1893. The first was a cartel agreement designed to regulate output, prices and sales. The second set up a new company called the Rhenish-Wesphalian Coal Syndicate. The capital was provided by the collieries which had signed the trust agreement. It was formed to buy and sell coal, coke and briquettes. In 1904 the functions of the syndicate were extended to include "the preparation of coal for the market and the acquisition of coal-lands and mining installations, the conduct of such undertakings as might aid in the storage, sale and transport of coal". The Syndicate controlled eighty-six per cent of the coal produced in the Ruhr in 1893. Each colliery firm which joined the cartel was given a production quota based upon its output in 1891–2. It had to deliver all its coal (with certain exceptions) to the Syndicate and all orders for coal had to be passed on to the Syndicate.

Between 1893 and 1914 the Syndicate came to be dominated by the larger concerns. Membership declined from ninety-six in 1893 to sixty-two in 1914. Over one-third of the output in 1904 came from the six largest companies. It may be added that a high proportion of the coal handled by the Syndicate—about seventy per cent—was used directly for industrial purposes.

When the Syndicate was first established nearly all of its members were purely coal-mining concerns. Most of the Ruhr steel companies which owned collieries did not join the Syndicate since they normally consumed all the fuel which their mines produced. Subsequently the output of these "tied" mines expanded and by 1900 it amounted to one-fifth of the total output of the Ruhr. Coal which was surplus to the requirements of the steel-plants was sold on the open market —sometimes at a price lower than that fixed by the Syndicate. In 1899 the steel companies which owned collieries joined the Syndicate on terms very favourable to themselves.

There were significant reactions on the part of wholesale and retail coal merchants and of large and small coal consumers to the price-maintenance policy of the Syndicate. Wholesale coal merchants and carriers soon formed associations of their own. The Syndicate, however, was generally represented on the boards of directors of these associations. Retailers formed associations to purchase and store coal on a co-operative basis. Finally coal consumers large and small took action to safeguard their interests. Many large consumers —not only steelworks but chemical companies, shipping firms and large municipalities—purchased coal-mines so as to be independent of the Syndicate. Householders often joined co-operative societies which handled large quantities of coal for sale to the general public.

On the whole the policy of the Syndicate was successful in eliminating seasonal variations in the output of coal and in substantially reducing the effects of cyclical fluctuations. From time to time the Syndicate was able to sell abroad stocks of coal which might otherwise have accumulated at the pithead and so caused a decline in output. Between 1893 and 1913 the Syndicate gradually raised coal prices from 7·50 marks per ton to 12 marks per ton. It was not possible to secure a more substantial price increase than this owing to the competition from other fuels and from power plants. The higher prices benefited the coal-miners and their wages rose more rapidly than coal prices.

## THE GREAT BANKS

The banks played a vitally important part in promoting the rapid expansion of German industry and trade. Between 1850 and 1870 the notes of the banks of issue increased the amount of money in circulation. The volume of bank notes in Germany increased from about 120 million marks in the early 1850's to 1,352 million marks in 1873. After the establishment of the Reichsbank in 1875 a number of banks gave up their right to issue notes.

In the two boom periods of the early 1850's and the early 1870's many joint-stock credit banks were established. Among the more important institutions founded in the earlier period were the Schaaffhausen Bank (Cologne), the Darmstadt Bank, the Discount Company (Berlin) and the Commercial Company of Berlin. In the latter period came the Deutsche Bank and the Dresden Bank. These banks, and many others, handled bills of exchange and made loans to industry. But they went much further than this. They helped to place the shares of new companies on the market. To secure the confidence of the investing public the banks took up blocks of shares themselves. The banks were often represented on the boards of directors of business firms. In this way the banks were intimately concerned with the progress of industrial and commercial enterprises.

Just as joint-stock companies expanded and became linked in cartels so great banks emerged which held a dominant position in German finance and industry. There were numerous bank mergers. The larger banks acquired a controlling interest in smaller private banks, joint-stock banks and savings banks. There were agreements between banks to exchange blocks of shares. By these means—and by other arrangements—great associations of banks were established. In 1908 the six major banks—other than the Reichsbank and a few federal State banks—were the Deutsche Bank, the Discount Company, the Schaaffhausen Bank, the Darmstadt Bank and the Commercial Company of Berlin. The largest was the Deutsche Bank with share-capital and reserves of over 300 million marks. A dozen major banks were associated with the Deutsche Bank. The capital of the whole Deutsche Bank group was 588 million marks and reserves amounted to 197 million marks. The total capital and reserves of the six great banks and their associated houses was over 2,500 million marks.

There were also groups of banks which regularly co-operated to raise public loans. A separate "consortium" of banks was set up for each loan but many financial houses appeared again and again in associations which were formed for this purpose. There was a Prussian Consortium, led by the Overseas Trading Corporation (*Seehandlung*) which was responsible for placing Prussian State loans on the market. The first occasion on which several banks co-operated for this purpose was when a loan was raised in connexion with the mobilization of the army at the time of the Italian war of 1859. There was a Reich Consortium, led by the Reichsbank, to handle Imperial loans. The Rothschild Consortium, to which several German banks belonged, raised loans for the Government of Austria-Hungary.

One way in which the joint-stock banks influenced the expansion of the German economy may be illustrated by examining the part played by the banks in bringing about the establishment of mergers and cartels in various industries. Bankers were very active in the coal and iron industries. The Darmstadt Bank, for example, stood behind the Deutsch-Luxemburg Mining and Iron-smelting Company. The Schaaffhausen Bank owned a majority of the shares of the *Internationale Bohrgesellschaft* and also operated the sales office and accounts office of the Union of German Wire Manufacturers. In 1904 the Commercial Company of Berlin and the finance house of S. Bleichröder successfully resisted an attempt by the Prussian Treasury to nationalize the Hibernia coal-mining company in the Ruhr. The banker Carl Fürstenberg declared that this was the greatest triumph of his career.

The electrical industry, too, owed a great deal to the financial support of the banks. In 1883 a group of banks supported the establishment of the first German joint-stock company in this industry—the German Edison Electric Company. By 1896 there were thirty-nine joint-stock companies in the electrical industry and practically every one of them had been started with the help of a bank or a group of banks. Cut-throat competition between these firms threatened to reduce the industry to chaos and it was largely due to pressure from the banks that two great associations of firms were set up—the Siemens-Schuckert group and the A.E.G. (*Allgemeine Elektrizitäts-Gesellschaft*). On the other hand the banks do not appear to have exercised any influence on the development of large firms and cartels in the chemical industry.

German banks were also closely associated with the promotion of foreign investment, the export drive and the expansion of Germany's economic interests overseas. The grandiose project for the construction of the Bagdad railway—which aimed at the "peaceful penetration" of the Ottoman Empire—was supported by great German financial houses. In 1889 the Deutsche Bank and the Dresden Bank co-operated to set up the Anatolian Railway Company while the Deutsche Bank, in association with a Vienna bank, acquired Baron von Hirsch's shares in the Oriental Railway Company. The Deutsche Bank also helped to finance various colonial enterprises such as the East Africa Company (1904). The Discount Company was associated with the reorganization of the German Commercial and Plantation Company of the South Sea Islands (1880) and with the founding of the New Guinea Company (1883-7) and the Otavi Mining and Railway Company of South West Africa (1900). German banks co-operated to set up the German Asiatic Bank (1889), the German East Africa Bank (1905), the German West Africa Bank (1904-5) and the Cameroons Railway Company (1906). And there was an Asiatic Consortium of German banks, led by the Discount Company, which handled State, provincial and public works loans in China, Japan and Korea.

Karl Helfferich's biography of Georg von Siemens (the man behind the Deutsche Bank) and the memoirs of Carl Fürstenberg (of the Commercial Company of Berlin) show how closely the great German financial houses were associated with the expansion of German industry, shipping, commerce and overseas investment between 1870 and 1914. Fürstenberg warned those of his colleagues who failed to appreciate the limitations of a banker's functions. He wrote: "I have never cherished the ambition to become an amateur business man. I am not the sort of bank official who thinks that he has the right to air his views on industrial problems on the strength of a visit to a coal-mine, the superficial examination of a technical handbook, or attendance at a meeting addressed by the director of a big firm. But I have tried—and I have often succeeded —in putting through important industrial deals by listening to the advice of experienced business men and technical experts. I have never wished to be anything more than the financial adviser of my friends in industry."

## INDUSTRIAL EXPANSION, 1888–1914

When Wilhelm II celebrated the twenty-fifth anniversary of his accession Karl Helfferich wrote an account of Germany's economic expansion between 1888 and 1913. This survey gives an admirable description of the industrial progress of the Reich from the age of Bismarck to the eve of the first World War.

The continued growth of the population—66 millions in 1913 as compared with 48 millions in 1888—increased both the labour force and the number of consumers. Industrial expansion and rising living standards were reflected in a sharp fall in the number of emigrants. Only 28,000 Germans left the country in the first decade of the twentieth century as compared with 134,200 in the 1880's. The population was becoming concentrated in large industrial towns and ports. In 1910 Germany had twenty-three great cities of over 200,000 inhabitants each. Their total population was 8,677,000. Three of them—Essen, Duisburg and Dortmund—were in the Ruhr. The occupational structure of the population was changing. In 1882 the number of persons engaged in industry and commerce on the one hand and in agriculture and forestry on the other were approximately equal but in 1907 there were nearly twice as many people engaged in industrial occupations as in farming. Nevertheless the value of the output of agricultural products was very considerable. In 1907, for example, Germany's milk production was valued at 2,600 million marks which was far greater than the value of the output of the entire mining industry (1,600 million marks).

Many factors helped to bring about the astonishing progress of German industry and commerce. The unifying influence of the Zollverein, the economic and social achievements of Bismarck, the growth of cartels, and the influence of credit banks have already been discussed. Scientific and technical progress played their part in carrying Germany forward on the road to industrial expansion. Werner von Siemens's electric dynamo, Otto's gas engine, Daimler's petrol engine, Diesel's heavy oil engine, the Haber-Bosch process for the fixation of the nitrogen in the air by electrolysis, and the discovery of alizarin dyes by Caro and others were but a few of the many inventions which contributed to Germany's rapid development as a manufacturing country. Much scientific research took place in laboratories maintained by large firms and by technical colleges.

The development of a highly efficient transport system contributed to the expansion of industry. It has been seen that Germany's railways came increasingly under public ownership. The nationalized lines of Prussia and other states were efficiently managed and were run at a profit. The railway network grew from 37,190 km. to 60,521 km. between 1885 and 1912.

The inland waterways were extended and improved in this period. The Kiel Canal (1895) linked the Baltic to the North Sea while the Dortmund–Ems Canal (1899) joined the Ruhr to Emden. A Prussian law of 1905 provided for a substantial expansion of Prussia's navigable waterways. The Rhine–Herne Canal and the Berlin–Stettin Ship Canal were both opened in 1914 while the Ems–Weser Canal (Bergeshövede–Minden) was ready for traffic in 1915. A quarter of the goods traffic of the Reich was carried by the inland waterways in 1910. In a report written at this time W. H. Lindley declared that the usefulness of the German waterways "has been greatly increased and the cost of transportation by water diminished by shortening as much as possible the time necessary for loading and unloading the boats. Some of the new harbours—for instance at Duisburg, Kosel and others—have been equipped with very complete arrangements for this purpose, consisting of coal chutes and tips, hydraulic steam and electric cranes, depots served by elevated lines of rail, fixed and movable grain elevators, granaries and sheds and all arrangements for handling bulk goods in the most rapid and cheap manner possible."

*Coal.* Keynes declared that "the German Empire was built more truly on coal and iron than on blood and iron". It was the coal, iron and steel industries which were the backbone of the German economy after 1870. Germany was catching up to Britain as a producer of coal in 1913. The output of the Reich was then 190 million tons as compared with 60 million tons in 1887. In addition Germany produced 87 million tons of lignite as compared with only 16 million tons in 1887. Net exports of coal and coke amounted to 20 million tons. The number of coal-miners in Germany had increased from 120,000 in the 1860's to over half a million in 1913.

The principal coal-fields were in the Ruhr, the Saar and Upper Silesia. By far the most important was the Ruhr. Over 114 million tons of coal were mined in this region in 1913 and this represented over half the total German output. Upper Silesia produced nearly 44 million tons in 1913 and the Saar produced 13 million tons.

The amount of coal mined in the valley of the River Ruhr itself had declined from half of the total output of the coal-field (1850) to only ten per cent (1900). The opening of the *Rheinpreussen* Mine (1875) on the left bank of the Lower Rhine and of the Werne Mine (1903) north of the River Lippe marked the extension of the mining area far to the north and to the west of the original coalfield. The Ruhr was dominated by a handful of great mining companies which had absorbed many smaller collieries. The Gelsenkirchen Mining Company and the Harpen Mining Company had each acquired fourteen mines between 1873 and 1907. Mines producing a fifth of the Ruhr's output were owned by steel works. After 1893 most of the Ruhr mining companies were brought together in the Rhenish-Westphalian Coal Syndicate. The great increase in the output of coal stimulated the expansion of the industrial economy. The steelworks, the railways, the merchant ships, the power stations, the gasworks and the factories all needed coal while many products of the chemical industry were derived from coal-tar.

*Iron and Steel.* The expansion of the iron and steel industries was also of fundamental importance. Before 1871 these industries were based upon scattered iron-ore deposits of which the most important were those of the Siegerland, Upper Silesia, Luxemburg and the Lahn-Dill and Ilsede-Peine districts. In the 1860's when total output amounted to two million tons Silesia's output of iron-ore had declined while that of western Germany had expanded. The annexation of Lorraine greatly increased Germany's iron ore resources since the output of the province was 684,000 tons (1872). This *minette* ore was phosphoric, but once the process invented by Gilchrist Thomas was introduced the output of iron-ore in Lorraine—and also in Luxemburg—rapidly increased. Germany's output of iron-ore grew from 6·7 million tons in 1887 to over 28 million tons in 1913. This volume of production was, however, inadequate for Germany's needs and in 1913 her net imports of iron-ore amounted to 11·4 million tons. In 1901 the Ruhr drew 43 per cent of its iron-ore from German mines while nearly 22 per cent was imported from Sweden and 17·5 per cent from Spain.

There were a few blackband deposits in Germany and Luxemburg, but normally iron-ore and coal were not found together. So it was necessary either to take the ore to a coal-field or to transport the coke to an ironfield. Some ironworks and steelworks were situated on the ironfields. The de Wendel works at Hayange (Lorraine), the Ilsede works by Peine (Hanover), and the Deutsch-Luxemburg Company at Differdange (Luxemburg) were examples of steelworks which used local iron-ore and secured coke for smelting from the Ruhr or other coal-fields. On the other hand many ironworks were established on the coal-fields, as in the Ruhr and Upper Silesia, and drew their ore from iron mines which might be hundreds of miles away. There were also some ironworks at the ports which smelted Swedish iron ore with English coal.

In 1860 Germany's pig-iron output was still only just over half a million tons as compared with Britain's 3·8 million tons and France's 898,000 tons. With the introduction of Bessemer converters and open-hearth furnaces the iron and steel industries expanded more rapidly. The annexation of Alsace and Lorraine gave Germany not only a new ironfield but also great ironworks and engineering establishments. Immediately after the Franco-Prussian war the iron trade experienced a great boom and a large number of new iron companies were established. In 1875 Germany's ouput of pig-iron had risen to two million tons.

A sharp recession followed this boom. In the 1880's however the industry recovered, although rival industries abroad were either stagnant or making little progress. A small import duty on pig-iron had been imposed in 1879 and the introduction of the Thomas process enabled the vast *minette* resources in Lorraine and Luxemburg to be fully exploited. By 1913 Germany's output of pig-iron had risen to 19·3 million tons of which 8·2 million tons were produced in the Ruhr and 6·4 million tons in Lorraine and Luxemburg. Germany was now the second largest producer of pig-iron in the world. In the same year Germany's output of steel ingots and castings amounted to 18·9 million tons of which 10·1 million tons came from the Ruhr. The iron and steel industry, like the coal industry, was dominated by very large firms (such as Krupp) and thirty of them—mainly in western Germany—were linked in a powerful cartel (the Steelworks Association).

The German iron industry was mainly based on the internal market. "Its development was closely connected with the increasing industrialization of Germany, with the growth of large towns and with building, with the extension of the network of tramways and railways, etc. The external market for raw materials and partly manufactured as well as foundry goods was very small." On the other hand Germany exported a quarter of her rolling mill products. Even more important were the exports of the finished products of the engineering industry. The value of the machinery exported rose from 52·8 million marks in 1887 to 680·3 million marks in 1913.

*Shipbuilding.* The very rapid expansion of shipbuilding and the making of marine engines at Hamburg, Bremen and Stettin was a particularly remarkable achievement. As late as 1886 there still appeared to be no challenge to Britain's position as the leading builder of modern iron and steel ships. Such was the view of the secretary of the British boiler-makers' trade union when he gave evidence before a Royal Commission. At that time Germany's mercantile marine amounted to 1·2 million tons of which only 470,000 tons were steam-ships. And most of these ships had been built abroad. Twenty-five years later the position had entirely changed. Great shipyards had been established such as Blohm & Voss of Hamburg, Rickmers of Bremen and the Vulkan yard at Stettin. On the eve of the first World War German shipyards could turn out 400,000 tons of shipping a year and fulfil naval orders as well. German ships were being sold abroad. Germany's mercantile amounted to 4·4 million tons in 1913 and about a quarter of her ships were less than five years old. Her greatest shipping concerns—the Hamburg-Amerika line and the North German Lloyd—challenged the Cunard Company and other rivals for passenger traffic on the North Atlantic route. The Hamburg-Amerika line, under the able leadership of Albert Ballin, had a fleet of 172 ocean steamers (one million tons) in 1913 as compared with only 22 such ships (60,000 tons) in 1886.

*Textiles*. The textile industries also expanded, though their progress was somewhat uneven. The number of persons employed in these industries did not change very much. In 1907 the number was just over a million as compared with 910,000 twenty-five years before. Yet the volume of output and the value of exports showed a considerable increase.

The manufacture of cotton had developed on modern factory lines at Elberfed-Barmen, Chemnitz and elsewhere in the 1850's and 1860's. After the Franco-Prussian war the annexation of Alsace substantially increased the number of spinning machines, power looms and factory operatives in the Reich. In the early 1870's Germany was importing over 100,000 tons of raw cotton a year. Power-weaving was introduced more slowly than mechanical spinning. In 1875 about two-thirds of the German weavers were still domestic outworkers. Twenty years later there were only 50,000 such workers left and the vast majority of the weavers were to be found in large factories. In 1913 the German cotton industry— measured in terms of raw cotton imports—was about half the size of the British cotton industry. German cotton mills drew much more of their raw material from India than was customary in Lancashire. Consequently the quality of much German cotton cloth was not so good as that manufactured in Britain. German spinners did not make enough yarn to satisfy the demands of the weaving establishments. Before the first World War the value of Germany's annual imports of yarn and twist—mostly fine English yarns—was about

100 million marks. Exports of German cotton piece goods and yarns were worth 500 million marks in 1913.

The manufacture of woollens also developed as a great modern industry. There were many woollen centres and few signs of geographical concentration. At one time German sheep farmers had produced enough wool not only to supply the home market but to sell abroad as well. The fine wools of Saxony had commanded a ready sale in foreign markets. In the 1860's, however, a fall in wool prices led to a sharp reduction in the home clip and to an expansion of imports from Cape Colony and the Argentine. The decline in sheep farming continued so that the German woollen industry came to depend almost entirely upon imported raw wool. By 1900 "no great nation was so dependent on the outside world for the raw material of its warm clothing". It was the modern spinning mills and weaving sheds that used imported wool while, for a time, domestic craftsmen continued to work up local wools. There were still 28,000 domestic weavers in Germany in 1895. In the woollen (as in the cotton) industry the weaving factories drew some of their fine yarns from Britain though at the same time coarser yarns were exported to Austria-Hungary and the Balkans. The worsted (or combed wool) branch of the industry expanded rapidly after 1870. The combing of wool became a specialized activity and the number of woolcombers increased. Both combing and worsted spinning mills were usually joint-stock companies and not family businesses. Germany's exports of woollen goods and yarns were valued at 361 million marks in 1913.

The silk industry, with exports valued at just over 200 million marks in 1913, had greatly changed since 1887 when exports had amounted to only 16 million marks. The rapid modernization of the industry can be seen from the growth of power-loom weaving in Crefeld which was the greatest silk centre in the country. In 1890 there were only 5,400 silk and velvet power looms in the town. But there were 25,000 handlooms. In 1909, however, there were only 2,700 handlooms left while the number of power looms had increased to 9,900. German silk manufacturers were now able to compete with their French rivals in the markets of the world.

The linen industry has been called "one of Imperial Germany's failures". In the eighteenth century German linens had been among the best in the world and they had been exported in large quantities. In the nineteenth century less flax was grown in Germany and more was imported. It was a long time before the linen industry was reorganized on a factory basis. The domestic spinners and weavers of Silesia and elsewhere persisted in their efforts to survive despite the competition of Irish and Belgian machine-made linens. Eventually modern heckling and spinning machines and power looms were introduced and factories were established. But in 1913 Germany was still an importer of both linen yarn and fine linens.

*Chemicals.* The chemical and electrical industries were two new branches of manufacture which developed with remarkable rapidity after 1870. As early as 1840 Dr. Bowring had declared that in Germany "chemical knowledge in its various branches is further advanced than with us" and since that time German scientists had played an important part in advancing chemical knowledge. There were three main branches of manufacture—the making of "heavy chemicals" such as sulphuric acid and alkalis; the manufacture of artificial fertilizers (such as phosphates); and the production of coal-tar and mineral dyes, explosives, pharmaceutical products, cosmetics and plastic materials.

The main centres for the production of sulphuric acid were the Ruhr and Mannheim-Ludwigshafen. The alkali industry was based on Germany's great deposits of potassium salts at Stassfurt, Halle an der Saale, Mansfeld, the valleys of the Werra and Fulda and Wittelsheim. Nitrogen fertilizers were imported from Chile, but during the first World War nitrogen was extracted both from the air and from by-products of coal distillation. Germany also produced a variety of coal-tar products. Three-quarters of the world's output of synthetic dyes came from Germany. In 1913 her exports of dye-stuffs were valued at 195 million marks.

Two great "communities of interests" dominated the German chemical industry after 1904. Each was composed of three major firms. The first (*Badische Elberfelder A.G. für Anilin-fabrikation*) consisted of F. Bayer of Elberfeld and Leverkusen, the *Badische Anilin- und Sodafabrik* of Mannheim-Ludwigshafen, and the *A.G. für Anilin-Fabrikation of Berlin.* Bayer's firm was known to the public since it made aspirin, while the Berlin firm (AGFA) manufactured photographic articles. The second "community of interests" (*Höchster Farben-Cassella*) consisted of Meister, Lucius and Brüning of Höchst am Main; Leopold Cassella of Frankfurt am Main; and Kalle & Co. of Bieberich am Rhein. In this group the Höchst firm was in a dominant position. In 1916 the main groups of chemical firms united to form a single "community of interests" which was later called *I.G. Farben.*

*Electrical Industry.* The electrical industry developed in the 1880's. As early as 1847 Werner Siemens and Georg Halske founded the Telegraph Construction Institute which, in the following year, laid a telegraph from Berlin to Frankfurt am Main where the National Assembly was in session. But Britain and the United States rather than

Germany took the lead in the 1850's and 1860's in the manufacture of telegraphic appliances and submarine cables. When Werner Siemens invented the electric dynamo (1866) and experimented with electric traction—a short electric tramway was opened at Lichterfelde (Berlin) in 1881—German entrepreneurs quickly appreciated the potentialities of the new form of power and light. The banks supported the new industry from its early days and they were behind the establishment of the German Edison Company in 1883. Companies were formed to provide German cities first with electric light and then with electric trams. In May 1884, for example, Emil Rathenau established the City Electric Works in Berlin with a capital of three million marks. Its first power station was in the *Markgrafenstrasse*. Before long a number of electric light and electric tramway companies were taken over by municipal authorities.

The great electrical boom of the 1890's was followed by a slump in the early years of the twentieth century. Excessive competition in the industry led to a fall in both prices and dividends. In an effort to remedy this state of affairs two great cartels were formed with the financial assistance of the banks. These combines were the A.E.G. (*Allgemeine Elektrizität Gesellschaft*) and Siemens and Halske. By 1907 the A.E.G., under Emil Rathenau's able leadership, had grown to be a huge concern with 10,000 employees. Clapham considers that "the creation of this industry was the greatest single achievement of modern Germany". "Her success was rewarded by a foreign trade in electrical appliances which no other nation could approach." Germany's exports of electrical goods were valued at nearly 220 million marks in 1913.

*Exports & Imports.* By 1914 Germany had become the second trading nation in the world. In the previous twenty-five years her overseas commerce had been expanding much more rapidly than that of her rivals. The imports and exports of the Reich (excluding bullion) had increased from just under 6,500 million marks in 1888 to a little over 20,000 million marks in 1913. The pattern of Germany's overseas trade was typical of an advanced industrial country. Over seventy per cent of the imports in 1913 consisted of industrial raw materials (such as cotton and iron-ore), food (cereals, fish and tropical fruits), drinks (wines and coffee) and tobacco. A quarter of her imports were semi-manufactured articles (such as textile yarns) and finished goods. Three-quarters of her exports were manufactured or semi-manufactured products, fifteen per cent were raw materials, and ten per cent were foods and drinks (such as barley and beet sugar).

The expansion of Germany's exports of manufactured goods had, to some extent, taken place at Britain's expense. In 1914

German goods were being sold in many markets in Latin America, Africa and Asia where English exporters had formerly not had to face much competition. Nevertheless "increased trade rivalry between Britain and Germany at the turn of the century did not—with few exceptions—produce political repercussions in either country. The Atlantic shipping pool, agreement on the continuation of the building of the Bagdad railway, the relations between British and German commercial firms in the Far East, and the activities of German, British and North American banks in South America, prove that at this time there were growing possibilities of trade and profit for all."

*Export of Capital.* Germany was exporting not only goods but capital as well. A country which Voltaire had thought would be condemned to everlasting poverty was now rich enough to invest money abroad. In the first two-thirds of the nineteenth century Germany was still a borrower rather than a lender. In the 1820's two loans raised on the London money market had put the Prussian Government on its feet after the Napoleonic wars. In the boom period of the 1850's foreign investors helped to establish new collieries and ironworks in the Ruhr while English financial houses extended generous "open credits" to Hamburg merchants and shippers. Even in the 1860's English capital was helping to extend the network of German railways. After the Franco-Prussian war the situation changed and Germany began to export capital. In an earlier period German financiers had invested in American railways. Professor Hyde states that by the 1870's "German interests were already very strong in Oregon, and the bondholders' committee in Frankfurt (am Main), by means of some 11 million dollars invested in the Oregon and California Railway, controlled practically all the transportation in the country west of the Cascade Mountains—a territory through which the Northern Pacific desired to run. Henry Villard, who was the agent of the German bondholders, had by a judicious purchase of the stock of the Oregon and California Railway made himself president of this company in 1876." Large German investments were made in Russia between 1870 and 1887. Many of these investments were sold in 1887 and the German great banks then began to lend money overseas on a large scale, heavy investments being made in Argentine securities and in loans to the Italian and Turkish governments (1887–90).

In 1913 Germany's overseas investments amounted to about 23,500 million marks over half of which were in Europe and the Ottoman Empire. Elsewhere Germany's largest investments were in North and South America and Africa. Herbert Feis states that "despite a prevailing conception to the contrary, substantially more

73

than half of the foreign investment was in fixed-interest-bearing securities, especially in the bonds of foreign governments. A large part of the investment of variable return was not in the hands of individual investors but of the Great Banks." Those German investments abroad which were not in government bonds were in the shares of railway companies, public utilities, mining companies, oil fields and colonial plantation and trading companies. Germany had an adverse balance of commodity trade (one million marks in 1913) but she paid her way in international commerce since she earned money by her "invisible exports" which included interest from foreign investments and payments received for banking, insurance and shipping services.

According to W. G. Hoffmann and J. H. Müller Germany's average annual national income increased from 15,100 million marks (364 marks per head of population) in 1871–5 to 47,300 million marks (716 marks per head) in 1911–13.[1] Prussia's national income rose from 8,200 million marks to 30,100 million marks in the same period. Karl Helfferich estimated that the Reich's total wealth increased from 200,000 million marks in the 1890's to 300,000 million marks in 1913. This increase in both national income and national wealth was reflected in rising living standards. Between the 1880's and 1914 there was a substantial increase in the consumption (per head of population) of meat, sugar, coffee, rice, cotton and many other commodities. Men with views so different as those of the socialist Bebel, the nationalist Treitschke and the industrialist Walther Rathenau agreed in condemning the accumulation of capital in the hands of a very few wealthy men. But Helfferich observed that statistics gave no support to the view that Germany was becoming a plutocracy in 1914. His investigations showed that many people whose income had formerly been so low that they had not paid income tax had now entered the lowest income group liable to direct taxation. The average annual wages of coal-miners had risen from 863 marks to 1,755 marks in the Ruhr between 1888 and 1913 and from 516 marks to 1,053 marks in Upper Silesia. Deposits in the German savings banks had risen from 6,800 million marks in 1895 to 17,800 million marks in 1911. In Prussia the deposits in public savings banks had increased more than tenfold between 1870 and 1910—from 20 marks per head of the population to 276 marks. Evidence of this kind suggested that the industrial workers shared in the national prosperity in the reign of Wilhelm II.

[1] The *real* average annual national income (adjusted by price index based on prices of 1913) was 14,600 million marks in 1871–5 and 48,100 million marks in 1911–13.

# CHAPTER IV

# THE INDUSTRIAL REVOLUTION IN FRANCE

## (i) 1789-1815

### THE LEGACY OF THE REVOLUTION

IN the ten years between the calling of the States General (1789) and the *coup d'état* of the eighteenth of Brumaire (1799) the French economy was weakened by the disorganization that followed the collapse of the *ancien régime*, the events of the Terror and the civil war, the totalitarian economy of the Committee of Public Safety (1793–4), the changes in landownership, the failure to maintain the highways and inland waterways, the inflation of the currency through the over-issue of *assignats* and the virtual repudiation of two-thirds of the national debt.

There was a drastic fall both in agricultural production and in industrial ouput. The war which broke out in 1792 led to the collapse of France's extensive colonial trade owing to the British blockade and the loss of San Domingo. On the other hand the iron, engineering and textile industries were stimulated by war demands, while the conquest of the Low Countries, the Rhineland and northern Italy brought rich booty to France—bullion, plate and art treasures—and gave her control over important new economic resources such as the coal-fields in the valleys of the Meuse, Sambre and Saar, the Dutch mercantile marine, and the varied industries of Holland, the Austrian Netherlands, the Bishopric of Liège and the territories on the left bank of the Rhine.

Many reforms of fundamental significance were achieved in the years of revolution. It has been observed that "with the exception of the Russian revolution of 1917 mankind has not experienced so quick and radical a change of social conditions as during the years from June 1789 to March 1791". Feudalism was liquidated. It is sometimes supposed that this great reform was achieved in 1789. At its historic meeting on the night of August 4, 1789, the National (or Constituent) Assembly agreed in principle to the redemption of feudal dues and to the abolition of feudal services and manorial jurisdiction. On August 11, 1789, an edict was passed which declared that "the National Assembly hereby completely abolishes the feudal system" and on March 15, 1790, another decree implemented the policy approved on August 4 and August 11, 1789. The decree of March 15, 1790, also abolished ecclesiastical tithes although five weeks later another decree postponed abolition until January 1, 1791. A law passed in March 1791 abolished the gilds and declared that everybody was now "free to do such business and to exercise such profession, art, or trade as he may choose". A law of September 1791 allowed farmers to grow what crops they pleased.

The National Assembly however had not really abolished feudalism in 1789–90 because the distinction between "seigneurial rights" and "real rights" was maintained. The seigneurial privileges included rights over hunting and fishing; the preservation of dovecots and rabbit warrens; the levying of tolls at markets, fairs and rivers; and the monopoly of the local mill, baking oven and winepress. These privileges were liquidated in 1789–90. But the so-called "real rights" survived. These were burdens falling upon a particular piece of land and not upon a particular individual. They included quit-rents on copyhold lands (*cens*), an annual tax upon cultivated lands (*champart*), and fines levied when land changed hands (*lods et ventes*). For three years the peasants strenuously resisted the attempts of the landlords to collect quit-rents and fines. It was not until the summer of 1793, when royalist risings in La Vendée and Brittany had assumed the proportions of a civil war, that the National Convention abolished quit-rents, fines, and similar feudal dues. The abolition of the feudal system and of all dues associated with it was one of the major advantages which the French peasants gained from the revolution. It was a permanent gain. When the Prussian and Russian serfs were emancipated many years later they had to make substantial redemption payments before they owned the land which they cultivated. French peasants made no such payments after 1793. The existence in France of a substantial group of independent peasant proprietors in the nineteenth century was due largely to the revolutionary settlement of the agrarian problem in 1789–93.

A reform of fundamental significance was the reorganization of local government. The National Assembly liquidated the historic provinces, the local estates and the lawyers' assemblies (*Parlements*) which were all considered to be too closely associated with feudalism to survive. The provinces were replaced by eighty-three departments of approximately equal size. At first the administration was decentralized since departments and municipalities were given wide powers of self-government, but this system did not last long and soon *députés en mission* from Paris were exercising a considerable measure of control over local affairs.

The National Assembly swept away the internal tariffs and tolls which had in the past seriously hampered the movement of goods from one part of the country to another. In 1790 the separate tariffs of the "five great farms", "the provinces regarded as foreign" and "the provinces foreign in fact" were abolished. Numerous provincial dues levied within these former customs regions were liquidated. The salt tax came to an end and with it the machinery for controlling the movement of salt in France. The tariff of the new customs area was of a protective character. In 1791, the National Assembly introduced a new tariff which prohibited the importation of thirty-four articles. On the outbreak of war in 1792 all commercial agreements were annulled. The brief experiment of a liberal commercial policy embodied in the Anglo-French treaty of commerce of 1786 had come to an end.

The system of taxation was overhauled at the time of the Revolution. Many direct and indirect taxes which fell mainly upon the unprivileged classes were replaced by taxes to which all citizens were liable according to their means. Excises (*aides*) on wines, spirits and playing cards and the salt and tobacco monopolies were abolished. Private taxes and tolls also disappeared. For a time the vast revenues lost in this way were replaced by printing paper money (*assignats*) and by selling sequestered estates. These could be only temporary expedients. New taxes on land (*contribution foncière*) and on industry (*contribution mobilière*) were introduced but no adequate machinery was devised for their collection and payments fell into arrears. Between 1790 and 1795 only about thirteen per cent of the Government's revenues was derived from taxation. Levies on capital and forced loans were imposed to reduce the budget deficit. The Revolution had swept away the unfair system of taxation of the *ancien régime* but no new satisfactory system had been devised to take its place.

Another financial reform was the establishment of the Great Book of the Public Debt. During the *ancien régime* the public finances had degenerated into so chaotic a state that the precise extent of the national debt was not known. In the first years of the Revolution the Assembly tried to reduce the floating debt and about 1,000 million livres were paid off in a little over two years. A considerable proportion of the early issues of the *assignats* were used for this purpose. The outbreak of war in 1792 made it impossible to continue the policy of reducing the national debt. In August of the following year the Convention decided that persons entitled to receive payments from the State must prove their claims. When the claims had been verified the names of the creditors were to be entered into the Great Book of the Public Debt.

The revolutionaries were determined to abolish the chaotic system of weights and measures which varied from province to province and from district to district. In May 1790 the National Assembly decided to adopt a new system of weights and measures and invited the Academy of Sciences to draw up a suitable scheme. In April 1795 the Convention adopted the metric system. In 1799 a standard metre of platinum and a standard kilogramme were deposited in the Paris Observatory. At first the old and new weights and measures existed side by side. It was not until 1840 that the metric system became the sole standard for weights and measures. The introduction of the new system greatly simplified commercial dealings in France and its advantages were so considerable that it was eventually adopted by most countries on the Continent. The decimal system was also used when the French coinage was reformed in August 1795. The livre was replaced by the franc, the two coins being practically the same in value. But while the livre had been divided into 20 sols (sous) of 12 deniers—just as the English pound sterling had 20 shillings of 12 pence—the franc was divided into 100 centimes.

Industrial expansion was fostered at the time of the Revolution by the passing of a patent law, the establishment of a collection of machines, and the encouragement of technical education. A decree of the National Assembly (January 1791) gave an inventor the exclusive right to exploit his invention for a maximum of fifteen years. In 1798 the Directory brought together three collections of modern machinery and established the *Conservatoire des arts et métiers* which was "the first museum of science and technology". An industrial exhibition, organized by Chaptal, the Minister of the Interior, was held in Paris at the Champ de Mars in 1798. It was the first of many similar exhibitions. In 1793 a Mining College was set up and in the following year the Polytechnic was established—both in Paris—for the education of government engineers.

France was the first Great Power to try to emancipate the slaves in its colonies. In 1793 the French slave trade was abolished and in February of the following year the Convention freed the slaves in the overseas possessions and gave them full rights of citizenship. No provision was made to compensate the slave owners and the white planters of San Domingo refused to recognize the decree. The island came under the control of Toussaint l'Ouverture. Napoleon, who sent an ill-fated expedition to recover the island, issued a decree which re-established slavery (1802). The natives rebelled again and San Domingo was lost to France for ever. In Réunion and Mauritius the white settlers were strongly opposed to setting the slaves free and the emancipation edict did not come into force in those islands. It was not until 1848 that the slaves in the French colonies were finally set free by the government of the Second Republic.

## THE LEGACY OF NAPOLEON

Although Napoleon was responsible for many reactionary measures in France—such as the re-establishment of slavery in the colonies— he was also responsible for a series of reforms which helped to lay the foundations of the economic and social progress made by France in the nineteenth century.

The system of local government was radically changed in 1800. The departments, which had replaced the former provinces, survived, but local self-government was abolished. Prefects with powers greater than those of the old Intendants were appointed to represent the central authority in each department. The departments were ruled from the capital and a highly centralized form of administration was established. Centralization had significant economic results. The initiative for the development of public works had to come from Paris. Local manufacturers tended to look to the central authority for assistance in starting new enterprises.

The policy of centralization, exemplified by the changes in local government, was seen also in Napoleon's reform of the law which gave France five legal codes at a time when the various German states were governed in accordance with many different legal systems. The laws of the *ancien régime* have been described as "an inextricable labyrinth of laws and customs, mainly Roman and Frankish in origin, hopelessly tangled by feudal customs, provincial privileges, ecclesiastical rights and the later undergrowth of royal decrees". Neither the Convention nor the Directory had brought order to this legal chaos. Napoleon was more successful. His codes[1] provided the legal framework of French society throughout the nineteenth century and they exercised a powerful influence upon the legal systems of many other countries.

The spirit that animated Napoleon's legal reforms may be seen from some of the provisions regulating economic affairs. The

[1] The five codes of 1804–10 were: (i) the civil code, (ii) the code of civil procedure, (iii) the commercial code, (iv) the *code d'instruction criminelle*, and (v) the penal code. Any appeal to the authority of the laws and customs of the *ancien régime* was expressly prohibited.

"sacred right of freedom" dear to the revolutionaries, survived in the Frenchman's liberty to enter any trade or profession. For the most part, however, freedom gave way to discipline. Napoleon saw an estate or a workshop with the eye of a soldier and he held that efficiency depended upon obedience to authority. He regarded the employer as an officer and the worker as a private soldier. The authority of the employer was maintained in various ways. The police kept a close check upon the activities of the working classes. After 1803 every artisan had to have an identity card (*livret*). The legislation of the Revolution which had banned trade unions—Chapelier's anti-combination law of June 1791—was reaffirmed. Associations of workers were declared to be illegal, while collective bargaining and strikes were prohibited. The evidence of employers concerning wages paid to workers was accepted by courts of law without question. On conciliation councils—the *conseils des prud'hommes* authorized by an edict of 1806—the representatives of the employers were always in the majority.

Napoleon was a firm believer in the virtue of private property. His codes safeguarded the rights of the owners of landed estates and industrial plant. On the other hand there were circumstances when the rights of society as a whole were regarded as being of even greater importance than the rights of private property. Hence private property could be expropriated—with fair compensation to the owner—if the interests of the State made it necessary that this should be done.

Napoleon's belief in the importance of discipline in social affairs and in the merits of private property was seen also in the strengthening of the position of the head of the family (in relation to his wife and children) and in the somewhat greater latitude allowed to testators in the disposal of their property by will. It was in keeping with the spirit of the codes that Napoleon should have adopted the reactionary course of re-establishing slavery in the French colonial empire.

The educational reforms of Napoleon had an indirect rather than a direct influence upon the industrial economy of the country. Though a mining school was established at Geislautern in the Saar, Napoleon appears to have taken little interest in improving facilities for vocational education. Indeed the Paris Polytechnic was turned into a military academy. But the curriculum of the new grammar schools (*lycées*) was such that the technicians of the future received a sound grounding in mathematics and science. Moreover the *Société d'encouragement pour l'industrie nationale de la France*, which was founded under Government patronage in 1802, tried to stimulate technical progress by offering prizes for inventions and for improvements in existing machines.

One of Napoleon's most important achievements was to establish an orderly financial system in France. The revolutionaries had destroyed the unfair financial system of the *ancien régime* but they had failed to establish permanent new sources of revenue and they had ruined the currency by the over-issue of *assignats*. In Napoleon's day the evils of inflation were avoided and a sound currency was maintained. Some taxes—on salt, wine and tobacco for example—were increased, but no income tax was imposed. The vast expenses of the long wars were to a considerable extent met by forcing the conquered peoples—the Dutch, the Germans and the Italians—to make substantial financial contributions towards the cost of Napoleon's military adventures. Local finance was also reorganized. Strenuous measures were taken to ensure that each commune lived within its means. But a price had to be paid for solvency. H. A. L. Fisher observes that "if we could revisit any great provincial town of France as it stood in any year from 1808 to 1815 we should find the schoolmasters and clergy starving upon miserable pittances, the schools empty of scholars, the public hospitals short of nurses and appliances, industry at a standstill, and the government of the town listless, incurious and sapped of all initiative".

Napoleon's financial reforms were crowned by the establishment of the Bank of France. Three banks of issue had been set up in the eighteenth century. The first was John Law's bank of 1716 which failed in 1720. The second was the *Caisse d'Escompte* of 1776. Excessive borrowing by the bankrupt Government in the last years of the *ancien régime* (1787–9) weakened the position of the bank to such an extent that it had to be wound up in 1793. The third was the *Caisse des Comptes Courants* of 1796 which issued notes to the value of twenty million francs.

The Bank of France was established under the Consulate in 1800 and absorbed the *Caisse des Comptes Courants*. The initial capital of the new bank was thirty million francs of which five million francs were subscribed by the Government. It acted as a banker for the Treasury and paid out the dividends on Government loans (*rentes*). In 1803 the Bank of France was given the monopoly of issuing notes in Paris. The smallest denomination was 500 francs. An attempt in 1808–10 to set up branches of the Bank of France in provincial towns failed, but after 1835 fifteen branches were successfully established. In 1803 authority was given for the establishment of provincial joint-stock banks under Government control. They were known as Departmental Banks. Nine such banks were in existence in 1848 when they were incorporated in the Bank of France.

Napoleon was determined to make good the neglect of the national system of transport which had characterized the revolutionary period. His decree of 1811 was the basis of road developments in the nineteenth century. Highways were classified as Imperial and Departmental. The main arterial roads were built and maintained by the central Government while the secondary roads were the responsibility of the local authorities. The highways from Paris to Strasbourg and from Metz to Saarbrücken and Mainz and the network of roads in Picardy were originally constructed for military purposes, but they were also valuable from an economic point of view. De Bourrienne wrote that "Paris is not the only city, nor is France the only kingdom which bears traces of the passion of Napoleon for great and useful monuments . . . At Turin a magnificent bridge was constructed over the Po, in place of the old one which had fallen to ruin. How many things undertaken and executed under a reign so short and so eventful! Communications were difficult between Metz and Mainz. A magnificent road was formed, as it were by magic, and carried in a direct line through impassable marshes and trackless forests: mountains opposed themselves, they were cut through; ravines presented obstacles, they were filled up; and very soon one of the finest roads in Europe was opened to commerce . . . A road, level as the walk of a garden, replaced in Savoy the precipitous passes in the wood of Bramant, and thus the passage of Mont-Cenis . . . became a pleasant promenade at almost all seasons of the year."

Karl Marx summarized Napoleon's achievements in the sphere of economic development as follows: "Napoleon established throughout France the conditions which made it possible for free competition to develop, for landed property to be exploited after the partition of the great estates, and for the nation's powers of industrial production to be utilized to the full. Across the frontiers he made a clearance of feudal institutions, in so far as this was requisite to provide French bourgeois society with a suitable environment upon the continent of Europe."

## THE CONTINENTAL SYSTEM

The pursuit of economic self-sufficiency had been France's traditional commercial policy in the eighteenth century. Prohibitions and high tariffs kept imports from abroad at bay and assured to French manufacturers a privileged position in their home market. It was probably only the imminent threat of bankruptcy that led Vergennes to favour a more liberal policy and to agree to the negotiations which led to the signing of the Anglo-French commercial agreement of 1786. The new arrangement did not last long since the French declaration of war against Britain in February 1793 brought the treaty to an end.

The introduction of the Continental System in 1806 was not a new policy. Napoleon applied on a far larger scale the weapons of economic warfare already used by the Jacobins, the Directory and the Consulate. The Jacobins had believed that Britain could be defeated if her commerce were destroyed and as the French armies swept into the Low Countries, the Rhineland, and northern Italy every effort was made to exclude English manufactured goods not only from France itself but from the newly conquered countries. By a decree of 10 Brumaire, an V, the French banned the importation of British goods into the territories under their control. When war broke out again after the Peace of Amiens this policy was resumed. From the middle of 1803 until October 1805 the French closed the mouths of the Elbe and Weser and English merchants had to use the ports of Emden and Tönning in order to trade with Germany. After Hanover had been handed over to Prussia in 1805 Napoleon insisted that the coast of north Germany should be closed to British goods (February 1806). The British Government replied by declaring the whole coast from Brest to the Elbe to be in a state of blockade. When Napoleon occupied the Prussian capital after his victories at Jena and Auerstädt he issued the Berlin Decree (November 1806) which forbade all commerce with the British Isles and prohibited any trading in goods produced in Britain or her colonies. The decree applied to France, Italy, Switzerland and the Confederation of the Rhine. By the treaty of Tilsit (1807) the Czar agreed to enforce the system in Russia. The Milan Decree of December 1807 declared that every ship trading with Britain or her colonies was liable to be seized if it entered a port under French control.

About one-third of Britain's exports of goods manufactured at home (such as the products of the textile and iron industries) were sold on the Continent. So at first two-thirds of this branch of Britain's foreign trade could not be injured by Napoleon's policy. But another third was sold in the United States and when that country closed its ports to British goods the position concerning the export of manufactured products became more serious. Strenuous efforts had to be made to increase illicit trade with the Continent through Heligoland, Malta and other loopholes in Napoleon's "iron curtain" and to open up new markets for manufactured goods in South America and elsewhere. Three-quarters of Britain's re-exports—mainly raw materials (e.g. cotton) and foodstuffs (e.g. sugar) from the colonies—were sent to the Continent and this sector of Britain's foreign trade quickly felt the effects of the Continental System.

The war does not seem to have checked the forward march of Britain's industrial expansion. Coal output increased steadily—if the increase in the shipment of coal from the Tyne and Wear ports may be regarded as typical of the production of all the coal-fields. A substantial growth in the imports of raw cotton throughout the war suggests that the cotton industry was flourishing. The expansion of power-loom weaving and puddling was evidence of technical progress in this period.

Napoleon hoped to injure Britain not only by depriving her of markets for her exports but also by cutting off essential imports. During the war Britain could not secure her normal supplies of wheat, wool, timber, and naval stores from the Continent, but timber could be imported from Canada and only one-tenth of the wheat and the wool normally consumed in England came from the Continent.

On the whole Britain weathered the storm surprisingly well. Despite the Continental System and the American Non-Intercourse and Embargo Acts Britain's industries continued to develop and were able to meet the increased demand for goods required to meet the war effort. Substantial financial aid was given by Britain to her allies. Nevertheless it might be argued that the rate of industrial expansion in Britain was checked somewhat by the Continental System. Britain's industries grew, but perhaps they might have grown faster if there had been no war. The inflation of the currency after 1809, the great commercial crisis of 1810–11, and the serious social distress of the early years of the nineteenth century showed that the British economy had not survived unscathed.

M. Crouzet, in his detailed survey of the Continental System, criticizes some of the generalizations made by historians concerning the effects of economic warfare upon British trade and industry at this time. He suggests that those who argue that Napoleon's policy failed because English goods were smuggled into the Continent on a large scale should remember that between July 1807 and July 1808 and again from the spring of 1810 to the failure of the Moscow campaign the Continental System was strictly enforced, illicit trading was reduced to a minimum, and the British economy was subject to severe pressure. M. Crouzet argues that Napoleon's mistake lay in failing to maintain his system rigorously for a sufficiently long period to ensure success. Above all Napoleon's blunders in his relations first with Spain and then with Russia made it impossible for him to unite the whole of the Continent against Britain. And so many of those responsible for enforcing the blockade were slack or corrupt while most of the satellite states failed to give Napoleon's economic policy their whole-hearted support. Moreover British traders proved to be remarkably quick in adapting themselves to a new situation. They seized every opportunity—in Buenos Aires in 1806, in Brazil in 1808, in the Baltic in 1810—to open up new markets or to re-establish themselves in former markets.

The Continental System had significant results on the Continent. The great ports lost valuable trades which had flourished in the eighteenth century. Continental industries, safe from English competition, were given an unexpected opportunity to expand even although their raw materials were sometimes difficult to obtain. There was a steep rise in the prices of tropical products and—as de Bourrienne remarked—this led to "countless vexations and miseries". The increase in unemployment, pauperism and vagrancy was noted by many contemporary observers. Yet there was a silver lining even to this aspect of the Continental System, because shortages were a spur to the production of substitutes which sometimes developed into new branches of manufacture. Beet sugar produced by Delessert of Passy (by Achard's process) began to replace colonial cane sugar. Soda, used in the manufacture of soap and glass, was made from sea salt by Nicolas Leblanc's method when Spanish soda (made from the barilla plant) was no longer obtainable. Chlorine, another product of sea salt, was made by the Oberkampf–Widmer apparatus and was used as a quicker way of bleaching cloth than the traditional method of exposing it to the sun. Indigo for dyeing textiles was produced from native woad when there was a shortage of supplies made from Indian or American indigofera. There were of course branches of manufacture on the Continent which were little affected by the Continental System. Certain craftsmen—masons, carpenters, ironworkers for example—who used local raw materials and sold their products to local customers might be able to carry on as usual in spite of the war.

The Revolutionary and Napoleonic wars fostered a new tendency in the evolution of the French economy. In the eighteenth century certain industries had found important markets overseas, particularly in the colonies and in the Levant. Manufacturers had not only supplied the needs of a large protected home market but had also made goods which were sent to the colonies and to the Near East. Transport and financial facilities—particularly in south-west France —were geared to handle this flow of goods. After Canada and India had been lost there was still a substantial trade with the West Indies and the Levant. The colonies sent tropical products to France and this trade too was important to the French economy. Sugar from San Domingo, for example, was the raw material of the French refineries. The prosperity of Bordeaux in the 1780's—upon which Arthur Young commented in such glowing terms when he visited the city—was due to its flourishing colonial trade. But during the Revolutionary and Napoleonic wars the colonial trade virtually disappeared since the French ports were blockaded by the British navy. Consequently a number of branches of manufacture, particularly in the south-west of France, declined and some disappeared altogether. The catastrophic decline in the overseas trade of Bordeaux, Nantes and Marseilles led to the collapse of a number of industrial establishments in the vicinity of these ports. Workshops which supplied ships with sailcloth and ropes; spinners and weavers who had once made cloth for the Levant trade; those who made barrels and bottles in which wine had been exported; the refineries which had handled the sugar imported from the West Indies—these and many others were forced out of business. In 1809 the German traveller Nemnich stated that there were only eight sugar refineries in Bordeaux as compared with forty in the 1780's. It was not only the industries on the coast of this part of France that were affected by the collapse of the overseas trade. Further inland came reports of the decline of the manufacture of cloth and gloves at Agen, of the production of silks at Montauban, of the making of ropes at Marmande and Tonneins, and of the output of the flour mills of the Tarn-et-Garonne district. In Languedoc the cloth industry collapsed. In the year IX the Prefect of the Aude Department reported that the output of coarse cloths at Carcassonne was only a quarter of what it had been during the *ancien régime*. Some 20,000 workers were unemployed in this district. At the same time it was stated that the production of paper in Angoulême had suffered seriously owing to the decline in France's overseas trade. In north-east France, however, the position was different. France had extended her frontiers to the Rhine, the Meuse and the Po and had established satellite states in Germany, Italy and Poland. While the trade routes from the industrial centres to the ports languished the trade routes to central Europe and Italy carried an increasing volume of traffic. Commerce with the annexed territories and the satellite states expanded. But it was not until the 1850's that the conquest of new colonies in Algeria and Senegal once more fostered the expansion of colonial and other overseas trades. By that time about three-quarters of France's external trade went by sea routes.

While the French ports languished owing to the lapse of overseas trade at the time of the Continental System certain branches of industry expanded in the early years of the nineteenth century under the stimulus of the situation brought about by the Napoleonic wars. The cotton industry made remarkable progress at this time particularly in Ghent and Mulhouse which had recently been incorporated in France. Encouraged by the French authorities Liéven Bauwens brought seventeen mule-jennies and some forty skilled operatives from England to Ghent. By 1803 he was employing over two hundred workers. His example was followed by other entrepreneurs and the cotton industry spread from Ghent to a number of old-established centres in Flanders where woollen cloth had long been manufactured. A coarse type of cotton cloth was generally made and many orders were received from the military authorities. It is stated that at the peak of the Ghent cotton boom some fifty factories and workshops existed in the town and 10,000 workers were employed. In Mulhouse the printing of fine calicos expanded rapidly after the Imperial City was annexed in 1798. The firm of Koechlin was a pioneer in the introduction of new dyes—Berlin blue and Adrianople red—at this time. The Alsace cotton industry concentrated on the finishing processes. Spinning and weaving, however, were not neglected and in 1812 Dollfus, Mieg et Cie set up a small steam engine at Mulhouse to drive a spinning machine. The industrial expansion of Mulhouse at this time was reflected in the growth of the population from 6,000 in 1798 to 9,300 in 1815. The cotton industry also expanded in the Paris region (over 130,000 spindles) and in Roubaix. Oberkampf's well-known calico-printing works at Jouy (near Paris) were among the leading French establishments of this kind and their owner was decorated by the Emperor for his services to French industry. The rapid growth of the French cotton industry during Napoleon's reign, however, was not based upon sound foundations. The raw material could not be obtained from the United States. Supplies from the Levant, Spain and Italy were uncertain and costly. French spinners were paying about three times as much for raw cotton as their Lancashire rivals. By 1813 the Ghent cotton industry had collapsed and soon after the end of the war the cotton industry of Paris declined.

The French woollen industry was encouraged by the Government. A clause in the Treaty of Basel of 1799 enabled large flocks of merino sheep to be imported into France. The greatest expansion in the manufacture of woollens took place, however, in the recently acquired Roer Department (on the left bank of the Rhine) and not in France within her traditional frontiers. The production of woollen cloth developed at Cologne and Aachen and these relatively new centres of production did not have to fear any competition from Yorkshire.

The silk industry of Lyons, too, made some progress in the first decade of the nineteenth century. This appears to have been due partly to improvements in manufacturing technique and partly to the assistance which the Government gave to the industry. Napoleon considered that even in time of war a luxury industry should be subsidized so as to keep the workers in employment. Nevertheless there was a serious crisis in the Lyons silk trade in 1811. Labasse has shown that this was due mainly to a poor silk harvest in Piedmont which greatly increased the cost of the raw material.

Progress was made by the French engineering industry, particularly in the manufacture of textile machinery. Greater advances were made in the annexed Belgian provinces than in France itself. In 1799 the elder William Cockerill established himself at Verviers as a manu-facturer of textile machines and in 1802 he was joined by James Hodson. Before long Hodson set up a machine-building business of his own. In 1807 the elder William Cockerill moved to Liège where—in association with his three sons (William, Charles James and John)—he made carding machines, spinning machines and mechanical looms for the woollen industry. In the heyday of the Napoleonic régime about half of Cockerill's output was sold in France. Another manufacturer of textile machinery at this time was William Douglas who was brought to France by Chaptal, Napoleon's Minister of the Interior, in the early years of the nineteenth century. Douglas introduced improved carding and spinning machinery into his clothworks in Paris and also built such machines for the manu-facturers. At the same time F. C. L. Albert—who had served a term of imprisonment in England for trying to persuade a cotton operative to migrate to France—was building textile machines in Paris.

Reference has been made to the development of the chemical industries in France in Napoleon's reign. Progress was made in the manufacture of soda, sulphuric acid, nitric acid, ammonia, alum and camphor. Textile dyeing, sugar refining and the manufacture of soap benefited from advances in chemical knowledge. The pioneer researches of Lavoisier and his pupils gave France a lead in the field of chemistry and its application to industry.

It has been pointed out that France's industrial development in Napoleon's reign "was essentially artificial". "It was the outcome, not so much of the enterprise of French manufacturers, as of the compulsion laid upon consumers to have recourse to them, and their undisturbed sway in the home market." And a French expert on the tariff stated that "after being kept apart for a quarter of a century from all regular contact with the products of the British manufacturers, we found ourselves at the establishment of peace even further behind them than before the war. Whilst machinery had gradually developed in England, in France it had made very little progress."

When considering the effects of Napoleon's economic policy upon continental countries other than France it must be remembered that the Continental System was a weapon of economic warfare directed against Britain and not a policy adopted in peacetime to promote the economic expansion of France or of her neighbours. Moreover Napoleon's motto in these matters was *la France avant tout.* The satellite states were expected to export what France required and to import what France had to sell. Their industries were not to presume to compete with those of France. Even states which were annexed might find that they were still being treated as foreign countries from an economic point of view. In 1811 it was decided to set up a Franco–Dutch customs union but this arrangement was not carried into effect. Many continental states suffered severely because they paid heavy war contributions to France, because they had to put up with grave shortages both of necessities and of luxuries, because there was a steep rise in the cost of living, because poverty increased to an alarming extent, and because their economic development was ruthlessly subordinated to the interests of France. Any advantages which the satellite states obtained from the Continental System were purely fortuitous.

The effects of the long wars and of the Continental System upon the various regions of Germany varied considerably. The legitimate trade of the North Sea ports came to an end. No manufactured goods from Britain and no supplies of British colonial goods might be imported by Hamburg, Bremen and other North Sea harbours. Coastal trade and smuggling from Heligoland were no adequate substitutes for the loss of normal overseas trade. The Prussian Baltic ports could no longer export grain and timber. At Memel vast stores of timber were left to rot. On the other hand Rostock flourished in 1809–10 as it had a lively trade with Swedish ports.

Some German industrial regions expanded because they supplied goods for the French military authorities or because the Continental System protected them from British competition. In the Roer Department on the left bank of the Rhine the output of woollens expanded. In the Kingdom of Saxony the production of muslins at Plauen and of calicoes at Chemnitz benefited from the absence of competition of machine-made Lancashire goods. The Ruhr and the Saar made little progress at this time. The Ruhr now lay in the Duchy of Berg and (by the Trianon Tariff) its products were barred from the French market. The inhabitants of Berg asked to be incorporated in the French Empire but Napoleon rejected the suggestion. The output of coal in the Ruhr was less in 1815 than it had been ten years before. The Saar had been occupied by the French in 1792 and remained in their hands for twenty-two years. No marked expansion of output occurred in that period either in the production of coal or of pig-iron. A hundred years later—after the first World War—when the French were again planning to annex the Saar, they claimed that the progress made in this industrial region in the nineteenth century was due largely to the pioneer efforts of the French between 1792 and 1814. No contemporary evidence supports this view.

In the Low Countries the Dutch lost both their colonial and carrying trades. Amsterdam and Rotterdam were as hard hit by the Continental System as Bremen and Danzig. The Dutch fisheries were adversely affected by the shortage of salt. The sale of Dutch gin declined. On the other hand in the Belgian provinces the cotton industry of Flanders, the construction of machines at Verviers and Liège, and the armaments industry of Liège were all stimulated by war demands and by the lack of English competition.

In Switzerland the Continental System gave the cotton industry a welcome respite at a critical time. Machine-spun English yarns were on the point of ousting Swiss hand-spun yarns from the market when Lancashire goods virtually disappeared from the Continent. The Swiss cotton manufacturers found that raw materials were difficult and costly to obtain. They lost their markets in Italy. But they found a new outlet for their products in Germany. At the same time progress was made at Schaffhausen in the construction of textile machines. Some Swiss handspinners and handloom weavers migrated to Alsace because there was a demand in Mulhouse for skilled labour.

Russia, on the whole, was little affected by the Continental System since so much of her industrial production was destined for the home market. But the export of timber from Russia's Baltic ports ceased for a time and the trade of St. Petersburg—dominated at that time by a few large English merchant houses—declined when the Continental System was adopted in the Czar's dominions. The destruction of Moscow during the campaign of 1812 checked the expansion of this important centre for the production of textile goods. Ivanovo on the other hand benefited from the misfortunes of Moscow.

It is not easy to assess the permanent consequences of the Continental System because many other factors influenced the development of the economies of the European countries during and immediately after the Revolutionary and Napoleonic wars. Some branches of manufacture which received their first stimulus at this time—even though they may have suffered a brief eclipse immediately after 1815—eventually established themselves on a permanent basis. The sugar beet industry was one of these. On the other hand some industries which flourished in the days of the Continental System did not long survive its disappearance. Indeed the cotton industry of Ghent showed unmistakable signs of collapse even before the fall of Napoleon. Some industries which would probably have been in difficulties but for the Continental System were reprieved owing to the absence of British competition and subsequently survived. The cotton industry of Saxony was an example. Sometimes an industry declined during the period of the Continental System—handloom weaving in Silesia for example—and never really recovered afterwards. The effects of the Continental System upon different manufactures and industrial regions obviously varied very considerably.

A generation after the Continental System had disappeared some Protectionists looked back to the days of Napoleon's empire as a period during which their policy had been put into force with satisfactory results. They argued that under the Continental System English manufactured goods were virtually excluded from the Continent and, as a result, many branches of manufacture in France, Germany, Belgium and Switzerland had an opportunity to expand. They claimed that Britain was so far ahead of the rest of Europe from the point of view of large-scale manufacturing enterprises that high—if necessary prohibitive—import duties and stringent navigation laws were necessary to save "infant" continental industries from extinction. In so far as the Protectionists used "historical" arguments to support their views they gave a picture of Europe in the days of the Continental System that was a travesty of the facts. They ignored the great hardships which the peoples of France and her satellites suffered because of the shortages of manufactured goods and colonial products. No one who lived through that grim period of austerity would have wished to see the re-establishment of the Continental System as a means of ensuring "prosperity" for the man in the street.

## (ii) 1815–1848

### FACTORS INFLUENCING INDUSTRIAL EXPANSION

In some respects the industrial revolution in France differed from similar developments elsewhere. The pace of industrialization was slower than in Britain or Germany. "The transformation accomplished in a century was in many ways less complete than that which Germany experienced in the forty years after 1871." Throughout the nineteenth century farming was of greater importance in the French economy than in those of other manufacturing countries. In 1881 two-thirds of the population still lived in villages and small market towns.

It has been seen that the French system of administration was highly centralized. In Germany before 1871 economic affairs were controlled by the federal states except that unity of tariffs had been secured by the establishment of the Zollverein. But France had been unified from an economic point of view between 1789 and 1815. The reorganization of local government under the Consulate placed virtually all effective power in the hands of the central authority. It has been pointed out that this "unwittingly created obstacles to the co-ordination of future economic developments. The economic and commercial domination of Paris had serious effects on the economic life of the provinces. The concentration of main lines of communication on the capital rendered inter-regional communication difficult. The competition of Paris shops and commercial houses stifled local commercial enterprises, and the drain of capital to Paris has brought about the decline of banks."

It was not until the latter years of the nineteenth century that the power of Paris over French economic affairs began to decline. By the 1890's some of the larger provincial towns had expanded to such an extent that they exercised considerable influence over a surrounding region. The improvement of transport facilities between provincial towns, the increased use of hydro-electric power, and the activities of local chambers of commerce and co-operative societies fostered economic developments on a regional basis.

Lack of coal was one of the main causes of France's relatively slow industrial progress. In the first half of the nineteenth century the scattered coal deposits of the central highlands were her main source of supply. In the 1860's the output of the coalfield in the Departments of the Nord and Pas de Calais overtook that of the central highlands. With an output of under five million tons in 1852, just over thirteen million tons in 1870 and 34·7 million tons in 1905 France was far behind the United States, Britain and Germany as a coal-producing country. France did not produce enough coal for her needs and had to import coal from Belgium, Germany and Britain. The cost of coal was high and this increased manufacturing costs and made it difficult for French industrialists to compete in world markets. E. Baines (the younger), writing in 1835, stated that in Paris coal was actually ten times more costly than in Manchester. The fact that it was rare to find coal and iron-ore close together in France hampered the development of the iron, steel and engineering industries. The absence of coal in the vicinity of the great ports hampered the growth of a modern shipbuilding industry.

The position with regard to pig-iron and steel was different. Until 1871 France had in Lorraine the largest iron-ore deposits in western Europe. The success of the Hayange ironworks showed what could be achieved in this region. But, on the whole, the French neglected to exploit the vast iron-ore resources of Lorraine. Soon after Lorraine was annexed by Germany the Gilchrist Thomas process was invented and this enabled the phosphoric *minette* of Lorraine and Luxemburg to be used to make basic steel. In 1914 France was not among the world's leading producers of pig-iron or steel.

The establishment of an adequate network of railways was essential to industrial progress in the nineteenth century. The main French railways were constructed more slowly than those of Britain, the United States or Germany. Railway construction was held up while the legislature debated on the routes to be followed by the principal lines and the extent to which the State should finance railway construction. It was not until the reorganization of the main railway companies under the Second Empire that France secured an efficient system of railways.

The expansion of France's main ports was also delayed by various unfavourable factors. After the Napoleonic wars the loss of the former trade with San Domingo adversely affected the development of Bordeaux and Nantes while the decline of France's share in the Levant trade hampered the revival of Marseilles. Eventually the establishment of a new colonial Empire in Africa and in Indo-China opened up new trade routes for French merchants and shippers. The growth of the ports was also hampered by the lack of industrial hinterlands. Only Le Havre had such a hinterland in the Normandy manufacturing region. Marseilles and Bordeaux had few great industries in the immediate vicinity.

The failure to attract sufficient capital was another reason why French industry did not make rapid progress. The French were a thrifty people but their savings tended to be invested in State bonds (*rentes*), commerce at home and abroad, and in foreign loans rather than in manufactures. Until about 1850 it was the notaries who held the purse strings in the rural districts. They acted as financial advisers, bankers and trustees for their clients and controlled the destinies of the savings of land owners, farmers and small holders. They were generally conservative in outlook and only occasionally recommended their clients to invest in industrial enterprises. In the first half of the nineteenth century both industrialists and farmers were hampered by lack of capital. Neither the *haute banque* of Paris nor the provincial banks invested directly in manufactures on anything like an adequate scale. The *Caisse Laffitte* (1837) was a pioneer attempt to set up a bank to promote new manufacturing enterprises, but it was not until the establishment of the *Crédit Mobilier* in Napoleon III's reign that savings began to flow into industrial undertakings.

Unlike most industrial countries France was slow to develop the technique of mass production. English merchants declared that "the Frenchmen work for the few, but we for the millions". The reputation of the French rested not on the manufacture of cheap articles on a large scale but on the production of luxury goods of high quality. Well-designed silks, carpets and tapestries; fashionable gowns, gloves and hats; superior glassware and porcelain and high-class jewellery and trinkets; vintage wines and brandies—these were the products for which France was world famous. When Chaptal showed Charles James Fox and Lord Cornwallis round the industrial exhibition at the Louvre in 1802 Fox remarked to his host that only luxury products appeared to be on view and nearly fifty years later at the Great Exhibition in London the French exhibits which visitors admired were the silks of Lyons, the porcelain of Sèvres, the tapestries of the Gobelins and the carpets of Aubusson. In 1860 the luxury trades of Paris alone gave employment to 63,000 workers. These trades catered for only a limited market of relatively wealthy customers at home and abroad. They were industries which were nearly always the first to suffer in times of war or commercial depression. The notorious fluctuations of the Lyons silk industry—and the chequered fortunes of those whose livelihood depended upon it—illustrate the drawbacks from which luxury industries suffer. Some luxury industries, however, expanded so as to produce cheaper goods for a larger number of customers. The manufacturers of glassware began by making high-quality articles for wealthy clients but later turned out large quantities of bottles and of other glass articles in common use.

The industrial policy of the French Government did not encourage a spirit of enterprise among manufacturers. Since Colbert's day successive governments had fostered, supervised and subsidized French industrialists and had protected them from foreign competition. Only during two periods—between 1786 and 1792 and between 1860 and the 1880's—was a more liberal fiscal policy adopted. Normally high import duties gave manufacturers a privileged position in the home market, navigation laws protected French shipping, and colonial trade was, as far as possible, monopolized by the mother country. Michel Chevalier declared that between 1814 and 1848 the tariffs "were more rigorous, more exclusive, more opposed to liberty than the tariffs of the Empire and were utterly without excuse". In the circumstances it was hardly surprising that some French manufacturers should show a tendency to conservatism and should lack initiative and enterprise. Without the spur of foreign competition they were frequently content to use traditional techniques without troubling to change with the times. This helps to explain why France was so slow to adopt modern techniques of industrial production. Important inventions such as the steam engine, the coke blast-furnace and hydro-electric power were introduced into France more slowly than in some other manufacturing countries.

In most manufacturing countries industrialization was accompanied by a rapid increase in population. In France, however, the rate of growth of the population was slow when compared with Britain, Germany or the United States. In the nineteenth century the population of France increased by only 10 millions—from 29 to 39 millions. But the population of Great Britain rose in that period from 10·5 millions to 37 millions although emigration from Britain was greater than from France. In the 1860's the live birth rate in France (per 1,000 of the population) was only 26·1 as compared with 37·2 in Germany and 35·4 in England. In 1910 French live births per 1,000 of the population were only 19·7 while the figures for Germany and England were 29·8 and 24·8 respectively.[1] Consequently French industry did not have the same stimulus of a rapidly growing home market and an expanding supply of factory workers that other great manufacturing states enjoyed. Only a few manufacturing and mining towns—such as Roubaix, Saint Etienne, Decazeville and Commentry—grew with anything like the rapidity of Chicago, Essen or Manchester. In 1910 both Britain and the United States had 50 cities each with a population of over 100,000, Germany had 48 cities of this size, and Russia had 22, but France had only 15.

## The Restoration, 1815–30

The period of the Restoration was one of reconstruction after the abnormal economic conditions brought about by the Revolution,

---

[1] When considering the growth of France's population it must be remembered that the provinces of Alsace and Lorraine were annexed by Germany in 1871. They were returned to France in 1919.

the Napoleonic wars and the Continental System. France had lost control over large territories on the Continent such as Holland, Belgium, northern Italy and the left bank of the Rhine. She had lost San Domingo and its rich sugar trade. The virtually complete failure of the harvest in 1816–17 led to great distress in many parts of France. In the Languedoc region economic depression inflamed religious intolerance and Catholic artisans attacked their Huguenot employers. The Government had to pay off the war indemnity and to fund the national debt. The output of some branches of manufacture—such as iron and textiles—declined when military orders ceased. France had long been cut off from Britain, the home of modern machinery, and French industry was relatively backward from the point of view of technical equipment.

Some writers have contrasted the economic development of France during the Restoration and the July Monarchy and have suggested that the former period was one of stagnation while the latter was one during which substantial economic progress was made. It is true that the long wars were followed by a period during which painful readjustments had to be made and that there were depressions in 1816–17 and in 1827–30. Nevertheless there were signs of some economic recovery in the 1820's and Henri Sée has observed that "notable progress in mechanization" took place at that time. There is evidence of vigorous entrepreneurial activity in France as may be seen by examining the achievements of men like Georges Dufaud (who established the Fourchambault ironworks for the Boignes family), François Cabrol (described as the "real founder" of the Decazeville ironworks), Schlumburger of Guebwiller and Koechlin of Mulhouse (cotton spinners and machine builders), Ternaux (the leading cloth manufacturer of Sedan), Marc Séguin (famous bridge builder and constructor of the first French railway), and the well-known bankers James Rothschild and Jacques Laffitte. Professor Leuilliot suggests that France's "pre-Industrial Revolution" should be dated from 1825 and not from 1830.

Progress in farming, improvements in transport, the introduction of new machines, the activities of French and foreign entrepreneurs, and the development of banking and insurance—these were factors which contributed to the revival of manufactures in the late 1820's. J. Kuczynski remarks that "agriculture emerged from the period of the Revolution and the Napoleonic régime as a strong and firmly based capitalist branch of national economy, surpassing in importance all other branches put together". The great landlords were politically powerful under the restored Bourbons. They obtained compensation for their losses during the Revolution and they secured the impositions of high import duties on cereals and livestock to protect the owners of great estates from foreign competition. Tooke and Newmarch denounced the French corn laws as "inexcusable—inasmuch as grain and provisions had been left free of entry even in the most violent enactments of the previous war".

Despite the large area of waste land and fallow land and the continued use of primitive tools and appliances, agricultural output increased. The urban and rural workers consumed cereals, potatoes, vegetables and livestock produced by French farmers. The textile industries used wool, flax and raw silk produced at home, though additional supplies had to be imported. The leather industry used hides from French farms. The sugar-beet crop provided the raw material for the refineries. Grapes from French vineyards were used to produce wines both for home consumption and for a great export trade. And as agricultural output expanded those who gained a livelihood from the land had more money to spend upon manufactured goods. Thus in various ways the gradual recovery of farming —the major economic activity in France at that time—promoted industrial expansion.

Economic recovery was to some extent dependent upon improved communications. In the years following the Napoleonic wars the maintenance of the roads was neglected. Becquey, the director general of the Department of Highways and Bridges, reported in 1825 that the condition of the roads in industrial regions, such as the Nord Department and the Saint Etienne district, was particularly unsatisfactory. Some French historians have criticized the Restoration governments for neglecting the highways, but A. L. Dunham argues that the central and local authorities made the most of their limited financial resources. In this period the first suspension bridges were built in France—such as Marc Séguin's bridges over the Seine (La Roche-Guyon) and the Rhône (Tournon) The Restoration governments improved and extended France's inland waterways. The Burgundy and the Berry Canals were improved and the Saône–Doubs section of the Saône–Rhine Canal was constructed. Several new canals were built in the north-east to facilitate the trade in coal. The regulating of the upper Rhine by J. G. Tulla—a scheme originally approved by the *Magistrat du Rhin* appointed by Napoleon—was carried out by agreement between the states through which the river ran. The project saved farm lands from flooding but did not greatly improve the navigation of the upper Rhine. At this time canals in France were generally constructed by joint-stock companies with some assistance from the State. The Government lent money to canal companies and the construction of new waterways was often undertaken by the engineers of the Department of Highways and Bridges. The first French railway—the line from Saint Etienne to Andrézieux—was built in Charles X's reign.

The activities of foreign—particularly English—entrepreneurs in France were of particular significance at this time. Aaron Manby and his sons established engineering plants and gas undertakings and operated river steamships. Aaron Manby and his partner Daniel Wilson set up an engineering establishment at Charenton near Paris. Pelouze, writing in 1827, stated that the plant included forges, foundries and rolling mills. He drew attention to "the extraordinary influence exercised by the Charenton ironworks upon all—or nearly all—the many manufacturers who, in the short period of four years, have established forges of the English type".

Manby and Wilson not only operated the Charenton works but also erected new engineering establishments for French firms. The machines installed in these works were of English design and, in the first instance, were often operated by skilled English artisans. In 1826 Manby and Wilson acquired an interest in the famous Le Creusot ironworks. Additional forges and rolling mills were erected and new shafts were sunk in the adjacent coal-field. The commercial crisis of 1830 led to the failure of this enterprise and the new owners —the brothers Schneider—secured the benefit of the recent modernization of the plant.

Manby and Wilson were responsible for the establishment of a gas company in Paris which successfully lit the Rue de la Paix on December 31, 1829. Aaron Manby was also interested in the introduction of iron steamships on the rivers of France. In 1822 an iron steamship named after him crossed the English Channel and sailed up the River Seine to Paris. Two years later a witness told an English parliamentary inquiry that Manby had "established iron steamboats on almost every river in France". Aaron Manby's four sons were associated with him in many of his enterprises.

Several other English entrepreneurs were active in France in the 1820's. Humphrey Edwards was the manager of an important foundry and ironworks at Chaillot (Paris) where skilled English artisans were employed. He introduced the Woolf high-pressure engine into France. John Collier constructed cloth-shearing machinery in Paris, while James Cockerill erected modern machines at Elbeuf, Louviers and other centres for the manufacture of woollen cloth. James Jackson set up a large plant near Saint Etienne to make cast steel by Huntsman's process. His four sons acquired new works at Assailly in 1830. Job Dixon, an English engineer, was employed by Nicholas Schlumberger of Guebwiller to build cotton-spinning machinery

(1818) and he later became a partner of Risler Brothers of Cernay, who constructed steam-driven machinery and locomotives (1820). Richard Roberts, who invented the self-acting mule, installed the machinery in André Keochlin's cotton mill in Alsace. In the 1820's skilled artisans from Nottingham introduced the manufacture of bobbinet-lace to Saint-Pierre-les-Calais. Swiss entrepreneurs also contributed to the industrial progress of France at this time. J. C. Fischer of Schaffhausen—inventor of a method of making crucible cast steel and a pioneer in the production of steel alloys—set up steel plants and engineering workshops for French industrialists at Badevel and Voujeaucourt.

The growth of the French banking system at the time of the Restoration contributed to industrial expansion. Several Jewish financiers established themselves in Paris of whom James Rothschild was the most important since he represented a family of international financiers who operated in Frankfurt am Main, Vienna and London. The Rothschilds handled public and foreign loans. Jacques Laffitte had established himself as a banker under the Empire and Napoleon had entrusted him with his fortune in 1815. A part of the loan raised by the French Government in 1817 to pay off the war indemnity was handled by Laffitte. He made a fortune in the 1820's, lost much of it during the commercial crisis of 1830, and then re-established his position in Louis Philippe's reign. Casimir Périer and Scipion Périer had combined banking with manufacturing activities in the days of the Empire when they controlled ironworks, sugar refineries, and textile mills. After the Napoleonic wars they extended their financial interests to floating public loans and dealing in *rentes*. The Syndicate of Receivers General was a finance company that was set up in 1826 to handle the large funds accumulated by tax collectors on behalf of the Treasury. It co-operated with the Bank of France and the Paris private banks to invest funds in public works and industrial enterprises. Some of its members eventually became private bankers. Several important insurance companies were founded during the Restoration such as the Royal (1816), the General Fire (1819), the Phoenix (1819), the Union (1828) and the Sun (1829). The Royal Insurance Company was responsible for the establishment of the Paris Savings Bank. The accumulation of capital at the time of the Restoration was sufficient to enable money to be invested in foreign countries. After the Napoleonic wars the French Government had to raise a loan to pay her indemnity but by 1830 France's investments abroad—in Spain and Italy for example—were estimated at 500 million francs. This money might perhaps have been more usefully employed at home to foster the expansion of French industry.

The gradual expansion of the output of French ironworks and textile mills and the growth of overseas commerce may serve to illustrate the development of industry during the Restoration. The iron industry used iron-ore mined in France. A large number of small iron-ore deposits, generally capable of being worked by open-cast methods, were exploited by individuals or partners who were often peasants for whom mining was only a part-time occupation. Chaptal stated that in 1819 France had 230 blast-furnaces, 82 Catalan forges and 860 refining works (*feux d'affinerie*). According to Flachart the output of pig-iron in 1819 was 112,500 tons and the production of steel amounted to 74,200 tons.

The typical French ironworks—like the typical iron-ore mine—at this time was a very modest establishment operated by a family or by a small group of partners. There were, however, some larger modern ironworks and their numbers increased between 1815 and 1830. It has been seen that the Le Creusot ironworks—"probably the greatest establishment in the French iron industry in 1815"—were modernized by Manby and Wilson who also ran the Charenton ironworks at Paris. The ironworks at Hayange (de Wendel), Chaillot (Périer), Assailly (Jackson), Decazeville (Guérin), Audincourt (Saglio, Humann et Cie), Châtillon-sur-Seine (Marmont, Duke of Ragusa), Saint Etienne (de Gallois-Lachapelle) and those run by the Isère and Loire Company were large progressive concerns. The capital value in 1829 of French ironworks using coal—and this would exclude hundreds of small works using charcoal—amounted to nearly forty-six million francs.

Some technical improvements were being made at this time. The first coke furnace in France had been set up by William Wilkinson at Le Creusot in 1785. It was not until 1819 that further furnaces of this type were erected by de Wendel at Hayange and by de Gallois-Lachapelle at Saint Etienne. At about the same time the puddling and rolling processes were introduced at Le Creusot, Grossource, Fourchambault, Hayange, and Saint Etienne. The hot blast was first used in about 1830. A large amount of capital was required to install modern equipment in ironworks; the price of coal and coke was high; and transport costs were a substantial item of expenditure. High costs were probably the main reason why coke smelting, puddling, rolling and slitting, the hot blast and other improvements in the manufacture of iron—though well known in France in 1830 —were not generally adopted. Side by side with a handful of modern iron works and steelworks were a large number of out-of-date furnaces and forges run on traditional lines.

The engineering industry—particularly the construction of machinery—made some progress at the time of the Restoration. Mule-jennies, looms, carding machines, cloth-cutters and various other appliances for the textile industries were made by such firms as Risler Brothers of Cernay, Nicholas Schlumberger of Guebwiller, André Koechlin of Mulhouse, John Collier of Paris and the Dyer family of Gemaches. Some advance was also made in the manufacture of steam engines, pumps, boilers, rails, iron ships and installations for ironworks and steelworks.

The textile industries were of considerable importance in this period. The cotton industry had expanded in the early years of the nineteenth century. Owing to the British blockade there had been difficulties in securing supplies of the raw material but cotton from the Levant had generally enabled the cotton mills to keep going. During the war French cotton manufacturers did not have to face competition from Lancashire as they had done while the Eden Treaty was in operation. Cotton spinning had developed in the Paris region and at the end of the Napoleonic Wars there were more spindles in the Seine Department (133,000) than in any other Department. The Paris mills declined soon after peace was declared. But the expansion of other centres of cotton production—Normandy, Alsace and the Nord Department—more than made up for this loss. The consumption of raw cotton amounted to 30 million kilogrammes in 1827 as compared with only 18 million kilogrammes in 1812.

The cotton industry in Normandy had developed in the eighteenth century. This province had excellent supplies of water power and could draw upon a labour force trained in the manufacture of woollens. Le Havre was Normandy's cotton port while Rouen was its main commercial and manufacturing centre. Some of the yarn and cloth was produced in fairly large workshops but the rural and domestic side of the industry was still of considerable significance. The expansion of the industry owed much to the pioneer work of the Englishman John Holker who had settled in Rouen in the middle of the eighteenth century. He was the manager of a factory at Saint Sever (Rouen) where mixed woollen-cotton fabrics were made. English machinery was installed and English foremen and skilled operatives trained French artisans in the weaving and finishing processes. In 1755 Holker was appointed an Inspector General of Factories and for thirty years he played an active part in spreading the knowledge of improved textile machinery throughout the country. In the 1820's calico prints and other cheap products were made in Rouen and adjacent towns. The spinning jenny was in general use but only a few power looms had been installed.

Alsace had developed rather later than Normandy as a centre

for the manufacture of cotton. The finishing processes—such as dyeing—had been introduced into Mulhouse in the eighteenth century when it was still an Imperial City. Weaving and spinning had come later. The industry had grown at the time of the Continental System and continued to expand after 1815. The number of spindles increased from 70,000 to 500,000 between 1818 and 1828. A group of able families—Koechlin, Schlumberger, and Dollfus, for example—had helped to lay the foundations of a great industry. The leaders of the cotton industry in Mulhouse were among the most progressive in France in the early nineteenth century. The publications of the Industrial Society of Mulhouse, which was founded in 1825, show how active these men were not only in promoting technical improvements in the textile industries but also in taking practical measures to ameliorate the social evils brought about by industrialization.

The larger cotton establishments in Alsace were generally engaged in spinning, weaving and dyeing and did not concentrate on one branch of the industry. Some were already developing workshops for the construction and repair of cotton machines. The cotton industry was more mechanized in Alsace than elsewhere in France. Handspinning had almost disappeared by 1820 and power looms were being rapidly installed. Mulhouse produced finer cottons than Rouen.

The Nord Department was the newest of the French cotton regions. Lille, Roubaix and Tourcoing had made woollen cloth in the eighteenth century. Despite the high cost of raw cotton during the Napoleonic wars the increased demand for cotton fabrics led to the development of the manufacture of fustians and calicos.

The woollen industry was carried on throughout France and there were as yet few signs of geographical concentration. Louviers, Amiens, Roubaix, Reims, Sedan, Elbeuf, Abbeville, Nîmes, Carcassonne and the Paris region were among the more important woollen centres. Several problems faced the industry after the Napoleonic wars. One was to secure an adequate supply of fine wool. It is true that the home clip was increasing and that the breeding of merinos was making progress. The first merino flock had been brought to Rambouillet by Louis XVI in the 1780's and some 5,000 merino sheep had been imported under the terms of the Treaty of Basel (1799). In the 1820's Polignac maintained a large flock of merino sheep—its size varied from 7,000 to 11,000 sheep—on his estates in the south of Normandy. But Baron Dupin stated that France's output of merino wool in 1827 was a mere 766,000 kgm. as compared with a clip of 4·5 million kgm. of wool from the sheep

of mixed breeds (*métis*). In 1819 Ternaux, the great cloth manufacturer of Sedan, imported a flock of Tibet goats (brought to France
by Jaubert) on his estate at Saint Ouen near Paris. The wool was
used to make cashmere shawls. Another difficulty facing the French
woollen industry at this time was the failure to invent a machine to
comb short wool. John Collier of Paris had invented such a machine
—and it was patented in England under the name of John Platt of
Salford—but it did not prove to be entirely successful. Equally
disappointing were the attempts to replace hand-carding by machine
carding for the appliances constructed by Douglas and Mercier
were used to only a limited extent. Spinning machines, on the other
hand, were available for carded yarn and for combed wool. In 1811
William Douglas and the Cockerills had spun carded wool and
Ternaux had used a machine for spinning combed wool in one
of his mills near Reims. In 1827 seven mills in Paris had 10,000
mechanical spindles for combed wool and one factory in Sedan had
9,000 such spindles. But these machines too were not very widely
adopted and much spinning was still done by hand. The weaving of
wool was done almost exclusively by hand.

Changes were taking place in the type of woollens produced in
France. The output of high-quality products—such as carpets,
tapestries, curtains, cashmere shawls, and fancy waistcoats—was
still important but a number of manufacturers were now turning
their attention to the production of cheaper types of cloth such as
*union* (woollen weft and cotton warp) and *drap de renaissance*
(shoddy cloth).

The French woollen industry was still run mainly on a domestic
basis. There were a few large establishments, such as those of
Ternaux and of de Neuflize in Sedan, but many of the prominent
entrepreneurs in the industry were merchants who controlled the
work of large numbers of village spinners and weavers who worked
in their own homes. Dupouilly of Paris is described by Dunham as
"a great organizer who developed the weaving of his cloths all
through Picardy and the Nord". "He was perhaps the greatest of
all creators of mixed cloths and one of the greatest creators of
novelties as well as one of the chief supporters of the new Jacquard
loom." Morin was "a leading designer of novelties" who did not
run a big factory but "employed hundreds of rural weavers in
Picardy as well as in the Nord".

The manufacture of silk was the one textile industry in which
France led the world. The Jacquard loom for silk weaving was one
of the few major textile machines invented in France. The loss of
Piedmont in 1815 made France more dependent than before upon

foreign raw silk. Strenuous efforts were made to increase the growth of mulberry trees and the production of cocoons in France itself. The greatest success was achieved in the Rhône valley (between Rive de Gier and Avignon) and in the Cevennes. The Gard Department produced most silkworms but the best raw silk came from the Ardèche Department. A contemporary, writing in 1831, remarked that "a merchant of Lyons states that foreign silk does not form more than one-tenth or one-eighth of the whole quantity now used in the French manufactories; thirty years ago one-half was foreign". But he added that "no very authentic information can, indeed, be obtained on this point".

The manufacture of silk was largely concentrated in the Lyons district though the industry was also making substantial progress in Saint Etienne and the nearby village of Saint Chamond. In 1825 it was reported that Lyons had 8,100 silkweaving workshops in which over 20,000 looms were installed. By 1832 the number of looms was estimated to be 42,000. The preliminary processes—reeling and throwing—were generally undertaken in workshops in the villages near Lyons. During the Restoration there was an increase in the types of silk products made in France. The silk ribbon industry of Saint Etienne made remarkable progress immediately after the Napoleonic wars. The manufacture of plush, crêpe, tulle and mixed cloths (cotton and silk waste) also deserve mention. Lyons suffered from the competition of new silk centres in France, and also from the spread of silk-weaving in the villages around Lyons. As in the other textile industries so in silk there were comparatively few large establishments. La Sauvagère's silkworks appear to have been the only big factory in Lyons in the 1820's. The leading entrepreneurs of the city—Arlès-Dufour, for example—were wholesalers who supplied French and foreign customers with raw silk and merchants who handled the silks made in small workshops. There was a serious depression in the Lyons silk industry in 1829 which has been ascribed to competition (particularly in cheap silks) both from abroad and from the new silk centres in France itself. One-third of the looms were idle, earnings fell and unemployment was rife. The stage was already set for the strikes and riots of 1831 and 1834.

The linen industry had been established in France for centuries. Chaptal states that 40,000 hectares of land were under flax in 1817 but this may be an underestimate. The acreage under flax probably increased during the Restoration but it did not expand sufficiently to meet the demand and some flax was imported from Belgium and Russia. The manufacture of linen was undertaken in many districts— in the north-east (Saint Quentin, Valenciennes, Cambrai, Douai,

Lille), in Normandy (Lisieux, Dieppe), in Dauphiné (Grenoble), in Brittany (Quimper, Saint Malo) and in Maine. The types of linen manufactured in France fall into two groups. On the one hand fine linens were made—at Cambrai for example—for domestic use as dresses, table-cloths and sheets. On the other hand coarse linen sailcloth and hempen ropes were made for the shipping industry at the Normandy and Brittany ports.

The manufacture of linens was still mainly a small-scale domestic industry and few large workshops or factories existed. Between 1810 and 1815 Philippe de Girard greatly improved an English flax-spinning machine invented by Kendrew and Porthouse but his machine was not immediately adopted in France. One of his associates betrayed his secret to John Marshall and Horace Hall who built the machine in Leeds where a new flax-spinning industry developed in the 1820's. It was not until 1830 that a Lille firm brought this machine back to France. On the whole in the period of the Restoration the manufacture of linens in France was backward in comparison with the Irish and Belgian linen industries.

There were many other French industries besides textiles and iron which were expanding at this time. The building trade, the leather industry, the sugar refineries, the flour mills, the chemical works, the glassworks, and the potteries showed signs of expansion. The development of soda factories in Marseilles was particularly significant in this period.

Although by the late 1820's a number of French industries were recovering from the effects of the Revolutionary and Napoleonic wars no similar recovery had taken place in France's overseas trade. France's position from the point of view of international commerce was perhaps better than that indicated by official trade statistics. A French consul reported in 1828 that owing to smuggling French exports to Spain were three times as great as those indicated by the statistics. Even if allowance is made for defects in the statistics it is still true to say that France's external trade did not expand very rapidly in the period of the Restoration. The shipping tonnage using French ports rose only from 600,000 tons to 800,000 tons between 1816 and 1830. There was an adverse balance of commodity trade in 1830 since France's exports of manufactured articles and wines did not balance her imports of raw materials and colonial goods. The failure of the colonial trade to revive after 1815 was one reason why France's overseas commerce did not expand as much as might have been expected. San Domingo had been lost but Guadeloupe and Martinique had been recovered. These two islands produced considerable quantities of cane sugar. But the attempt to revive the old colonial system of the *ancien régime* was doomed to failure. The mother country was not in a position to insist that the whole of the commercial sugar crop should be sent to France. As Dunham observes: "The colonies no longer appreciated the old system. They had grown accustomed to selling sugar elsewhere and to obtaining their food and manufactures from other sources that were nearer and cheaper." As far as its sugar policy was concerned the Restoration Government was in a cleft stick since it wished to afford protection both to cane sugar from the colonies and to beet sugar grown at home. The two objects of French policy were incompatible since measures taken to favour one type of sugar inevitably reacted unfavourably upon the other type of sugar. By fostering home-grown beet sugar the French Government was no longer in a position to guarantee the sugar colonies a market in which there was no competition. This made it impossible to insist that the colonies should buy manufactured goods only from France. The French also lost a considerable part of their former markets in the Mediterranean (particularly the Levant) and in South America. When the Spanish colonies in South America secured their independence and opened their ports it was English merchants who secured the lion's share of the new trade.

Moreover, the system of high protection made it difficult, if not impossible, for France's foreign trade to expand. Those who restrict their purchases from foreign countries inevitably find it difficult to sell their goods abroad. The protective system gave many French manufacturers a virtual monopoly of the home market. Their profits were assured and—with certain striking exceptions—they did not trouble to try to sell their goods abroad on a large scale. According to Dunham the root of the trouble was that "most French manufacturers had no interest in foreign trade, knew little or nothing about foreign markets or the needs and wishes of foreigners, and sold goods for exporting only when they could not sell them at home".

Some of the social consequences of industrialization were already in evidence in France in the 1820's. Immediately after the Napoleonic wars the introduction of new machines led to outbreaks of violence among the workers. Early in 1819 there were riots at Vienne (Isère Department) when a cloth-cutting machine (*tondeuse*) was brought to the workshop of Gentin, Odoard et Cie. In May 1821 a similar machine was destroyed in Faulguier's workshop near Lodève (Herault Department). There was much unrest in various cloth-making centres at this time owing to the installation of the mechanical cloth-cutter.

There were complaints that both adult and young wage-earners were being ruthlessly exploited by their employers. Two examples may be given—one from Alsace and the other from the Nord Department. In 1821 the Council of the district (*arrondissement*) of Colmar in Alsace severely criticized local manufacturers who had recently introduced new machines into their factories and workshops. The Council stated that:

"several of the manufacturers—not content with having by the aid of these machines expanded their output beyond all measure— have given much greater scope to their cupidity by making children of either sex and of any age work day and night in their workshops to keep their machines going all the time and so double their profits. This policy has been made possible by the poverty of the inhabitants of this district. And so the poor children and young people, handed over to this new species of slave labour, lose their health and hardly retain a human appearance. This is a generation sacrificed to the cupidity of the manufacturers, a generation that shows no physical growth and displays unex- ampled moral corruption. And the inevitable consequence will be that in a few years great difficulty will be experienced in finding men capable of bearing arms and of cultivating the land."

In 1826 M. Brunot of Le Cateau in the Nord Department wrote as follows to the Minister of Ecclesiastical Affairs:

"The greed of the manufacturers knows no limits; they sacrifice their workers to enrich themselves. They are not content with reducing these poor creatures to slavery by making them work in unhealthy workshops from which fresh air is excluded, from 5 a.m. to 8 p.m. (and sometimes 10 p.m.) in the summer, and from 6 a.m. to 9 p.m. in the winter; they force them to work a part of Sunday as well. From bed to work and from work to bed—that sums up the life of their victims. Many workers have to go half a league to their work—sometimes even a whole league. In summer they have to rise at 4 a.m., and, in the evening, after a hard day's work, they do not get home until 9 p.m. In winter it is even worse. Then they are exposed to the rigours of a severe season and they are often drenched to the skin. Yet on the following day they have to put on their damp clothes once more. A worse slavery cannot be imagined. They never have a moment for their private affairs; they always breathe a polluted atmosphere; for them the sun never shines. The children employed in these workshops become

107

stunted and weakly, and the men—deprived of wholesome air—lose all their vitality."

## THE JULY MONARCHY 1830–48

When the July Monarchy was established in 1830 France was in the middle of a slump which had started in 1827 and which continued until 1832. Prices were rising, grain was in short supply and several industries—textiles, building and the wine trade—were in a depressed condition. The new régime was immediately faced with the problem of stimulating the economic development of the country. There can be no doubt that the pace of industrialization in France was accelerated in Louis Philippe's reign. Some of the factors which had promoted the expansion of manufactures during the Restoration continued to influence industrialization during the July Monarchy. Agricultural progress, mechanization, new factories and improved banking facilities played their part in promoting greater industrial activity.

Two factors of major importance were the policy of the government in stimulating economic developments and the improvement of communications. There was in France a long-standing tradition that it was the duty of the State to promote industries by every means at its disposal. The *ancien régime*, the Revolutionary governments and Napoleon had all been active in this respect. The Restoration governments had been dominated by the landed aristocracy and had favoured the landlord and the farmer rather than the industrialist. And financial stringency had made it inevitable that the authorities should adopt a policy of strict economy and should hesitate to finance industrial developments.

On the other hand the July Monarchy "represented the victory of the finance bourgeoisie over the landed capitalists. During the following eighteen years up to 1848 the financial oligarchy reigned supreme in France, subordinating to their own interests those of the rest of the capitalists. They joined with the railway kings in exploitation; in fact they partly became railway kings themselves. They entered into alliances with some sections of the iron, steel and coal industries—alliances which were based to some extent on the rapid development of joint-stock companies—and with sections of the defeated landed aristocracy. The majority of the industrial capitalists, however—especially the textile industry, the strongest single industry at that time—came by degrees into even stronger opposition to them."

Louis Philippe's governments financed a programme of road building and canal construction. Above all the 1840's saw France's first railway boom. By 1847 some important main lines were in operation such as those from Paris to Le Havre, Lille, and Orleans and that from Strasbourg to Basel. Railway construction stimulated the iron industry and made it possible for French manufacturers to serve much wider regions than before. The forward policy of the July Monarchy with regard to the construction of roads, bridges, canals and railways—coupled with heavy military expenses in Algeria—led to financial difficulties. In the period 1840-7 budget deficits and government loans together amount to nearly 1,500 million francs.

The government of the July Monarchy greatly improved France's network of roads. Levasseur states that 578 million francs were spent on the highways in Louis Philippe's reign. A Highway Law of 1836 provided that able-bodied taxpayers should either give three days' labour a year on the roads or should pay a tax instead. The construction of many secondary (*vicinal*) and local (*communal*) roads linked farms to villages and market towns. An impetus was given to the expansion both of farming and of craft industries by the building of these roads. There was no very striking increase in the length of the network of main roads but much repair work was done. Some 240 bridges were built or repaired by public authorities and 31 were constructed by private persons or companies. More travellers and more goods were using the roads at this time and they were moving faster than before. The increase in the number of travellers by coach may be seen from the rise in the receipts of the tax on passenger tickets from 5·4 million francs in 1828 to 9·5 million francs in 1846. Two important stage-coach companies—the *Messageries Royales* and Jacques Laffitte's *Messageries Générales*—controlled about one-third of the traffic. They carried both passengers and parcels and they came to an agreement on fares and on the sharing of the main routes. The post office was handling more letters and printed matter at this time.

There was also considerable activity in canal building in Louis Philippe's reign. The Saint Quentin Canal was constructed and the Rhine–Marne and Aisne–Marne Canals were begun. Altogether over 2,000 km. of canals were built between 1830 and 1848 at a cost of 300 million francs. A law of 1836 regulated the dues to be levied on the new canals. English capital, technical knowledge and skilled engineers played an important part in promoting the development of steam-shipping on France's inland waterways at this time. The efforts of English entrepreneurs, however, do not seem to have been uniformly successful. In 1844 Jules Burat stated that "enormous losses" had been suffered by certain English river-steamship companies.

The French mercantile marine—about 680,000 tons in 1848—was the largest on the Continent and the third largest in the world. But it was far smaller than those of its nearest rivals, for in the middle of the nineteenth century Britain had a merchant navy of 3·5 million tons and the United States had one of 1·5 million tons. Attempts of the French Government to establish new steamship lines in the Atlantic and Mediterranean were unsuccessful and France did not become one of the great ocean carriers of the world.

By far the most significant development in transport in Louis Philippe's reign was the construction of the first railways. At the end of the eighteenth century wooden and cast-iron tramways had been built in various mines (such as the Montcenis and Anzin collieries and the Poullaouen copper mines) and in industrial establishments (such as the Indret foundry). During and immediately after the Napoleonic wars articles in the *Annales des Arts* and the *Annales des Mines* showed that experts appreciated the significance of the colliery tramways in Britain.

It was not, however, until 1827 that France's first railway was completed. Marc Séguin—bridge builder and inventor of a tubular boiler—had inspected the Stockton to Darlington line and had discussed problems of railway building with George Stephenson and his son. Séguin was responsible in 1827 for the construction of a single-track line linking the industrial centre of Saint Etienne and the little port of Andrézieux on the Loire (18 km.). Horse traction was used at first. Next Marc Séguin and his brother built a line from Saint Etienne to Lyons (58 km.). The first section from the Rive de Gier coalfield to the Givors Canal was opened in October 1830 and the line was completed in 1832. The first French train to be drawn by a locomotive ran on this railway. In 1833 the line from Saint Etienne to Andrézieux was extended to Roanne.

This early railway network—which was not a financial success at first—was built to serve the needs of a mining and industrial region. The lines radiated from Saint Etienne and formed a link with the main waterways of the region—the Rhône, the Loire and the Givors Canal. They were designed to carry freight rather than passengers. They were built by private companies and much of the capital was raised locally.

The significance of these lines was not at first appreciated by the public. It was not realized that the future development of the French economy made it essential for a great network of railways to be built radiating from Paris to the main industrial centres and to the great ports. Only a small group of people—mainly followers of Saint Simon such as Enfantin, Michel Chevalier and Emile Pereire —tried to arouse public interest in railways. Eventually they achieved some success and influential persons such as Legrand (Director of the Department of Highways and Bridges) and the international banker James Rothschild began to appreciate the need for the construction of a national network of railways.

In 1833 the French legislature took two decisions which ultimately had important results upon the development of railways in France. The first was that all future railway concessions should be made by the Chambers and not by the Crown. The second was that 500,000 francs should be set aside to defray the cost of planning the country's future railway system. With these funds at its disposal the Department of Highways and Bridges sent its engineers to Britain and to America to examine the lines already built in those countries. Then detailed surveys of some of the major railway routes in France were made.

The legislature proceeded to consider the details of a master plan for the country's railways and also examined the merits of nationalization and private enterprise. The network of lines envisaged for the future was largely determined by geographical factors. It was planned that the principal lines should start from Paris and should radiate to the main ports (Le Havre, Calais, Bordeaux, Marseilles), to neighbouring countries (Spain, Belgium, Switzerland, Germany and Italy), and to the chief industrial regions (the Nord Department, Alsace-Lorraine and the Loire basin). The needs of the army and navy had also to be considered. Fortresses such as Verdun and Metz and naval bases such as Brest clearly had to be linked by rail with the capital.

The problem concerning the construction and future ownership of the railways was more difficult to solve. In Britain and in the United States lines were being built by private joint-stock companies while Belgium was constructing a network of State lines. Eventually a compromise was adopted. The Railway Law of 1842 (for which Teste, the Minister of Public Works was largely responsible) provided that the State should pay for the land on which a railway was built as well as one-third of the cost of the "infrastructure"—the track, the bridges and the tunnels. Local authorities were to pay the remaining two-thirds of the cost of the "infrastructure". Private companies were to receive concessions for a limited number of years and were to pay for the "superstructure"—the rails, the stations, the signal boxes and the rolling stock. The companies, of course, would

111

have to meet the cost of running the railway—the fuel, the wages, the maintenance of the track and so forth. These arrangements did not work satisfactorily and soon had to be changed. The departments and communes objected to contributing towards the expenses of building railways and their obligation to pay for two-thirds of the "infrastructure" was transferred to the State. Moreover since promoters were not prepared to build lines which appeared unlikely to yield a profit the Government soon found that it had to shoulder substantially greater financial burdens than those laid down by the Law of 1842. Sometimes the State paid not only for the "infrastructure" but also for much of the "superstructure" before asking promoters to tender for a concession. Sometimes the State took up a block of shares, granted a loan or a subsidy, or guaranteed the payment of the interest on the company's shares. On the other hand if a line seemed likely to become a highly profitable enterprise the Government imposed on the company terms which might be less favourable than those laid down in the Law of 1842. This happened in the case of the Northern Railway from Paris to Lille. Lardner declared that the Railway Law soon became "in a great degree a dead letter". Nevertheless certain principles embodied in this enactment survived. First, the building and running of the railways was to be a partnership between public and private enterprise. The State provided some of the initial capital—the proportion varied from line to line—and in return secured the right to take over the lines when the concessions expired. The State also had the right to appoint its representatives to sit on the various boards of management. Secondly, the State laid down the geographical plan of the country's railway network. Private interest was not allowed to be the sole criterion governing the decision to construct any particular line. Proper weight was given to economic, strategic and other considerations of a national character. Thirdly, the State made regulations to ensure the safety of those who travelled by rail. Passenger fares and freight rates were subject to Government supervision.

While the French chambers were discussing various aspects of the railway problem between 1833 and 1842, the actual construction of new lines was delayed. Uncertainty concerning the terms of future concessions made it difficult for promoters to raise money for building railways. It was not until 1837 that Paris secured its first line. This was the railway from Paris to Le Pecq which was eventually extended to St. Germain. It took Emile and Isaac Pereire three years to raise six million francs and even then the line might not have been built if a group of bankers headed by James Rothschild had not subscribed a further three million francs. The financial success of this line was unfortunately overshadowed by the difficulties encountered by the two lines from Paris to Versailles. The first (built along the right bank of the Seine) was another Pereire-Rothschild venture and was opened in 1839 while the second (on the left bank) was supported by the banker Fould and was completed in 1840. Largely because they competed with each other neither of these lines made a profit. Moreover there was a serious accident on the left-bank railway and over seventy passengers were killed. This disaster, coupled with the poor financial returns of the Paris-Versailles lines, alarmed railway promoters and delayed the building of further lines. The railway from Paris to Corbeil was, however, opened in 1840. It was built by a company which had been formed to construct a railway from the capital to Orleans. When the promoters ran into financial difficulties the Government came to their aid by guaranteeing four per cent interest on the company's shares for forty-five years. Meanwhile two railways were being constructed in Alsace. The first was a short line from Mulhouse to Thann (1839) and the second ran from Strasbourg along the Rhine valley to Mulhouse and Basel (1841). The cotton magnate Nicholas Koechlin took the initiative in promoting the Strasbourg–Basel railway and eventually secured a substantial Government loan which enabled the line to be completed.

In 1842 France had only 885 km. of railways as compared with Britain's 3,600 km. and Germany's 2,800 km. Between the passing of the Railway Law (1842) and the commercial crisis of 1847 there was a boom in railway construction and lines were built from Paris to Rouen, to Orleans and to Lille. The construction of the Paris–Rouen line to link the capital with the Normandy industrial region and Le Havre was an Anglo-French enterprise. British capital, technical knowledge and labour contributed to the success of this project. In 1840 a company, founded by the Anglo-French banking house of Laffitte and Blount,[1] obtained a concession to build the line and secured the support of the directors of the London and Southampton Railway who wished to improve communications between London and Paris. Much of the company's capital was in English hands though the French Government bought some shares and made a substantial loan to the company. The engineer (Joseph Locke) and the contractors (Thomas Brassey and William Mackenzie) were British. British materials were used and the line was built by an international force of navvies. Brassey's son later declared: "When my father went over to France, as the pioneer of the

---

[1] The Laffitte who was a partner in the firm of Laffitte and Blount was Charles a nephew of the well-known banker Jacques Laffitte.

business of the railway contractor in that country, he owed his success, in a great measure, to the superior qualities of a body of 5,000 English workmen who followed him to the Continent." An English firm (Buddicom and Allcard) was established to build locomotives and rolling stock and some fifty English engine drivers were employed on the railway. The line reached Rouen in 1843 and Le Havre in 1847.

English railway contractors and engineers subsequently built many other lines in France such as those from Mantes to Cherbourg and Le Mans, from Amiens to Boulogne, from Orleans to Bordeaux, and from Valence to Avignon. English capital poured into the coffers of French railway companies and by 1847 about half of their shares were in English hands. In the same year that the Paris–Rouen line was opened the railway from Paris to Orleans was completed. The construction of the lines from the capital to Rouen and to Orleans marked a turning point in French railway history. The long period of experiment and hesitation was over. Promoters now went ahead with new projects and investors were ready to put their savings into railway shares.

Both the Government and private promoters were active between 1843 and 1847. Plans were made to build lines from the capital to Lille, Strasbourg, Marseilles and Bordeaux. The Northern Railway —Paris to Lille, the Channel ports and the Belgian frontier—was built by the Department of Highways and Bridges at record speed with the aid of American steam shovels and was opened in 1846. A company formed by James Rothschild secured a concession for this line for thirty-nine years and repaid the Government the money that had already been spent on the railway. The line prospered since it linked the industrial districts of the Nord Department and Mons (in Belgium) with the French capital and also provided a quicker service between Paris and London than that maintained on the Le Havre–Southampton route. The opening of the Northern Railway greatly stimulated the industrial expansion of heavy industries and textiles in both the French and the Belgian manufacturing districts which it served. Within a few years the cost of bringing coal from Mons to Paris had been halved. The Government decided that the railway joining Paris and Marseilles should be built in three sections —Paris–Lyons, Lyons–Avignon, and Avignon–Marseilles. All three companies however were soon in financial difficulties and two of them ceased operations. The Paris–Orleans Company was refused a concession to continue its line to Bordeaux. A new company was formed for this purpose and the contract to build the line was secured by William Mackenzie. Several promoters were interested in a plan to construct the Eastern Railway (Paris–Strasbourg) and James Rothschild succeeded in bringing them together into a single company which secured a concession from the State. The Government stipulated that a branch line should be built to Forbach (near the Saar industrial region in Prussia).

By 1847 France had about 1,830 km. of railways in operation. There was a commercial crisis in that year which—though less serious than the one in Britain—held up railway construction. Holders of railway shares generally paid for them by instalments and in 1847 many English investors could not afford to pay fresh instalments when called upon to do so. Some French investors were in a similar position. Speculation in railway shares aggravated the situation. Several lines had only a small part of their track open for traffic and therefore were unable to earn much revenue at this critical time. A number of French railways were already in a difficult position in 1847 and were in no condition to face the disastrous economic consequences of the revolution of 1848.

Industrial expansion in Louis Philippe's reign was fostered by the development of banking facilities. It is said that when the July Monarchy was established Jacques Laffitte declared that "from now on the bankers will rule". Apart from the central bank (the Bank of France) and a few chartered banks (the Departmental banks) it was the metropolitan and the provincial private banks which were of importance in France at this time. They varied from wealthy institutions of international fame to modest local banks serving the needs of farmers and traders. These banks administered the financial affairs of landowners and other capitalists; lent their own funds and those of their clients to various types of borrowers; assisted in the flotation of public loans and industrial securities and accepted drafts from correspondents abroad. Some banks specialized in particular types of business. The Rothschilds were best known as international bankers who handled State loans though they were also interested in financing railway companies. The Paris house of Hottinguer specialized in financing foreign trade. Jacques Laffitte was a pioneer in the financing of industrial enterprises.[1] His *Caisse Générale pour commerce et l'industrie* (1837)—generally called the *Caisse Laffitte*—performed the functions of both a commercial and an investment bank. It discounted promissory notes and bills of exchange and lent money on the security of merchandise, *rentes* and commercial paper. Jacques Laffitte helped to organize both public utilities (such as railway companies) and manufacturing

---

[1] For the earlier career of Jacques Laffitte under Napoleon and the Restoration, see above p. 94 and 99. For his nephew Charles see above, p. 113.

enterprises (such as sugar refineries and ironworks). He made plans to float industrial securities but it is doubtful if he ever did so. When he issued notes payable at the *Caisse Laffitte* the Bank of France objected to this infringement of its own exclusive right of note issue and Laffitte then issued promissory notes payable on a fixed date—a device used by Nicholas Biddle in the United States.

Banking in France was still somewhat rudimentary in comparison with banking in England. Tooke and Newmarch observed that the financial transactions of French industry and commerce at this time "were essentially of a retail character, and but a very small part of them called into existence any form of transferable credit. The purchases and sales were effected by the employment of an enormous mass of metallic money; and the great central banking institution of the country at Paris was enabled to maintain a uniform course, and practically a uniform rate of discount at four per cent, for the four sufficient reasons—(i) of the comparatively limited external trade of France; (ii) of the slow and retail nature of the mercantile transactions of France; (iii) of the very small extent to which those transactions were carried on by means of any form of transferable credit; and (iv) lastly, of the employment upon the largest scale of metallic money for all purposes of sale and purchase." Claude Fohlen's account of the banks serving the Lille district during the Restoration and the July Monarchy shows how meagre were the financial facilities available to the merchants and industrialists of this important manufacturing region. The establishment of the Bank of Lille was authorized by a royal edict of June 29, 1836. There were also a few private banks, the most important being those founded by the elder L. Pollet (1829), Auguste Scalbert (1837), T. Ronzé-Mathou, and H. Cuvelier-Brame. A few examples may be given to show how some French banks assisted industry in Louis Philippe's reign. The Seillière bank provided capital for the ironworks at Le Creusot (Schneider), Hayange (de Wendel), and Bageilles as well as mines at Montchanin. The Vassal bank gave financial support to the Doubs and the Epinac ironworks, to a spinning mill at Saint Quentin and to a sugar refinery. Delante, one of the Receivers General, formed a small banking syndicate to put up the capital to establish the *Compagnie des Mines de la Loire* which was an amalgamation of the coal-mines in the Loire basin.

More accurate information concerning France's development as a manufacturing country is available for the reign of Louis Philippe than for the Restoration. Statistics for sixty-three departments collected by Moreau de Jonnès show that in 1847 the value of France's industrial output was about 4,000 million francs. If Dupin's estimate that industrial output in 1827 had been 1,340 million francs was correct it is clear that substantial progress had been made in twenty years. In 1847 the Nord Department appears to have been the most prosperous manufacturing region. The district (*arrondissement*) of Lille alone had over 900 industrial establishments producing goods to the annual value of over 230 million francs. Some 62,000 workers were employed in this region. But the large industrial establishment was still the exception and not the rule. The average factory in the textile industries at this time employed only about fifty operatives.

Apart from railway construction the most significant feature of France's economic development during the July Monarchy was the increased use of machinery driven by water power and by steam power. Most of the steam engines drove machinery in the textile mills or pumps in the mines. The cotton industry made the greatest progress from the point of view of mechanization. The consumption of raw cotton rose from 32 million kgm. in 1830 to 65 million kgm. in 1846. Alsace had 1·2 million mechanical spindles in 1846. In weaving the machines were introduced much more slowly and there were still only 31,000 mechanical looms in France in 1846. In the woollen industry the mechanical spinning of carded wool made more rapid progress than the spinning of combed wool. Josué Heilmann's invention of a combing machine in 1845—originally intended for the cotton industry—marked the introduction of mechanization into the preparatory processes. Josué Heilmann's patent rights were acquired by Nicholas Schlumberger of Guebwiller. In the silk industry the improved Jacquard loom was at last being widely adopted and Lyons had 60,000 mechanical silk looms in 1847. Even the rural silk-workshops were starting to use more machinery. In the linen industry some factories with up-to-date equipment were established at Saint Quentin and Amiens. The number of mechanical flax spindles in France rose from 14,800 in 1838 to 120,000 in 1845 but much flax continued to be spun and woven on traditional lines in village workshops.

The iron and steel industry was also expanding. Rails for the new railways and sheet-iron for constructional purposes were required in increasing quantities. New furnaces (some using the hot air blast), steam hammers, puddling equipment, and rolling and slitting mills were erected. The production of steel was increased by the introduction both of the traditional German cementation process and the newer English process invented by Huntsman, the greatest progress being made in the big establishments at Le Creusot (Schneider brothers), at Hayange, at Fourchambault, at Decazeville, at Assailly and at Denain. The output of pig-iron in France was nearly 600,000 tons in 1847. In the same year 13,000 tons of steel were produced. But in the 1840's about nine out of ten French furnaces were still burning charcoal and were operated in small plants. Various branches of the metal-working industries were also expanding —general engineering, the construction of railway locomotives and marine engines, the manufacture of cutlery, and the making of tools. Most of the production was still in the hands of relatively small workshops and the large establishments were the exception and not the rule. In other industries, too, some machinery was now being introduced. Flour mills, sugar refineries, paper works, glassworks and potteries were among the manufactures in which engines driven by steam or water were being installed.

The expansion of manufactures in France in the latter part of the Restoration and in the reign of Louis Philippe did not affect the whole of France. Industries developed to a much greater extent in the Paris basin, in the north-east, and in the eastern provinces than in the central highlands and in the south-west of France. It has been seen that south-west France—which had some flourishing industries at the time of the *ancien régime*—suffered severely from the Revolutionary and Napoleonic wars, the Continental System, the loss of the French colonies, and the decline in France's overseas trade. This part of the country did not share in the revival of industry after about 1826. The ports of the south-west—Bordeaux and Marseilles —gradually recovered but the industries of the hinterland remained depressed. A few new manufacturing establishments—the ironworks at Decazeville and the scythe factory at Saut-du-Tarn—did not relieve the general decline of industry in south-west France in this period. Stendhal in his *Mémoires d'un Touriste* contrasted northern France with the Midi. The former was "the modern and civilized France, the land of the steam engine" while the latter showed few signs of economic progress except that the trade of Marseilles was reviving owing to the conquest of Algeria. At the same time Michel Chevalier in his book on *Des Intérêts Matériels en France* (1838) drew a similar contrast between the regions north and south of a line drawn from Paris to Perpignan. The industries of the north-east and of the eastern provinces were expanding but the south-west was "an almost exclusively agrarian region". Crouzet has examined the reasons for the relative backwardness of the south-west at this time. He does not think that the alleged lack of coal was a factor of great importance. Supplies of coal could be secured from the collieries of the central highlands and the Loire basin while Bordeaux could import coal cheaply from Wales. Crouzet points out that

Stendhal and Chevalier both criticized the Government for failing to improve communications in south-west France. In 1836, for example, the legislature voted large sums for the construction of roads and canals but sixty million francs were spent upon the northern districts while only twelve million francs were allocated to the Midi. Stendhal also suggested that racial differences—and differences of character—helped to explain why one part of France made more rapid progress in industry than another. He considered that the Frenchman of the Midi "fait ce qui lui fait plaisir au moment même, et non pas ce qui est *prudent*. Cet homme n'est pas fait pour la civilisation qui règne depuis 1830".

In considering some of the economic and social consequences of increased industrialization in France reference may be made to the decline of rural manufactures, the increased employment of women and children, and the social evils that followed in the wake of the establishment of large factories. The decline of rural industries is generally a characteristic of an industrial revolution. This occurred to some extent in France in Louis Philippe's reign. There was for example a marked decline in the linen industry in the country districts of Maine and Brittany. In the rural domestic cotton industry of Normandy and the Paris region hand spinning had disappeared by about 1830 and hand weaving had disappeared by the middle of the century. The inability of the part-time rural textile workers to compete with the more efficient factories in the towns was no doubt the main reason for their decline. A report on the rural canton of Sobre-le-Château (1848) explained why nail-making and clothmaking were declining branches of manufacture in the villages.

"There are two reasons for the decline of nail-making—the manufacture of cold-forged nails, the cost of which is less than hand-made nails, and the production of nails by ironmasters whose costs are those of labour added to the wholesale price of iron. These factors are ruining the nailmakers who cannot possibly compete except at a loss. The manufacture of coarse cloths . . . inevitably tends to decline. The quality of these cloths—which are made from rags and waste-wool—is not good enough. People prefer Roubaix products which are more showy, no more costly, and often of superior quality."

But there were other factors—besides competition from large-scale urban industries—which influenced the fate of rural industries. The decline in the quantity and quality of French flax, for example, contributed to the fall in output of the domestic linen workers.

Moreover progress in agriculture encouraged certain small holders to devote all their time to farming and to drop their part-time industrial activities. In France, as in England, some of the village spinners and weavers closed their workshops and became factory operatives in a nearby town. But other rural artisans became full-time workers on the land either as small holders or as farm labourers. C. H. Pouthas's investigations into changes in the population of France in the first half of the nineteenth century show that rural districts were overpopulated in the 1830's. The "surplus" lived by means of supplementary industrial work and when rural manufactures declined some of the peasants had to seek work in the towns. It has been said that "the rural inhabitants were forced from the country-side rather than attracted by the cities".

Grave discontent among both urban and rural workers was a serious social problem in Louis Philippe's reign. There were several types of industrial workers in France at this time. First, there were workers in small establishments in which fewer than ten persons were employed. In the middle of the nineteenth century 1·5 million masters employed 2·8 million workers in these workshops. These artisans were the typical French industrial workers of the period. Secondly, there were workers in the villages who were engaged partly on farmwork and partly on industrial work. The rural spinners and weavers, the village cutlers, and the rural iron-ore miners and charcoal burners belonged to this group. Thirdly, there were the factory operatives and the miners. In 1851 "large-scale" industry in France—establishments with ten or more workers—employed 1·3 million persons. Many of these establishments, though officially described as "large-scale", were in fact comparatively small work-shops. Only a small proportion of the workers were employed in really large establishments such as the Anzin coal-mines or the Le Creusot ironworks and engineering plants.

The grievances of different types of workers varied to some extent. The craftsmen in small workshops still opposed the intro-duction of new machines that appeared to threaten their livelihood. In the 1830's, for example, there was much agitation among the printers who objected to the installation of mechanical presses. The operatives in large establishments resisted the harsh discipline of the factory. But some complaints were common to all—or nearly all—types of workers. These included the exploitation of the labour of women and children, the long hours of work, the low wages, the wretched housing conditions, and the prohibition of trade unions and of strikes. Large numbers of women and children were employed at low wages in both large-scale and small-scale industry. According to Moreau de Jonnès 389,000 women and children worked in "large establishments" in sixty-three Departments in 1847. In the two industrialized Departments of Haut Rhin (Alsace) and Seine Inférieure (Normandy) nineteen per cent of the factory workers were children. A similar situation existed in small workshops. In 1848 in the rural canton of Sobre-le-Château, for example, there were 3,372 wage-earners and 1,534 of them were women and children.

An extensive inquiry made by Dr. Villermé in 1840 on behalf of the Academy of Moral and Political Sciences contained detailed information about the social condition of French factory workers. He stated that in Alsace some 100,000 factory operatives normally worked for 15 hours a day with breaks totalling 1½ hours for meals. Schlumberger's factory at Guebwiller, however, worked only a 13½-hour day. Housing conditions in Mulhouse were deplorable and the infant mortality rate was very high. Wages were low and there was a depressed class of unskilled workers who had migrated from Baden. In the Nord Department, too, the normal day's work at this time was 15 hours. Not only Dr. Villermé but other observers— such as Blanqui and Villeneuve-Bargemont—have given descriptions of the shocking conditions under which the workers lived in the insanitary courts and cellars of Lille. The Etagnes district was a notorious slum where living conditions were particularly revolting. One writer stated that in the 1840's nearly one-third of the inhabitants of Lille were in a permanent state of poverty. In the Nord Department the poor law authorities had one-sixth of the population on their books. In the Normandy industrial region the condition of the working classes was no better. One Rouen manufacturer admitted that sixty per cent of his workers did not earn enough money to satisfy their basic needs. In Lyons many of the workers who produced fine silks to adorn ladies of fashion lived in abject poverty. The slums of Croix-Rousse and Saint-Georges were among the worst in the country. In view of the conditions under which operatives and miners worked and lived it is not surprising that there was much vice, drunkenness, prostitution and ill-health in France at this time. Mortality rates—particularly of infants—were high and epidemics of infectious diseases were not uncommon. In some of the industrialized Departments nearly half of the conscripts were rejected by the army doctors.

These social evils, of course, were not confined to the new factories and the growing industrial towns. Paris was a great city of small workshops but the conditions under which the artisans worked and lived were certainly no better than those of the factory workers in the big manufacturing centres. There is ample evidence for this in the reports of the Paris Board of Health (*Conseil de Salubrité*) which had been established in 1806 by Dubois, the Prefect of Police.[1] Nantes was a port with small industrial establishments but Dr. Guepin's description of how some of its workers were housed in 1835 was very similar to accounts of slums in the larger manufacturing towns. Dr. Guepin stated that in the Rue des Fumiers it was necessary to pass through "an opening like a drain below street level" to reach the cold dark rooms in which the workers lived. "Foul water oozes out of the walls . . . the floor is uneven, unpaved and untiled." The furniture often consisted only of two or three rickety beds, a loom and a spinning wheel. Dr. Guepin declared that it was heart-rending to observe a street full of "pale, flabby and sickly" children. "They seem to belong to a different species from the healthy children—so shapely and robust—who play in the Henri IV Boulevard." It may be added that in the building trade—which was run by small masters employing only a few men—hours were worked which were even longer than those in the factories. Agricole Perdiguier stated in his memoirs that his day's work as a builder began at 5 a.m. and did not finish until 8 p.m.

Several writers give information concerning wages in France in the 1840's. The industrial statistics of 1847 confirm Dr. Villermé's view that the average wage of a factory workers was 2 francs a day for a man, 1 franc a day for a woman, and between 50 and 75 centimes for a child according to age. Apart from regional differences, wages varied according to the occupation and the skill of the worker. Skilled men employed in coal-mines, ironworks, engineering establishments and glassworks could earn 3 francs a day or more while in Paris bakers and carpenters were paid as much as 5 francs a day. On the other hand labourers, farm workers, and domestic servants received very low wages. The wages paid in Paris and in large manufacturing and commercial centres were higher than those paid in the smaller market towns and villages. In the rural canton of Sobre-le-Château the average earnings in the workshops were only between 1 franc and 1 franc 50 centimes a day for men. Glassworkers, however, could earn up to 5 francs 50 centimes a day according to the type of work performed. Factory wages in "large-scale" industry rose somewhat between 1835 and 1847. In Mulhouse in those years the increase was seventeen per cent. A worker with a large family

---

[1] A summary of the reports of the Paris Board of Health for the ten years 1829–39 is given in an appendix to Edwin Chadwick's *Report from the Poor Law Commissioners on an Enquiry into the Sanitary Condition of the Labouring Population of Great Britain*, July 1842 (Parliamentary Papers, 1843, Vol. XII, pp. 409–23).

often did not earn enough to support himself and his dependents. He frequently had to be content with a meagre diet of bread and potatoes. He had to put up with very poor accommodation. Even when fully employed—and certainly when out of work—he had to rely upon the poor law authorities and upon private charity for clothes and medical attention.

The workers were naturally restive under such conditions. Although trade unions were illegal at this time[1] some workers' associations appear to have been formed quite openly and were not always immediately dissolved by the police. Some old-established journeymen's gilds (compagnonnages) survived—particularly in the building and allied trades—and they seem to have been allowed to function unmolested. But since membership was confined to unmarried journeymen these gilds represented the interests of only one group of craft-workers and, in any case, they were largely concerned with helping the travelling journeyman (the compagnon du tour de France) who was completing his training by gaining experience in his trade in different parts of the country. Many towns had a "gild-mother" who provided accommodation for travelling journeymen. The activities of the journeymen's gilds contributed little to the growth of trade unionism among workers in factories or mines. In France as in England friendly societies sometimes provided cover for trade-union activities. As early as 1819 the watermen of the Loire port of Roanne were organized in a benefit club which was virtually a trade union. Strikes occurred in factories and collieries but labour unrest was particularly rife among craftsmen such as printers, hatters, shoemakers, tailors, carpenters, masons, and handloom weavers. Despite the difficulties under which trade unions operated strikes were not uncommon in Louis Philippe's reign. They were often organized by committees which sprang up on the eve of a strike and disappeared when the strike was over. Workers demanded higher wages, shorter hours, measures to prevent unemployment, the limitation of police supervision, and the withdrawal of new machines. The statistics issued by the Office du Travail show that there were over 1,000 strikes in France between 1830 and 1847 which led to legal action being taken against the workers. The total number of industrial disputes was greater than this since not all strikes were followed by the prosecution of those taking part in them.

Shortly after the establishment of the July Monarchy the grievances of the silk workers concerning rates of pay led to a great rising in Lyons in November 1831. The weavers of this city had been

[1] Associations of employers were also illegal but were not suppressed by the authorities.

organized since 1823 in a friendly society called the *Devoir Mutuel* which was made up of cells each containing less than twenty members. In this way the workers engaged in trade-union activities without breaking the law. In 1831 the workers gained effective control over the city of Lyons at a cost of some 600 casualties among the soldiers and the workers. Marshal Soult had to bring an army of 20,000 men to Lyons to restore order. The Socialist writer Tarlé has declared that "the insurrection in Lyons in 1831 was a turning point in the history of the working classes not only in France but in the whole world". Within two years the *Devoir Mutuel* had been re-established and had 3,000 members. The Government was alarmed at this revival of working-class activity and brought forward a bill to restrict workers' associations even more rigorously than before. This led to a new rising in Lyons in April 1834. Again the military had to be called out to maintain order. A law was now passed (1834) which prohibited the forming of associations even if they had under twenty members and for five years there was relatively little labour unrest. Bad trade and unemployment in 1839–40 led to a revival of the working-class movement in France. Workers' newspapers—such as *l'Atelier* (1840)—were founded, new unions were established, and a few industrial co-operative societies were set up. Despite these activities in the early 1840's only a small minority of the French workers could be described as class conscious at this time.

At the same time that some of the craftsmen and factory workers were starting to unite to resist capitalist exploitation the early French Socialists were analysing the evils of the new industrial system and were putting forward remedies of their own. The French Revolution of 1789 had swept away certain abuses of private property but the institution itself had been preserved and strengthened. Babeuf with his demand for complete State ownership of all property was a lone figure in the closing years of the eighteenth century. After the Napoleonic wars the socialist views of Saint-Simon gained currency only in the last ten years of his life (1815–25). He advocated State control over the production and distribution of goods and held that what a man received in the shape of goods and services should be precisely equal to the work that he had performed. His disciples propagated his ideas after his death but some of them (such as the Pereires) eventually came to terms with modern capitalism and made names for themselves as successful entrepreneurs. Fourier advocated the establishment of communist societies (*phalanges*) in which the members should work together for the common good and all property should be held jointly. Attempts in France and later in the United States to establish socialist communities on these lines met with little success. Human nature fell short of the idealist behaviour postulated by Fourier. Proudhon has been called "the father of modern anarchism". In his book *Qu'est-ce que la Propriété?* he declared that "property is theft, because it enables one who has not produced to consume the fruits of other men's labours". He was a powerful critic of the evils of early capitalism but he had little to offer in the way of an alternative social order. Louis Blanc, on the other hand, did have an alternative scheme. In his book on the *Organisation du Travail* (1839) he suggested that production should be in the hands of industrial co-operative associations. The distinction between the capitalist employer and the propertyless wage earner would disappear if the workers—with some initial help from the State—themselves jointly owned the premises, tools and materials necessary for industrial production. Since the typical unit of production was still the small workshop, Louis Blanc's plan was not so far-fetched as it was when Lassalle revived it in Germany twenty years later. Louis Blanc's views spread among the workers and he achieved considerable popularity. When Louis Philippe was overthrown Louis Blanc was the acknowledged leader of the workers.

Most French employers were indifferent to the sufferings of the workers. Those who investigated social conditions at this time were shocked at the callousness of the masters towards the men. There were of course honourable exceptions. Many of the textile manufacturers in Alsace were progressive in their outlook and introduced their own welfare services—model dwellings and factory schools—at a comparatively early date. Louis Philippe's régime, dominated by reactionary bankers and industrialists, had no rememdy for social unrest except repression. Almost the only social reform passed in this reign was the Factory Law of March 1841, which prohibited the employment of children under the age of 8 in the factories. Children from 8 to 12 years might not work for more than 8 hours a day and had to have some schooling. Children aged between 12 and 16 years were not to work for more than 12 hours a day. Children under 13 years of age were forbidden to work at night (9 p.m. to 5 a.m.). But this law applied only to those establishments which employed over 20 persons or which used steam power. Children employed in workshops where less than 20 persons were employed and no steam power was used were not covered by this enactment. Even the factory children did not in practice enjoy the protection to which they were entitled by the new law. Night work was still allowed in special circumstances such as the need to repair a machine. Unscrupulous employers took advantage of this provision to evade the law. The maximum penalty for infringing the law was only 500 francs. Unlike the English Factory Act of 1833 the French Law of 1841 contained no provision for the appointment of inspectors to enforce the law. No wonder that Karl Marx declared that the law was never carried into effect. Yet, except for the Apprenticeship Law of 1851, French factory children had for many years no other legal protection save that embodied in the Law of 1841.

Social discontent in the 1840's was aggravated by the rise in the cost of living and the lack of employment which followed in the wake of the crises in both agriculture and industry in 1846–7. Labrousse considers that the rise in the price of cereals and of bread was a major factor in bringing this crisis to a head. He states that prior to 1873 depressions in France originated in the agrarian sector of the economy and spread to industry and commerce. The cereal harvests failed in 1845 and in 1846 and the potato crop was affected by blight. The commercial crisis in London had repercussions in France since English promoters had been investing heavily in French railways and industrial enterprises. French railway expansion was halted and the demand for rails declined. As M. Fohlen asks: "Might not the crisis of 1846–8 have been due to an excess of railway investment, followed by a lack of liquid funds at the moment of tension?" In the Nord Department and in the textile regions production declined and unemployment increased. Studies sponsored by Labrousse show, however, that the various regions and industries of France were not affected in the same way by the agrarian and commercial crises of 1846–8. As at the time of the Continental System, so in 1847, there were "sheltered" and "exposed" sectors of the economy. While some parts of the country were short of grain lower Alsace and the Caen district had a surplus. Marseilles and the Var district experienced industrial and commercial prosperity at a time when some other regions of France were in a very depressed condition. Moreover it seems clear that the rural domestic craftsmen were much more seriously affected by the crisis than the factory workers. The social distress of 1847 helped to bring about the revolution of February 1848. Henri Sée observes that although the apparent cause of the rising was the demand for electoral reform—the franchise was limited to the few citizens who paid 200 francs a year in direct taxation—the fundamental cause was the economic crisis of 1847.

### (iii) 1848-1870

THE SECOND REPUBLIC

The Second Republic, though of brief duration, was important from the point of view of the economic development of France because a number of important reforms were introduced. The abolition of slavery in the colonies survived the reaction that soon followed the revolution of February 1848 but most of the other reforms (such as the National Workshops, the Luxembourg Commission and the fixed working day) had a very short life while some projects (such as the nationalization of the railways) were not passed into law at this time. Nevertheless the ideas and experiments of 1848 were not forgotten and provided reformers with objectives to be achieved in the future. The Second Republic had two distinct phases and the reforms of the two periods were different in character. The first phase began with the overthrow of Louis Philippe in February 1848 and ended with the collapse of the rising of the workers in Paris in June 1848. The second phase was dominated by Louis Napoleon who was elected President of the Republic in December 1848, overthrew the constitution by the *coup d'état* of December 1851 and assumed the Imperial title in the following year. The first phase of the Second Republic (February–June 1848) saw the introduction of far-reaching reforms inspired by radical and Socialist ideas. The second phase (June 1848–December 1851) saw the passing into law of a somewhat miscellaneous assortment of reforms much less radical in character. These reforms were introduced largely at the instigation of Louis Napoleon himself in the hope of securing the support of the "little man"—the craftsman, the factory worker, the shopkeeper, the black-coated worker—for his plan to establish himself as Emperor.

The fall of the July Monarchy was brought about partly by middle-class liberals who demanded the extension of the franchise, the ending of corruption in the administration, the freedom of the press, and trial by jury, and partly by Republicans and Socialists who believed that the distress of the lower classes should be alleviated not by half-measures but by a radical reform of society. At the political banquets which were the signal for the rising of the Paris mob in February 1848 the main demand was for electoral reform and this to some extent disguised the fact that the Republicans and the Socialists were just as much responsible for the overthrow of Louis Philippe as the middle-class liberals.

The Provisional Republican Government of February 1848 was a coalition of the two groups which had brought the previous régime to an end. They were ill-assorted bedfellows and had little in common except that both had been opposed to Louis Philippe's administration. The liberals—or Moderates—would have been satisfied with comparatively modest measures of reform. The Republicans (inspired by the ideas of 1789) and the Socialists (inspired by a vision of a new society) hoped to end the influence of the classes who had supported Louis Philippe and to introduce a new social order.

The Moderates, fearing a new and more violent revolution, realized that some concessions must be made to their left-wing allies. They agreed to three reforms—the guarantee of work, the National Workshops and a "parliament of industry" known as the Luxembourg Commission. A decree was passed on the Organization of Labour which guaranteed work to all citizens and so established the principle that it was the responsibility of the State to provide employment for those who were out of work. The decree did not, however, include any provisions for carrying this principle into effect.[1] The same decree legalized trade unions by stating that "workers may associate to enjoy the legitimate benefits of their labour".

The establishment of the National Workshops in Paris has given rise to some misunderstanding. It has been alleged that the workshops were an experiment in State management of industry on a large scale and that their failure was conclusive proof of the folly of Socialism. Presumably the fact that Louis Blanc was a member of the Government which established the workshops gave rise to the notion that they were a Socialist experiment. Actually the workshops were simply public works for the unemployed and had nothing in common with the co-operative workshops advocated by Louis Blanc. Indeed Louis Blanc denounced the National Workshops as "the regimentation of thousands of workmen of different trades, thrown together pell-mell, and set upon a kind of labour less profitable than ridiculous".

While the Moderates appreciated that something had to be done to carry out the promise to guarantee work to the unemployed they were not prepared to introduce dangerous Socialist experiments. Their plan for dealing with the unemployment problem was the conventional one of setting up public works of the type that had recently been established in Ireland on a large scale to relieve the distress caused by the potato famine. When the Government announced that public works would be started in Paris such large numbers of men applied for admission that the machinery for enrolment virtually collapsed and a chaotic situation arose. Émile Thomas, a young engineer who had recently graduated at the *École Centrale*

[1] Article 13 of the Republican Constitution of 1848 stated that the Government would foster economic expansion by promoting industrial and agricultural credit institutes and by starting public works.

*des Arts et Manufactures,* submitted a scheme for the reorganization both of the arrangements for admission to the workshops and for the conduct of workshops themselves. He proposed that the men should be organized on semi-military lines and that strict discipline should be enforced. Early in March 1848 Émile Thomas was asked to submit his scheme to a meeting of the mayors of the twelve districts into which Paris was divided. He told the mayors that his scheme simply provided for the efficient running of the public works. He warned them that his plan could succeed only if sufficient construction projects were authorized by the Government.

Émile Thomas's plan was accepted and on March 9 the first men reported for work. They were engaged on outdoor "pick and shovel" tasks such as levelling ground in preparation for the construction of new roads and buildings. Their wages were two francs for a working day and one and a half francs (soon reduced to one franc) for an idle day. In addition welfare services were provided. There was a family allowance for needy workers in the form of bread, meat and soup allocated on a sliding scale according to the size of the family. A medical service was maintained and 14,000 workers were treated gratuitously by twelve doctors. One of the four assistant directors of the National Workshops was a personnel officer who listened to the workers' complaints and tried to remove their grievances.

The National Workshops in Paris were attacked on two grounds. First, it was alleged (by Lamartine for example) that most of the men were "idlers and wasters". This criticism has been exaggerated. While Émile Thomas was not able to operate his scheme as smoothly as he wished, nevertheless a reasonable standard of discipline was generally maintained among the men and a good deal of useful work was done. Of course there were some idlers on the public works and there were men who adopted "go-slow" tactics to make the work spin out as long as possible. Craftsmen, accustomed to doing a skilled job indoors, could not be turned into efficient navvies overnight.

Secondly, it was asserted that Émile Thomas never set more than a small proportion of the unemployed to work. The largest number of men employed on any one day was about 10,000 while the maximum number of men enrolled in the workshops was 110,000. The responsibility for this situation lay not with Émile Thomas but with the Government which did not provide an adequate programme of works on which the men could be employed. The scheme for the construction of a circular railway in Paris was turned down by the Government because it was too expensive. Public works were costly and nearly 14·5 million francs were spent on the National Workshops in three months. The Government's failure to give Émile Thomas enough construction work to enable him to keep employed the men enrolled in his workshops was due partly to the refusal of the Department of Highways and Bridges to co-operate with the National Workshops. The engineers employed by the Department of Highways and Bridges were civil servants who had been trained at the Polytechnic and had wide experience of constructing roads, bridges, canals and railways. They were critical of the National Workshops which were controlled by an independent organization and were to a great extent run by graduates and students of the *École Centrale.*

At the general election of April 23, 1848, the Moderates gained a complete victory over the extremists. The new Constituent Assembly was predominantly middle class in character and it viewed the National Workshops with some concern. It was feared that the men employed in the workshops might become an organized political force supporting the radicals and the Socialists. The fact that large numbers of these men took part in a great demonstration in Paris on May 15, 1848, in favour of Polish independence confirmed many members of the Assembly in their belief that Émile Thomas's organization was highly dangerous from a political point of view. On May 17 the Government declared that no new members were to be admitted to the National Workshops and on May 24 Émile Thomas received instructions concerning various measures to be taken to reduce the number of men on his books. Men from the provinces, for example, were to be sent to their own Departments where public works would be provided under the direction of the Department of Highways and Bridges. When Émile Thomas objected to these instructions his resignation was demanded and the authorities—acting in a grossly arbitrary and illegal fashion— virtually placed him under arrest and made him leave Paris. Lalanne, a distinguished government engineer, replaced Émile Thomas as director of the National Workshops and took steps to reduce the number of workers employed.

On June 22, 1848, several hundred members of the National Workshops demonstrated against the deportation of unemployed workers from Paris and the calling up for army service of young members of the National Workshops. The authorities refused to change their policy concerning the reduction of the number of men employed on the National Workshops. This was followed by the erection of barricades in the workers' quarters in the eastern districts of Paris. The workers rose in revolt. General Cavaignac was given dictatorial powers to restore order. Seven generals and 1,500 soldiers fell in the fighting. Civilian casualties included the Archbishop of Paris and two deputies. The workers suffered heavy casualties and subsequently over 3,300 insurgents were transported to Algeria.

General Cavaignac declared that the National Workshops were a menace to the safety of the Republic and they were dissolved. It is true that a demonstration of men employed in the National Workshops was the spark which fired the conflagration, but the vast majority of those who manned the barricades had nothing to do with the National Workshops. The workshops provided the Government with a convenient whipping boy at a time when the public—panic-stricken at the thought of possible revolution—were demanding strong measures to restore law and order.

The establishment of the Luxembourg Commission was an interesting early attempt to solve industrial problems through a "parliament of industry" in which both masters and men were represented. It was set up as an advisory body on February 28, 1848. It was not a national organization since only the Paris trades were represented. At full meetings of the Commission three workers' delegates from each *corporation* and three masters from each *corps de métiers* met together. In addition to the full Commission there were two committees. The first consisted of one representative of the workers from each trade and one representative of the employers. The second committee was a permanent executive of twenty members—ten workers and ten employers. The two committees sometimes met jointly. The Luxembourg Commission performed a useful function at a critical time by bringing masters and men together to discuss common problems. Some strikes were avoided owing to its intervention. The Commission recommended that a new Factory Law should be passed to reduce the daily working hours of adults to ten in Paris and eleven in the provinces. A decree to this effect was passed by the Assembly on March 2, 1848. This was the first enactment in France to restrict the hours of work of adults. The reform, however, was short-lived. In September 1848, when the right-wing groups were in the saddle again, the hours which might legally be worked were increased from ten (or eleven) to twelve. The Luxembourg Commission also recommended that sub-contracting in the building trade (*marchandage*) should be abolished and the Assembly passed a decree to this effect. But it is doubtful if the decree had any practical effect. A few producers' co-operative societies—on the lines long advocated by Louis Blanc—were established by the Luxembourg Commission in 1848. One was an association of tailors which made uniforms for the national guard. This society—and one or two others sponsored by the Luxembourg

Commission—were wound up after the workers' rising of June 1848. The co-operation between masters and men on the Luxembourg Commission did not last long. The employers became alarmed when the workers' delegates not only aired Socialist views on the organization of labour and on equal pay but actually engaged in propaganda in favour of workers' candidates at the forthcoming general election. The "Luxembourg candidates" however were not very successful for in the elections to the Constituent Assembly (held in March 1848) they gained only six seats out of thirty-four in the Seine Department. The new Assembly disliked the Luxembourg Commission as much as the National Workshops. The Luxembourg Commission was not dissolved but no meetings were held after May 13, 1848.

Meanwhile Garnier-Pagès, the Minister of Finance from March 5 to May 11, 1848, had taken steps to alleviate the financial difficulties caused by the revolution and the commercial crisis. The Bank of France and the nine Departmental Banks suspended cash payments but their future total note issue was limited to 452 million francs. Discount banks (*comptoirs nationaux*) were set up in Paris and leading provincial towns. State warehouses (*magasins généraux*) were also established. Goods might be stored in these establishments and the receipts issued to depositors passed into general circulation by endorsement. Garnier-Pagès also proposed the sale of the Crown diamonds, the alienation of the domains of the civil list, the alienation of State forests (though this was found to be impracticable), and the issue of *rentes* to replace deposits in savings banks.

Two other projects for reform were discussed in the period before the rising of the Paris workers in June 1848. These were railway nationalization and the reform of the industrial conciliation councils. The railways, already in difficulties owing to the trade depression of 1847, suffered from the unrest and economic disturbances caused by the revolution of 1848. Unruly mobs—perhaps instigated by cab-drivers and innkeepers who fancied that the railways would threaten their jobs—attacked some bridges and stations. In addition to the fact that railway property was damaged the companies were faced with labour unrest. Strikers demanded higher wages and the dismissal of English drivers of locomotives. The companies found it impossible to raise new capital to complete their lines. Nobody would invest money in the railways at this critical time. Faced with strikes, rising costs, and falling revenues some of the railway companies were clearly heading for bankruptcy. Some members of the Government considered that the solution to the problem lay in the nationalization of the whole railway network. On May 17, 1848, Duclerc, the Minister of Finance, presented to the Assembly a plan for the purchase of the railways by the State. He summarized in an able manner all the arguments in favour of nationalization. He attacked the companies as dangerous monopolies and claimed that the railway system should be operated in the interests of society as a whole and not for private profit. The Finance Committee of the National Assembly, however, rejected the proposal mainly because of the high estimated cost (over 620 million francs) of nationalizing the railways.

The industrial conciliation councils (*conseils des prud'hommes*) were reformed in May and June 1848. Hitherto the representatives of the employers had always been in a majority on these councils. The new law made provision for equality of representation for masters and men. Since foremen were classed as masters the new arrangement was sometimes favourable to the men since the representatives of the employers would be in a minority if the delegates of the workers and of the foremen voted together. In the circumstances many employers tended to try to settle disputes with their men by direct negotiation rather than refer them to a conciliation council. Under the Second Empire a new law on conciliation councils (June 4, 1853) changed the method of electing the *conseils des prud'-hommes* but maintained the principle of equality of representation between masters and men. A new provision was that the president and the vice-president of each council were to be appointed by the Emperor while the secretaries were to be appointed by the local Prefect. The government nominees on the conciliation councils often favoured the workers and this was one way by which Napoleon III hoped to secure support for his régime from the working classes.

The suppression of the workers' rising in June 1848 brought the first phase of the Revolution to an end. It was not until Louis Napoleon was elected President in December 1848 that new reforms were introduced. There was, however, one interesting experiment which fell in the second half of 1848. This was the Law of July 6, 1848, which set up a fund of three million francs to subsidize the establishment of industrial co-operative associations. Under the scheme nearly sixty societies were established. Nearly all of the Paris associations consisted of masters only. In the provinces eleven associations included workers only while fifteen were run jointly by masters and men. Many of the societies failed owing to lack of judgement in selecting members and inexperience on the part of directors. C. R. Fay observes that "societies sprang up merely to enjoy the subventions and then looked for employment from the institution which had called them into being. The right to work was interpreted as a right to have work found for them. The State indeed made conditions but they were conditions which ensured democracy rather than stability of constitution."

During the period when Louis Napoleon was President (December 1848–December 1852) he was responsible for the introduction of several reforms of an economic or social character. He was genuinely interested in social problems and had written a pamphlet on the extinction of pauperism. He realized that some concessions must be made to the workers to secure their support for his régime. An important reform of this period was the Apprenticeship Law of 1851. Apprentices under the age of fourteen were not allowed to work for more than ten hours a day and they were not allowed to work at night. Apprentices aged between fourteen and sixteen now had a maximum day of twelve hours. Sunday work was forbidden except that apprentices might have to sweep out a workshop on a Sunday afternoon. Illiterate apprentices were to have two hours schooling a day. This enactment gave some protection to certain young persons who had not come under the provisions of the Factory Law of 1841 but it does not appear to have been very effectively carried out. Other laws passed at this time which affected the workers concerned the proper management of savings banks, friendly societies, hospitals and common lodging houses. The careful management of the country's finances, coupled with a welcome revival of trade at home and abroad, enabled the Bank of France to resume cash payments in August 1850.

On the other hand there were two enactments of a reactionary character which deserve mention. A law of November 1849 once more forbade workers to form trade unions or to strike. And a law of May 1851 continued the existing arrangements whereby every worker had to have an identity card (*livret*). The workers objected to the *livret* and demanded its abolition. The only concession made to the workers was that in future advances on wages recorded in the *livret* were limited to thirty francs and the amount which might be deducted by an employer to secure the repayment of such debts was limited to ten per cent of the workers' wage.

## THE SECOND EMPIRE

Some historians have seen in Napoleon III no more than a shoddy adventurer whose reign ended in defeat and disgrace. He betrayed those who trusted him, as Cavour and Maximilian learned to their cost. He had an insatiable appetite for other people's territory. He secured Savoy and Nice and at one time or another coveted Belgium,

Luxemburg, the Saar and the Bavarian Palatinate. His misjudgements and miscalculations were legion. At home he gained power by overthrowing the Republican constitution and he retained office by suppressing all opposition to his régime. Only at the end of his reign did he agree to the experiment of a "liberal Empire".

In his economic policy on the other hand Napoleon III was more successful. He took full advantage of the fact that the early part of his reign coincided with a rise in prices which was brought about by an increase in the amount of gold coming to Europe from the United States and Australia. Rising prices encouraged manufacturers to expand production and stimulated the development of all branches of the economy. The industrial boom of the early 1850's was fostered by Napoleon III's Government in various ways. Important public works were constructed, the establishment of a "Greater Paris" was begun, credit banks were founded to foster both industrial and agricultural expansion, and the railway network was extended and reorganized. When the feverish industrial expansion of the 1850's was checked by the commercial crisis of 1857 Napoleon III tried to stimulate economic recovery in various ways. Additional financial help was given to the railway companies. Low-tariff commercial treaties were concluded with Britain, Belgium and the Zollverein which gave French manufacturers new opportunities to sell their products abroad and forced them to introduce modern machinery so as to meet new foreign competition at home. A government loan to industry helped some manufacturers to modernize their factories and the policy of constructing public works was continued. Moreover the extension of France's overseas possessions enabled manufacturers to sell more goods in Algeria, Senegal and Indo-China. These were significant achievements and Napoleon III and his ministers played an important part in bringing them about. Some progress in the establishment of modern manufactures had already been made in Louis Philippe's reign but in the period of the Second Empire the pace of industrialization was speeded up. All sectors of the economy expanded and the influence of French capital and technical knowledge was felt throughout the Continent and also in Egypt, where the construction of the Suez Canal was a monument to French entrepreneurial activity.

Napoleon III, like his uncle, came into power at a time when the French economy was depressed after a period of revolution. Just as Napoleon I's reputation rested not only on his military achievements but on the reforms of the Consulate which helped to restore law and order and to revive agriculture and industry, so Napoleon III realized that not merely the vigorous handling of foreign affairs but also a policy of economic reconstruction, was needed to establish his position as the leader of the French people. Napoleon III saw that, as an industrial country, France was behind Britain and Belgium and was being challenged by the German states united in the Zollverein. He believed that vigorous State action was essential if France were to maintain her position as one of the leading manufacturing countries in the world. Industrial expansion and capital accumulation would enable France to extend her influence in relatively backward regions on the Continent and in the Levant. A prosperous France would be able to lend money and supply technical knowledge to Austria, Italy, Russia, and Egypt, and so increase her prestige in those countries. The progress of manufactures, commerce and agriculture in France would improve the standard of living of the peasants, factory workers, the craftsmen and the middle classes and so secure greater support for the Bonaparte dynasty. Napoleon III had already shown his interest in social questions by writing a pamphlet on the problem of poverty. In an address to the Bordeaux Chamber of Commerce in October 1852 Louis Napoleon declared: "We have immense uncultivated regions to improve, roads to construct, harbours to dredge, rivers to render navigable, a railway and canal network to complete." Ably supported by Rouher (Minister of Public Works), Franqueville (Director of the Department of Highways and Bridges), Fould (Minister of State) and Haussmann (Prefect of the Seine Department) Napoleon III made strenuous efforts to carry out the policy outlined in his Bordeaux speech.

*Railways.* Of the many public works constructed at the time of the Second Empire the rebuilding of Paris and the expansion of the railway system were probably the most important. The disorders of February 1848 had caused serious damage to railway property. Unsettled conditions during the early months of the Second Republic coupled with the threat to nationalize the railways brought railway building to a standstill. Strikes and depressed trade drastically reduced traffic on the railways and many railway companies were in serious financial straits. When Louis Napoleon became President order was restored, grants were made to railway companies to compensate them for recent losses and the Government assumed responsibility for the construction of some lines that had been abandoned. In 1852, however, the position was still far from satisfactory. France was building her railways too slowly and there were too many independent companies for the system as a whole to work efficiently. Napoleon III and his advisers decided that new railways must be built quickly and that the French lines must be reorganized so as to increase their efficiency. The amalgamation of existing lines, the granting of long concessions to new companies, and the guaranteeing of the interest on railway shares—this was the keynote of Napoleon III's railway policy. The State encouraged the amalgamation of lines so that each major region of France should be served by one main railway company. The granting of concessions for ninety-nine years and the guaranteeing of a minimum rate of interest to railway shareholders encouraged the formation of new railway companies and attracted much needed capital from investors at home and abroad.

The new railway policy was initiated in 1851 when the Government granted concessions for ninety-nine years to the Versailles–Rennes and the Lyons–Avignon lines and guaranteed the interest on the shares of the two companies. In January 1852 similar terms were granted to the Paris–Lyons railway company. In July of that year Louis Napoleon opened the Eastern Railway from Paris to Strasbourg. This line had cost over 200 million francs to build and half of this sum had been contributed by the State. The line was of great benefit to the cotton manufacturers of Mulhouse who could now secure their raw material from Le Havre more speedily and at a lower cost than before.

The leading railway promoters in France at this time—men like the Pereire brothers, James Rothschild, Enfantin and Arlès-Dufour —realized that greater efficiency and greater profits could be secured if the existing railways were brought together into a few large lines. The grouping of relatively short lines into bigger networks would reduce excessive competition, improve facilities for through traffic, increase revenues, and attract new capital. The State, which had formerly forbidden amalgamations because it feared the growth of railway monopolies, now changed its policy and gave every encouragement to the fusion of railways into larger units. Between 1852 and 1857 nearly thirty companies controlling about half the track in operation were brought together into six great companies. The reorganized lines were the Northern Railway, the Eastern Railway, the Western Railway, the Paris–Orleans–Bordeaux line, the Paris–Lyons–Mediterranean railway, and the Midi company. A seventh amalgamation—the Grand Central Railway—was established in 1853 but failed to prosper as it served only thinly populated districts in the central highlands of France and in 1857 its lines were divided between the Paris–Orleans and the Paris–Lyons–Mediterranean railways.

The nucleus of the Northern Railway was the line from Paris to

Lille and the Channel ports. By building branch lines and by absorbing other companies it secured control over a network of lines serving the coal-fields and the manufacturing districts of north-east France as well as adjacent industrial districts in Belgium. The company was a financial success and good dividends were paid. The Paris–Orleans Railway Company was the nucleus of a network of lines serving the basin of the Loire and linking the capital with Orleans and Tours as well as the ports of Bordeaux and Nantes. The Paris–Lyons–Mediterranean railway network, which controlled the lines in the Rhône valley, had been formed in two stages. In 1852 five lines were amalgamated to form the Lyons–Mediterranean Company which linked Lyons and Marseilles. In 1857, largely owing to the efforts of Rouher (Minister of Public Works), the Paris–Lyons Company and the Lyons–Mediterranean Company were joined together to form the Paris–Lyons–Mediterranean Company which controlled the lines between the capital and Marseilles. The new company absorbed half of the short-lived Grand Central system, as well as the line from Lyons to Geneva where contact with the Swiss railway system was made. In 1859, when France joined Sardinia in the war against Austria, the Paris–Lyons–Mediterranean Company conveyed large numbers of troops and horses to Marseilles for embarkation to Italy much more quickly and efficiently than would have been possible by any other means of transport. The Eastern Railway began as the Paris–Strasbourg line, absorbed the Strasbourg–Mulhouse–Basel line and the Ardennes Railway, and secured permission to extend its network. The Western Railway, with the Paris–Rouen line as its nucleus, was an amalgamation of six railways. It linked Paris with the Channel ports of Le Havre and Cherbourg and extensions were planned to St. Malo and to Brest. Many of the lines which were joined together to form the Western Railway had been largely financed by British investors and had been constructed by English contractors and engineers. The first chairman of the new Western Railway Company was the English banker Edward Blount. The Midi Railway owed much to the initiative of the Pereire brothers who had long been among the leading promoters of railways. They had family connexions with Bordeaux and they planned to make the city the centre of a network of lines to serve the south-west of France. They secured concessions to construct lines from Bordeaux to Toulouse and Sète (linking the Atlantic and the Mediterranean), from Bordeaux to Bayonne and from Narbonne to Perpignan. The creation of these great railway companies gave France a much more unified railway system than those of Britain, Germany or the United States. Each big company dominated a particular region. Five joined the capital to important industrial regions—the Nord (Lille), Normandy (Rouen), Alsace (Mulhouse), Lyons and the Loire basin. The sixth served the relatively under-developed region of south-western France.

Hardly had the amalgamations been completed than the French railways faced their most serious crisis since 1848. The trade slump of 1857 caused many commercial houses to close their doors. The railways suffered from the depression and their net revenue fell from 30,861 francs (per kilometre of track) in 1855 to 23,587 francs in 1858. Investors lost confidence in the railways and several lines were unable to raise the capital to construct extensions which had to be completed by the terms of their concessions. Napoleon III was determined that the completion of the railway network should not be unduly delayed. The Government negotiated agreements with the six big railway companies in 1858 which amended the terms of the existing concessions. The new agreements—called "conventions"—were later embodied in a new Railway Law of 1859. The conventions made a distinction between the "old" and the "new" railway networks—i.e. lines built under concessions granted before and after 1857. As far as the old network was concerned the conventions aimed at stabilizing dividends at about the rate paid in 1857. No additional financial assistance from the State was granted in respect of the old network. On the other hand the Government guaranteed the interest and the amortization payments (4·65 per cent together) on the new network. Profits from the operation of the old network which exceeded an amount fixed for each railway by its convention were to be paid to the Government which used the money to meet its obligations under the guarantee of interest in the new network. In other words the more prosperous lines relieved the taxpayer of some of his obligations under the guarantee to help the less prosperous lines. The Northern Railway and the Paris–Lyons–Mediterranean Railway earned sufficiently high revenues to cover their interest and amortization payments on their new networks. But the other four big lines did, at one time or another, secure financial assistance from the Government to pay the interest guaranteed to shareholders under the conventions of 1857. Since railway dividends were now virtually pegged, railway shares no longer interested the speculator but were attractive to the small saver who wanted a safe investment but was content with a modest return on his money.

In the 1860's the French Government gave substantial financial assistance to ensure the construction of lines which, for various reasons, would not otherwise have been built. Some served rural districts where the traffic was unlikely to earn enough money to attract the private promoter and the speculative investor. Some were lines called "railways of public utility" which served the needs of the army or the navy. Some were "railways of local interest" which were constructed under a law of July 1865 by local authorities (departments or communes) as well as by private companies. These were inexpensive, narrow-gauge steam tramways which linked villages and small market towns.

French railway policy differed from that of other continental countries. Belgium and some German states had nationalized railways, some lines being built and operated by the State while others were private ventures which were taken over by the Government. In Prussia and in Saxony several important lines were built and run by joint-stock companies. But in France, almost from the first, the building and the administration of railways was a partnership between public and private enterprise. The railways were operated by joint-stock companies in which the Government had a substantial financial interest. The State had generally paid for the "infrastructure" and had sometimes given further financial help through the purchase of shares, the guaranteeing of interest on shares, and the granting of subsidies and loans. The Department of Highways and Bridges had built—or had helped to build—certain lines. Consequently in 1860 the six great railway companies were already semi-public concerns. It was, however, not until the period of the Third Republic that a network of nationalized railways was established in addition to the lines operated by joint-stock companies.[1]

*Inland Waterways and Ports.* The improvement of the navigable rivers and the extension of the network of canals proceeded at a somewhat leisurely pace under the Second Empire. The investing public was more interested in railways than in canals so that funds to improve the inland waterways had to come mainly from the State. In 1860 the Government decided to nationalize several canals and freight rates on all State canals were substantially reduced. Navigation dues were again reduced in 1867 and were now so low as to be insufficient to pay for the upkeep of the waterways. Although some important works were undertaken to increase the efficiency of the navigable rivers and canals it was not until the period of the Third Republic that improvements of a radical character were undertaken. The most important new waterway constructed in Napoleon III's reign was the Saar Coal Canal which linked the Marne-Rhine Canal with the canalized River Saar. Coal from the Saar region could now

[1] For the French State railways see below, pp. 172–4.

be conveyed more easily to the industrial districts of Alsace and Lorraine.

Considerable improvements were made to the great ports to enable them to deal with larger vessels. At Marseilles the construction of the Gare Maritime basin and the Imperial basin was authorized although the Department of Highways and Bridges drastically modified Napoleon III's grandiose plans and reduced the estimated costs of harbour improvements from 37 million francs to 15 million francs. Similarly the original scheme to spend 40 million francs on the harbour of Saint-Nazaire was amended to one costing 18 million francs. At Bordeaux a quay, 700 metres in length, was built in 1856 and a new dock was ready in 1869. At Cherbourg both naval and commercial docks were constructed and at Brest a new commercial port at the mouth of the Porstein creek was begun in 1865 though it was not completed until 1876. Improvements were also made at Le Havre and at the inland port of Rouen. The Government gave financial grants and postal subsidies to foster the establishment of new services to the United States, the West Indies, the Far East and Indo-China as well as in the Mediterranean. The *Messageries Impériales* and the *Société Générale Maritime Transatlantique* were France's leading shipping companies at this time. The latter had been founded by the Pereire brothers (through the *Crédit Mobilier*) and had sixty vessels when first established. But in spite of all the help given by the Government the French mercantile marine was only one of a million tons in 1869. This was about one-sixth of the tonnage of the British merchant navy. Only a small proportion of French vessels were steamships. Moreover the shipbuilding industry showed few signs of expansion. One reason for this was that France's coal-fields and engineering works were not favourably located from the point of view of the development of modern shipbuilding yards.

*Rebuilding of Paris.* The greatest achievement of the Second Empire from the point of view of the construction of public works was the rebuilding of Paris. As an exile Louis Napoleon had dreamed of creating a capital worthy of his dynasty. He wanted to pull down slums notorious for outbreaks of cholera; he proposed to relieve the traffic congestion that was becoming more serious every year; and he was determined to get rid of the narrow streets in working-class quarters where barricades were erected when the mob rose in revolt. When he was elected President trade was stagnant owing to the depression of 1846–8. The National Workshops inaugurated in the early months of the Second Republic had been wound up and Louis Napoleon believed that the introduction of a great programme of public works would revive the building trade and give an impetus to economic recovery. A contemporary observer comments upon the striking difference between the years 1848 and 1852:

"No longer did bands of insurgents roam the streets but teams of masons, carpenters, and other artisans going to work; if paving stones were pulled up it was not to build barricades but to open the way for water and gas pipes; houses were no longer threatened by cannon or fire but by expropriation for which generous compensation was paid."

In G. E. Haussmann the Emperor found an ideal collaborator in the task of rebuilding Paris. Haussmann was Prefect of the Seine Department from 1853 until 1869 and he wielded far greater powers than those exercised by the provincial prefects. In addition to the normal duties of a prefect, Haussmann was responsible for the administration of Paris which, unlike other great cities, had no elected municipal council and no mayor. Both the Paris Municipal Council and the General Council of the Seine Department were appointed by the Minister of the Interior on the recommendation of the prefect.[1]

The planning of a new Paris was an immense undertaking. It involved the creation of a "Greater Paris" by extending the municipal boundaries from the *octroi* walls to the outer fortifications so that eight new districts (*arrondissements*), with a population of 234,000, were added to the city. It involved the demolition of slum property, the building of roads, the laying out of parks, the provision of markets, the erection of various public buildings, the construction of shops, department stores and blocks of flats, the provision of additional supplies of water, the introduction of more efficient street lighting, and the building of a circular railway round Paris. Problems of town planning and design, public health, landscape gardening, traffic, finance and the organization of building labour had to be solved. And all this was done at a time when the population of Paris was nearly doubled in twenty years. The Paris of 1851 had about one million inhabitants but the "Greater Paris" of 1870 had nearly two million inhabitants.

There were three new networks of highways. The first network included the Rue de Rivoli, the Boulevard du Centre (later Sebasto-pol), and the Boulevard Saint Michel lying in the heart of medieval

---

[1] On the other hand Paris had a Prefect of Police—an official not found in the provinces—who was responsible for the control of the police both in the capital and in the Seine Department.

Paris within the inner boulevards. Many slums, including those in the densely populated Ile de la Cité, were swept away. This network included all the projects authorized before 1858. The second network consisted of the streets listed in an agreement made in March 1858 between the City and the State. The municipal authorities and the Government agreed to share the cost of constructing twenty-three miles of new roads between the inner boulevards and the *octroi* walls. The development of the Place de l'Étoile and the avenues radiating from it formed part of the second of Haussmann's undertakings. The third network included the new roads not already approved in either the first or the second network. The municipal authorities were responsible for defraying the cost of the third network. In planning his great thoroughfares Haussmann accepted the traditional rules of French "official" town planning and architecture. He followed the classical formula of a wide, straight, symmetrical highway lined with buildings of the same height and uniform façades and having a vista of an imposing public building at the end. Buildings erected by private persons usually had to conform to the general plan of the new streets though they were not required to adopt the same style of architecture.

The construction of the new thoroughfares involved the demolition of nearly 20,000 houses. More than twice that number were built to house the families who had lost their homes and the newcomers who were streaming into Paris at this time. Many imposing public buildings were erected such as the new opera house, the new Hôtel Dieu (a famous hospital), the central markets and important extensions to the Louvre and the National Library. The civil and ecclesiastical authorities erected churches, hospitals, schools and so forth while private enterprise was responsible for the construction of large hotels, department stores and blocks of flats. Numerous buildings were erected by the *Compagnie immobilière de Paris* which was one of the many enterprises in which the Pereire brothers had a financial interest.

Several open spaces were added to the amenities of Paris. To the west of the city the Bois de Boulogne, a State forest, was transferred to the municipal authorities and was laid out as a public park and woodlands. The plain of Longchamps was added to this park and here France's leading racecourse was established by the Jockey Club. To the east of Paris another State forest, the Bois de Vincennes, was also handed over to the municipality and was converted into a park. Several smaller parks, such as those of Monceau and of Montsouris, were established at the time of the Second Empire.

A great improvement was made in the provision of water for the capital. Various waterworks were united in the *Compagnie Générals des Eaux* which was granted the sole right to supply Greater Paris with water. Two aqueducts were constructed to carry to Paris the waters of the River Dhuis (a tributary of the Marne) and of the River Vanne (a tributary of the Yonne). The sanitary arrangements of Paris were completely overhauled by the laying of nearly 320 miles of new sewers and the construction of a huge "collector sewer" to carry the entire sewage of the city to the River Seine twelve miles downstream.

The means adopted by Haussmann to pay for the rebuilding of Paris aroused violent controversy. When the plan was in its early stages the total cost could not be foreseen. In 1869 Haussmann stated that 2,500 million francs had been spent on the reconstruction of Paris. The municipal authorities, even with State subsidies, could not hope to raise sufficient revenue every year to pay for the new boulevards and public buildings that were being erected. The money had to be borrowed. Haussmann argued that money spent upon urban improvements was "productive expenditure" which would increase the wealth of the city. The necessary funds should therefore be raised by using the surplus of the city's "ordinary" budget as security for loans. Haussmann believed that the new public works would lead to an increase in the city's revenues and to an increase in the budget surplus so that further loans could be raised for further improvements. Haussmann gambled on the future. He was confident that Paris would share in the general economic prosperity of the early 1850's and that its revenues would expand so that old loans could be paid off and that, if necessary, new loans could be raised.

Haussmann's critics alleged that he was guilty of serious financial irregularities. He recast the city budget and moved certain items from the "ordinary" to the "extraordinary" budget so as to secure as large a surplus as possible on the "ordinary" budget. And this "surplus" was used as security to tempt investors to put their savings in municipal bonds. In 1858 a Paris Public Works Fund was set up for ten years. It handled the funds of special schemes, particularly works, which fell outside the city's normal financial operations. Bonds called *bons de délégation*, were given to contractors engaged in public works. These bonds could be redeemed when the works was finished. They were actually cashed, at a discount, by various banks—particularly the *Crédit Foncier*—long before they were redeemable at the City Hall. Eventually certain contractors, such as Ardouin and Ricardo, issued bonds of their own with Haussmann's permission. These methods of raising money were attacked by Jules Ferry in his pamphlet called *Les Comptes Fantastiques d'Haussmann*

(1868). Haussmann stoutly maintained that his financial dealings were perfectly legal but eventually Rouher, speaking on behalf of the Government, admitted that they had been "irregular". Towards the end of his official career Haussmann had to drop many of the methods of borrowing money that he had used in the past. The result was that in his last budget statement to the Municipal Council he observed that it would be possible to undertake "only very modest projects in the year to come".

*Banking.* The rebuilding of Paris and the construction of new railways and harbours was greatly facilitated by the existence of the *Crédit Mobilier*. In 1852 a scheme was put forward by the Pereire brothers with the support of Achille Fould (Minister of Finance)[1] for the establishment of a credit bank on the lines of the *Caisse Laffitte* and the Belgian *Société Générale*. In November of that year —a fortnight before the proclamation of the Second Empire—Louis Napoleon issued a decree which gave Isaac Pereire, Emile Pereire, B. L. Fould and Fould-Oppenheim a concession to establish the *Crédit Mobilier*. Associated with the four original "promoters" were several "founders" including several foreign bankers such as Prince Torlonia of Rome, Solomon Heine of Hamburg and Solomon Oppenheim of Cologne. The funds at the disposal of the new bank were the initial share capital (60 million francs divided into 120,000 shares of 500 francs each), the money paid in by depositors, and the proceeds of the issue of debentures (*obligations*). When the directors proposed to issue 240,000 debentures of 250 francs each in 1855 "the government became alarmed and forbade the definitive announcement of the plan". The *Crédit Mobilier* was dominated by the wealthy investors since only the 200 largest shareholders could attend the annual meeting and a holder of 200 shares had five votes.

The objects of the new bank were set forth by the board of directors in their first report:

> "The idea of the *Crédit Mobilier* is born of the insufficient credit available for the organisation of business on a large scale in this country, of the isolation in which the forces of finance are placed, of the lack of a centre strong enough to draw them together.
>
> It is born of the need to bring upon the market the regular support of new capital designed to aid in the development of public and industrial credit.

[1] Achille Fould held office as Finance Minister on three occasions: October 31, 1849, to January 24, 1851; April 10, 1851, to October 27, 1851; and December 3, 1851, to January 25, 1852. He was a brother of the banker B. L. Fould.

It is born of the exorbitant conditions under which loans are made upon the public funds and the difficulties which arise therefrom for the definitive placement of even the best securities.

It is born of the need to centralise the financial and administrative activities of the great companies, especially railway companies, and so to utilise for the greatest advantage of all, the capital which each in turn has available . . .

It is born of the necessity of introducing into circulation a new agent, a new fiduciary currency, carrying with it daily interest and enabling the humblest savings to fructify as well as ample fortunes."

Jenks has pointed out that the aim of the *Crédit Mobilier* was "to infuse life and organisation into an industrial and business society which was anarchical and moribund. It proposed to assemble resources for the purpose of the extensive sale of its shares and obligations to small investors. The Pereires thought of it as socialising the Rothschild business. They did not intend to enter commercial banking. Theirs was to be no agency for commercial discount, although it deserves credit for introducing the cheque-and-deposit system into France in a small way. Nor was it to be merely a holding company, although it retained share-control of some of the more important companies it promoted. But its resources were to be used chiefly as a basis for generous advances and "reports" upon securities, which would give encouragement to speculative investors and incite others to promote public utility undertakings. In this way the Pereires hoped to make their bank the major instrument in the great task of making France prosperous by means of public works."

The *Crédit Mobilier* had been established with the support of the Emperor and was under a measure of government control. It immediately gained the support of investors and on the day when its shares were first quoted on the Paris Bourse they changed hands at twice their face value. Foreign support was quickly forthcoming and at one time about a third of the shares were in English hands. At the height of its influence the *Crédit Mobilier* handled nearly one-third of all the new securities issued in Paris. It invested in government loans (particularly during the Crimean war) and it helped to finance many important undertakings such as the rebuilding of Paris (through the *Compagnie Immobilière de Paris*), the establishment of the Paris Central Gas Company and the Paris General Omnibus Association, the amalgamation of the French railways, the promotion of overseas trade (through the *Société Générale Maritime Transatlantique*), the building of harbours, the expansion of agriculture (through the *Crédit Foncier*) and the establishment of many public utilities in the provinces such as the Marseilles gas company. It was in the field of public works and public utilities that the *Crédit Mobilier* was most successful. By 1864 the capital of the companies which the *Crédit Mobilier* had helped to promote was over 125 million francs.

The *Crédit Mobilier* was also active outside France particularly in the promotion of new credit banks and railways. It played a part in establishing the Darmstadt Bank in Germany. Some of its officials, with money borrowed from the *Crédit Mobilier*, took up a block of shares in the Darmstadt Bank at the time of its foundation. The *Crédit Mobilier* was a leading member of a syndicate which secured a concession to operate the State railways of Austria as well as other former nationalized concerns such as a steamboat service on the Danube and certain mines and ironworks. In Spain the *Crédit Mobilier* was behind the *Credito Mobiliaro Español* which fostered the establishment of many public utilities and industrial enterprises including the Madrid gasworks, an insurance company and several railways. In Switzerland the *Crédit Mobilier* gained control of the Western Railway and held shares in the Central Swiss Railway but it failed to secure the amalgamation of all the Swiss lines into a single company. In Russia the Pereires and their associates gained an important share of the concession to establish the Great Russian Railway Company though the *Crédit Mobilier* itself was not directly concerned with the enterprise. In Italy the *Credito Mobiliare Italiano* —which was for a few years entirely under the control of the *Crédit Mobilier*—reorganized the Turin gas company, underwrote government loans, and had a share in the management of four railways. In many of these activities outside France—certainly in Austria, Spain and Switzerland—the Pereires and their associates had to face the implacable hostility of the Rothschilds. The rivalry of those financiers to some extent weakened the influence which French financiers and entrepreneurs enjoyed in those parts of the Continent where modern industries were just beginning to develop.

In its early years the *Crédit Mobilier* was able to achieve many of the ambitious aims of its founders. It paid high dividends and was a profitable investment for the shareholders. In the 1860's, however, it declined. The *Crédit Mobilier* tried to do too much with the capital at its disposal. Not until 1866, when it was too late, was its capital raised to 120 million francs. Too high a proportion of its capital was tied up in companies which it had helped to establish and when some of these undertakings—such as the *Compagnie Immobilère de Paris*— ran into financial difficulties public confidence in the parent company was shaken. Throughout its career the *Crédit Mobilier* had to face opposition from the Rothschilds and from other private bankers who detested the Pereire bank as an upstart rival. Moreover the *Crédit Mobilier* foolishly alienated the Bank of France by challenging its monopoly of the note issue. The Pereires supported an application by the Bank of Savoy to issue its own notes. A lively public controversy ensued and the proposal was eventually turned down. When the crash came in 1867 the Bank of France refused to help the *Crédit Mobilier* unless the Pereire brothers were excluded from all share in its management. The *Crédit Mobilier* was reorganized as a deposit bank. Levasseur has observed that the *Crédit Mobilier* "succumbed through being over ambitious, through immobilising too much of its capital, and through indulging in unwise speculation".

The *Crédit Mobilier* had taken a leading part in fostering the industrialization of France in the 1850's and had helped to extend French economic influence to many parts of the Continent. It was largely owing to the activities of the Pereires—and their rivals the Rothschilds—that, as C. K. Hobson has observed, "the French capital market was rapidly advancing towards the position, which it came to occupy during the 1860's of co-equality with London in a great part of the foreign investment business". The bank established by the Perieres found imitators all over the world. Among the more important of these institutions were the *Crédit Lyonnais*, the *Société Générale*, the Austrian *Kreditanstalt* (founded by the Rothschilds), the *Credito Mobiliaro Español* and the *Credito Mobiliare Italiano*. In Germany the Bank of Darmstadt was to some extent modelled upon the *Crédit Mobilier*, while the Discount Company of Berlin followed the model of the Paris *Comptoir d'Escompte*. The English consul-general in Leipzig reported in 1856 that "the favourite enterprises of the day are credit institutions or banks upon the plan of the French *Crédit Mobilier*".[1] It has been estimated that prior to 1870 about a quarter of the capital invested in the coal and heavy industries of the Ruhr and Rhineland was of French origin. In the 1860's firms under French control produced virtually all the zinc as well as half the lead and a quarter of the pig-iron and copper of western Germany.

Another important financial institution established in France at this time was the land mortgage bank (*Crédit Foncier*). When a decree of February 1850 authorized the establishment of land banks Wolowski set up the *Banque Foncière de Paris* which was subsequently reorganized as the *Crédit Foncier de France*. This bank had a capital

[1] For the new German banks of the 1850's, see above, p. 30.

of 60 million francs as well as a government subsidy and it received a monopoly of land mortgage business. Its original object was to assist landowners and farmers by granting them loans at five per cent interest for the improvement of their property. Before long, however, the *Crédit Foncier* was investing money in urban property and was granting loans to municipalities which were making on a small scale the sort of improvements for which Haussmann was responsible in Paris.

*The Suez Canal.* The construction of the Suez Canal was the greatest achievement of French entrepreneurs abroad during the Second Empire. The opening up of the overland route from Europe to India had been largely a British achievement. In the 1830's and 1840's Lieutenant T. Waghorn, R.N., established an agency which forwarded letters and parcels from London to Bombay by the quickest available route. This was generally by way of Marseilles (or Trieste), Alexandria and Suez. In the 1840's the Peninsular and Oriental Steamship Company made its own arrangements to convey passengers across Egypt. Waghorn then concentrated his attention upon getting letters and parcels across Europe to Alexandria as quickly as possible. In the 1850's the Peninsular and Oriental Company supported the plan for the construction of a railway from Alexandria to Cairo and Suez. Said Pasha decided to build the line partly from his own resources and partly with the aid of a loan of £285,000 from the Peninsular and Orient Company and its associates. He allocated forced labour to the contractors as was usual on all public works in Egypt at this time. Robert Stephenson was appointed the engineer in charge of the construction of the line. The railway from Alexandria reached the Nile in 1853, Cairo in 1855 and Suez in 1858. The Cairo–Suez section of the railway was closed in 1866 when a new line from Cairo to Ismailia and Suez was opened.

The French were also interested in the opening up of Egypt and in improving communications between Europe and India. When Napoleon invaded Egypt in 1799 the engineer Le Père was given the task of reporting on the possibility of constructing a canal through Egypt. For centuries there had been proposals to cut a canal from the Red Sea to the Nile and so provide a new waterway to the Mediterranean. Le Père, however, examined the possibility of constructing a salt-water—as distinct from a fresh-water—canal to join the two seas by the most direct route. Unfortunately he made a mistake in his calculations and came to the conclusion that the level of the Red Sea was nearly five metres below that of the Mediterranean. He believed that a ship canal would have to be provided with locks. Nothing came of Napoleon's plans for a Suez Canal but the scheme was not forgotten. Mehemet Ali improved communications between the Mediterranean and the Red Sea by constructing the Mahmoudieh Canal from Alexandria to Afteh on the Nile. Forced labour was employed and some 15,000 workers died before the canal was finished. Livant de Bellefonds, who was Mehemet Ali's chief engineer, made careful surveys of a direct canal route between the two seas. "It is to Livant more than to any other individual that the original plan of the Suez canal is due." In France Prosper Enfantin set up an international committee of engineers in 1847 to study the project of a Suez canal but no practical results were achieved at this time.

Ferdinand de Lesseps now came on to the scene. He had spent seven years at Cairo and Alexandria as a consul in the 1830's and had long dreamed of building a canal across Egypt. His father had been a personal friend of Mehemet Ali and de Lesseps himself had taught Said (Mehemet's son and heir-designate) to ride and to fence. Two circumstances gave de Lesseps the chance to turn a dream into reality. In 1853 his cousin Eugénie de Montijo married Napoleon III and in the following year his friend Said became Viceroy of Egypt. Ferdinand de Lesseps was now in a unique position both in Paris and in Cairo to press forward with his plan. He hurried to Egypt and in November 1854 the new Viceroy granted him a ninety-nine year concession to found a company to build the Suez Canal. Since Egypt was part of the Ottoman Empire the concession would have to be confirmed by the Sultan.

For years de Lesseps struggled to overcome obstacles that appeared to be insurmountable. Britain tenaciously opposed a scheme to open a new route to India over which she could not exercise complete control and her influence was sufficiently powerful in Constantinople to ensure that the Sultan would veto the scheme. The merchants of Alexandria opposed a project which would lead to the construction of a rival port at the Mediterranean end of the canal. Napoleon III would have liked to be the instigator and patron of so grandiose a scheme but he also wanted to remain on good terms with Britain and hence he adopted a vacillating policy which exasperated de Lesseps. In 1855–6 an international commission of experts examined the site of the proposed canal and reported that de Lesseps's scheme was perfectly practicable. The commission suggested, however, that the Mediterranean end of the canal should not be at Tineh (Pelusium) but 28 km. farther west (i.e. the future Port Said).

In 1858 de Lesseps decided to take the plunge and to float a canal company even though the Sultan had not confirmed the concession and the British Government opposed the project. Of the 400,000 shares offered at 200 francs each 220,000 were taken up, mostly in France. A large block of shares was booked to the account of the Viceroy in view of a verbal undertaking that he had given. In 1859 the excavation of the canal was inaugurated at Port Said. Ferdinand de Lesseps was acting in defiance of the Sultan and the well-known hostility of the British Government but he was confident that as the various sections of the canal were completed he would be able to defeat his enemies by presenting them with a *fait accompli*. He suffered many reverses and disappointments. At first he had to rely upon free workers since the Viceroy would not make forced labour available. In February 1862 the Freshwater Canal from the River of Moses (a tributary of the Nile) to Serapeum was completed and it was now much easier to supply drinking water to those working on the ship canal. In March 1862 the Viceroy at last decided to call men up for forced labour on the Suez Canal. This greatly speeded up the construction of the canal even though the peasants worked only with picks and baskets and would not even use wheelbarrows. In November 1862 the El Guisr (le Seuil)–Ismailia section of the canal was completed so that the waters of Lake Manzaleh flowed into Lake Timsah.

Said Pasha died in January 1863. His successor Ismail took office at a time when the economy of Egypt was booming owing to the Cotton Famine at the time of the American civil war. Egypt's exports of cotton were expanding and high prices were being obtained. The new Viceroy granted two new concessions to de Lesseps in March 1863. Ismail accepted on behalf of the Egyptian Government all the Suez Canal shares standing in Said's name and he agreed to complete the Freshwater Canal (parallel to the salt-water ship canal) to Suez at his own expense. In 1864 the Sultan of Turkey declared that it was illegal for the Suez Canal Company to use forced labour. Once more de Lesseps had to use free labour, but now he was able to make use of mechanical excavators which were far more efficient than manual labour. A dispute concerning the amount of compensation due to the Suez Canal Company from the Egyptian Government for the loss of forced labour and for the surrender of certain lands formerly ceded to de Lesseps was submitted to Napoleon III's arbitration. The Suez Canal Company was awarded 84 million francs (payable in instalments) which was a welcome addition to its depleted resources. Ferdinand de Lesseps's persistence was at last rewarded. Early in 1866 a convention was signed between Ismail and the Suez Canal Company which settled all outstanding questions in dispute. The British and French Governments approved the new arrangements and the Sultan confirmed them. Three years later the work was completed and the waters of the two seas met on August 15, 1869. The Empress Eugénie was present when the canal was opened on November 17, 1869. In the first year only 486 ships (654,915 tons) passed through the canal. In 1890 the number of ships using the canal was 3,389 with a total tonnage of 9,749,129 tons. By that time the British Government had acquired all the Khedive's shares in the canal—176,602 in number—and an international agreement had provided that "the maritime canal of Suez shall always be free and open, in time of war as in time of peace, to every vessel of commerce or of war without distinction of flag".

*The Cobden-Chevalier Treaty.* There was nothing original in the efforts of the Government of the Second Empire to hasten the pace of industrialization in France by improving communications, undertaking great public works, and fostering the establishment of new credit banks. These methods had often been used before, though Napoleon III and his advisers deserve credit for the energy with which they carried through their plans. But the attempt to promote the expansion of manufactures by adopting a policy of low tariffs was something that had not been tried since the days of the Eden-Reyneval Treaty of 1786. The amalgamation of railways, the rebuilding of Paris, and the founding of the *Crédit Mobilier* were criticized in some quarters but public opinion on the whole supported the policy of the Government as far as these measures were concerned. But the reversal of France's traditional fiscal policy aroused a storm of protest. Frenchmen firmly believed in Protection and were strongly opposed to Free Trade. Napoleon III showed considerable courage in pressing forward with a fiscal policy which he believed would benefit France but which was bound to lessen his popularity.

Since Colbert's day France had followed a policy of prohibitions and high tariffs to protect industry, agriculture, shipping and colonial trade. French manufactures were accustomed to enjoying a privileged position in both the home market and the colonial market. The brief interlude inaugurated by the Eden Treaty only confirmed Frenchmen in their belief that Protection was essential to the economic prosperity of their country. In the years following the Napoleonic wars Free Trade views were held only by a very small minority. Some of the merchants in the great ports, however, realized that it would be in their interests to secure the removal of tariff restrictions upon international trade. In 1833 the merchants of Bordeaux presented an address to the legislature in which they condemned "the fatal system" of Protection which was responsible for "the poverty of our internal commerce, the immense tracts of our soil devoid of culture, that listlessness in intercourse which, for a long time, will render it impossible to build any railways in our country". "Might we not also impute to this the absence among us of a spirit of association, the dislike of great capitalists to embark upon public enterprises, their backwardness in investing capital either in manufactures or in simple commercial affairs?" "Is it not the exclusive spirit of our legislature which encourages them to be exclusive themselves, and to reserve their riches and their credit either for the gambling of the Stock Exchange, or for privileged investments, such as purchases of forests, manufacturies of sugar from beetroot, and extensive ironworks?"

In the 1840's Bastiat wrote several Free Trade pamphlets and edited the journal *Le Libre Echange*. When Louis Napoleon secured power he cautiously moved towards a more liberal fiscal policy. He believed that—in conjunction with his other economic reforms —the lowering of duties on imported manufactured goods would force relatively backward French industrialists to introduce more efficient methods of production in order to meet foreign competition.

In 1853 when many railways were being constructed there was a shortage of rails in France. So import duties on iron and steel were twice reduced by decree. Since the Protectionists raised no objection, the Government submitted to the Chamber a Bill to replace certain import prohibitions by import duties. This time, however, there was a storm of protest from the Protectionists and the Government agreed that no prohibitions should be abolished before 1861. The Government stated in the *Moniteur* (October 17, 1856) that the proposal to abolish certain prohibitions had not been dropped but had merely been postponed. The official announcement added that "French industries, warned of the firm intentions of the government, will have ample time to prepare themselves for the new commercial régime". The Protectionists, however, did not take seriously this clear statement of the Government's intentions and made no preparations to meet foreign competition in the future. In 1859 the French Government proposed to abolish the corn laws which had been suspended for nearly six years. Again there were vigorous protests from the Protectionists and the Government re-imposed the sliding-scale of 1832.

Napoleon III realized that in view of the strength of Protectionist sentiment it would be useless to submit to the legislature any further proposals for the removal of prohibitions or the reduction of high import duties. There was, however, a means by which this difficulty could be overcome. Under the constitution the Emperor had the power to sign and to ratify commercial treaties without submitting them to the legislature. Tariff changes embodied in a commercial treaty could therefore be carried out without reference to the views of the deputies. In 1859 several of the Emperor's advisers suggested to him that the time had come to reduce import duties. Persigny, the French ambassador in London, suggested that a reduction of the tariff—brought about by a commercial treaty with Britain—should form part of a comprehensive plan for the economic revival of France through the investment of two million francs of public money in agriculture and transport. The Pereire brothers submitted a memorandum to Napoleon III on the stagnation of trade after the Italian war. They too suggested reductions in import duties to stimulate international trade and the raising of a State loan to provide money for investment in industry. Rouher and Chevalier put forward similar proposals for the Emperor's consideration.

In the summer of 1859 Chevalier suggested to Richard Cobden that an Anglo-French commercial agreement between Britain and France would kill two birds with one stone. On the one hand it would enable Napoleon III to make substantial reductions in the French tariff without consulting the legislature. On the other hand it would reduce political tension between the two countries. Public opinion in France had been inflamed because Orsini's plot to murder the Emperor had been hatched in England while public opinion in England was alarmed lest the annexation of Savoy and Nice should prove to be the prelude to further territorial demands by Napoleon III. Cobden discussed Chevalier's suggestion with Gladstone (Chancellor of the Exchequer). At this time many English Free Traders objected to commercial treaties and argued that France should be prepared to abolish prohibitions and reduce import duties without reference to the tariff policy of any other country. Gladstone and Cobden came to realize, however, that France was in an exceptional position, and that unless the proposed reductions in French tariff were embodied in a trade agreement they would probably never be made at all.

Lord Palmerston (the Prime Minister) and Napoleon III agreed that Cobden should have informal conversations with Chevalier concerning future reductions in the level of British and French import duties. These discussions took place in Paris in the autumn of 1859 and great secrecy was observed. Not even the French Minister of Finance was aware that preliminary negotiations for an Anglo-French commercial agreement were in progress.

So successful were these unofficial discussions that on January 5, 1860, Napoleon III wrote a letter to Achille Fould (Minister of State), in which he announced a far-reaching programme of economic reforms of which the tariff reductions to be included in the forth-coming commercial agreement would form a part. Napoleon III argued that the future economic progress of France depended upon an expansion of her foreign trade. If France were to sell more of her goods abroad she must be prepared to buy more from foreign countries. The tariff must be reformed. Import duties on raw materials necessary to French manufacturers would be repealed. Import prohibitions would be replaced by import duties. The duties on foods and drinks—such as sugar and coffee—would be gradually reduced. A government loan would be made to industry and to agriculture and this would enable manufacturers to buy new machines and so meet foreign competition at home and abroad. The letter to Fould was published in the *Moniteur* on January 15, 1860, and the Anglo-French commercial treaty was signed on January 23.

The chief concessions made to France by Britain were the abolition of the silk duties and the reduction in the import duties upon wine and brandy. A maximum import duty on wine of 5s. 9d. per gallon was replaced by duties ranging from 1s. per gallon on wine up to 15 degrees of alcohol to 2s. per gallon on wines of 40 degrees. The duty on brandy was reduced from 15s. to 10s. 5d. a gallon. These concessions were embodied in the budget of 1860 and came into force immediately except for the wine duties which were reduced on April 1, 1861. They applied to all countries and not to France alone.

The French agreed that the maximum rate of import duties would be thirty per cent *ad valorem* for four years and then twenty-five per cent. The actual rates were fixed in two supplementary conventions signed in October and November 1860 after the French authorities had made an exhaustive inquiry into the cost of producing various goods in France and in England. The new French import duties were generally much lower than the maximum rate of thirty per cent. Many were only ten per cent. Cast iron in future paid 25 francs per 100 kgm., machinery 15 francs and most types of cloth 15 francs. These concessions—which came into effect between July 1, 1860, and June 1, 1861—were made only to Britain. Other states still paid the old rates of duty. Belgium, Prussia (for the Zollverein), Italy and various other countries, however, soon signed similar commercial agreements with France so as to gain the advantage of the lower French duties.[1] These treaties all contained a most-favoured-nation clause. The network of low-tariff commercial agreements, inspired

[1] For the Franco-Prussian commercial agreement of March 1862 see above, pp. 27–28.

by the Cobden-Chevalier treaty of 1860, greatly facilitated the expansion of international trade in western Europe.

Napoleon III had to face strong opposition from the Protectionists. No sooner had the new commercial policy been announced than 165 manufacturers signed a petition to the Emperor (January 20, 1860) in which they complained bitterly of measures that were "nothing more nor less than an economic and social revolution" which would endanger "the very existence of a by no means insignificant number of our national industries". But the Emperor weathered the storm. In the hope of placating his critics a law for a State loan of forty million francs to industry was promulgated on August 1, 1860. It offered loans at five per cent interest to manufacturers who wished to borrow money to modernize their plants. In April 1861 it was reported that 200 applications for loans had been approved. Textile firms had secured 88 loans (15 million francs), while ironworks and engineering establishments had secured 45 loans (10·5 million francs). The loans reconciled some manufacturers to the new commercial policy. The progress of a number of French industries in the 1860's—particularly the iron industry—suggests that by forcing manufacturers to face a certain amount of foreign competition Napoleon III succeeded in making them introduce more efficient methods of production.

*Latin Monetary Union.* Another aspect of the efforts of the government of the Second Empire to extend French economic influence abroad was the conclusion of the Latin Monetary Convention in 1865. It came into force three years later. Just as the German states endeavoured to foster mutual trade by securing a fixed relationship between the thaler of Prussia and the guldens (florins) of South Germany and of Austria, so the French hoped to facilitate international commerce by giving the same value to the gold and silver francs of France, Belgium and Switzerland and the Italian lira. It was agreed that these coins should be of identical value and should be accepted as legal tender by all members of the Monetary Union.

INDUSTRIAL EXPANSION IN THE 1850's AND 1860's

The unusually rapid rate of expansion of manufactures in France at the time of the Second Empire—particularly in the boom of 1852–7 —was due partly to a favourable environment and partly to State encouragement. The influx of gold, the rise in prices, the growth of colonies, the improvements in world transport promoted the growth of industries in many countries. The government of

Napoleon III took advantage of this situation and promoted industry and agriculture by granting loans and subsidies, by constructing public works, by promoting the establishment of credit banks, and by adopting a liberal commercial policy. There were of course unfavourable factors such as the Crimean war, the cholera epidemic of the early 1850's, the commercial crisis of 1857, the war in Italy in 1859, the shortage of raw cotton during the American civil war, and the recessions of 1863–4 and of 1867. Goschen, writing in the *Edinburgh Review* in January 1868, remarked that "the French have been sharply checked in that victorious advance on the road of commercial and industrial development, by which they were asked, not quite in vain, to console themselves for many serious reverses in their military and political supremacy. All the heart has been taken out of business in Paris as in London. Rouen and Liverpool have been exchanging condolences; and the wreck of Overend, Gurney and Co. in England, found its parallel in the grounding of the *Crédit Mobilier* in France." The setbacks of the 1850's and 1860's did not have adverse consequences upon all branches of French manufacture. Wars stimulated ironworks and the armaments industry, while the shortage of cotton between 1862 and 1864 stimulated the woollen and linen industries. But in the closing years of Napoleon III's reign "the tempo of industrial expansion slowed. The hammers faltered and were silent on Haussmann's palaces. The forces which the Second Empire had released, which had made possible its long survival, had lost their initial impetus and were already being driven back by the new forces implicit in their forward drive."

*Coal.* Both the output and the consumption of coal increased between 1852 and 1870. Production rose from 4·9 million tons to 13·3 million tons, but this was insufficient to meet the needs of French industry and 5·5 million tons were imported in 1870 The relatively high cost of coal forced some French industrialists to continue to use water power although steam power would have been more efficient. And efforts were made to use coal as economically as possible. In 1859 the Industrial Society of Mulhouse offered prizes for devices to reduce the amount of coal used to heat steam boilers.

Over half of France's coal came from the Nord, the Pas de Calais and the Upper Loire. The Departments of the Nord and Pas de Calais together produced one-third while the upper Loire produced a quarter of all the coal mined in France. In the Nord new mines came into production at Lens and Béthune and in the Pas de Calais virtually the whole coal-field was opened up between 1850 and 1870. The output of these two departments rose from 1,000,000 tons in

1852 to 4·3 million tons in 1870. The most important coal-mining concern in the Nord was the Anzin Company which produced one-tenth of France's total output. The coal-field of the upper Loire—lying between the Loire and the Rhône—had the second largest output in France at this time. The most important centres of production were Saint Etienne and Rive de Gier. The output of this coal-field rose from 1·6 million tons in 1852 to 3·2 million tons in 1870. All the mines in the upper Loire coal-field had at one time been united in the *Compagnie des Mines de Loire*. But the miners were hostile to the combine and in 1854 the Government ordered the company to be split up into four smaller units. There were several smaller coal-fields in France including the Grand' Combe mine (developed by Paulin Talabot), the Le Creusot mines (Schneider), the Commentry mine, the Decazeville mine, the Carmaut mine and the Saint-Avold collieries. The rapid expansion of some of the coal regions may be seen from the growth of the mining towns of Commentry and Decazeville with a population of 10,000 each. A few great firms—such as Le Creusot and Denain-Anzin—operated both coal-mines and ironworks.

*Iron and Steel.* The production of iron-ore in France under the Second Empire was about three million tons a year. The most important ironfield was that of Lorraine which produced nearly 1·5 million tons in 1869 but its vast resources of *minette* ore were still inadequately exploited. Coke smelting was at last making real progress in France and the proportion of pig-iron produced by the old charcoal method declined from fifty-seven per cent of the total in 1850 to only eight per cent in 1870. There was also considerable progress in the making of wrought iron. The puddling process was now very widely used and the output of puddled iron increased in the 1850's. The production of steel increased with the introduction of the Bessemer and Siemens-Martin processes in some of the larger steelworks. The first experiments in France with Bessemer's con-verter were conducted by the firm of Jackson at Saint-Seurin sur l'Isle (by Bordeaux) in 1858 and the converter was subsequently intro-duced into steelworks at Assailly, Imphy, Terre Noire (Saint Étienne) and Châtillon-Commentry. Between 1863 and 1869 the amount of Bessemer steel made in France rose from 1,826 tons to 52,400 tons. In 1864 the brothers Pierre Martin and Émile Martin of Sireuil (Charente) invented the open-hearth process which incorporated a device discovered by William Siemens by which the gases were heated before entering the furnace. The Siemens-Martin process was introduced into Le Creusot steelworks. In time steel made by the new processes came to take the place of puddled iron.

The introduction of new processes in the production of iron and steel involving the use of coal or coke stimulated the expansion of ironworks in regions close to coal-fields (such as the Nord Department) and led to a decline of output in districts (such as the Haute Marne Department) which were not favourably located from the point of view of coal supplies. The chief regions in France for the smelting of iron and the manufacture of iron and steel products at the time of the Second Empire were Lorraine, Alsace, the Nord Department, the Central Highlands, and the Haute Marne Department. Lorraine produced nearly twelve per cent of France's pig-iron in 1860, the largest plants being those of the old established firm of de Wendel at Hayange. The Lorraine ironmasters secured their coal from the Saar and from Saint-Avold. Charcoal smelting had almost disappeared from this district by 1870. In the neighbouring province of Alsace two of the most important ironworks and engineering establishments were those of Dietrich (Niederbronn) and Thierry-Mieg (Mulhouse). In the Nord Department, although coal was more easily available than in Alsace or Lorraine, the transition to the new methods of production proved to be surprisingly difficult. The Nord Department still had a number of small ironworks which were scattered in remote wooded valleys where charcoal could be secured more easily and more cheaply than coal. But in the 1850's the iron industry of this region became concentrated in larger plants using coke blast furnaces. Two of the most important ironworks and steelworks in the Nord Department were the *Forges de Denain et d'Anzin* and the *Hautes Fourneaux de Maubeuge*. The ironworks of the Nord felt the effects of English and Belgian competition when the more liberal commercial policy inaugurated by the Cobden Treaty came into force. In the central highlands of France there were several large ironworks and engineering establishments including those at Le Creusot, Fourchambault, Saint Étienne, Commentry and Decazeville. The ironmasters of the Haute Marne Department complained bitterly in the 1860's that they were losing trade owing to English competition when the low iron import duties of the Cobden Treaty came into force. In fact their difficulties were due to a decline in iron-ore reserves, a shortage of timber, and increased competition in the Paris market from iron products made in Lorraine and in the Nord Department. Some of the small ironmasters of the Haute Marne went out of business while others survived for a time by adopting modern methods of production. The increasing concentration of production in the hands of large plants led to the establishment in 1864 of the *Comité des Forges*—with Eugène Schneider of Le Creusot as its first president—which was one of the earliest and one of the most powerful federations of employers in France.

*Textiles.* In the middle of the nineteenth century the most important textile centres were on the periphery of the country. Cottons were no longer manufactured in Paris but were produced at Mulhouse and at Rouen. Woollens were made in Sedan and Reims, linens in Anjou and Maine. Only Lyons and Saint Étienne, where silks were made, had a central location. In several textile towns— Lille, Roubaix, Tourcoing, Mulhouse—both cotton and woollen cloths were produced. There was comparatively little geographical specialization in spinning, weaving, dyeing and printing. It was not uncommon for large firms to engage in all branches of production from the preparatory to the finishing processes and some of them maintained their own engineering workshops for the construction and repair of textile machinery. In the woollen industry, however, firms which specialized in carding were established in the 1850's. France also had an important industry devoted to the manufacture of men's suits and women's dresses and accessories. Paris became the centre of *haute couture* at this time and the Second Empire was called the Age of Fashion. Worth, the former apprentice at Swan and Edgar of London, who designed dresses for the Empress, was the leading *couturier* of his day.

At the time of the Second Empire the French cotton industry was the largest on the Continent. In 1860 it had 5·6 million spindles, employed nearly 380,000 operatives, and worked up 100,000 tons of raw cotton most of which was imported at Le Havre. A report of C. Thierry-Mieg to the Mulhouse Industrial Society on Alsace's industrial development in the 1850's shows the remarkable progress that was being made in the cotton industry of this province. The number of steam engines in the factories of Alsace rose from 163 (of 3,565 h.p.) in 1851 to 473 (of 11,000 h.p.) in 1860. The spinning of short-staple cotton had been greatly improved by the general adoption of self-acting mules while the spinning of long-staple cotton had been revolutionized by the use of carding machines invented in Mulhouse by Heilmann and Hübner. Moreover, the spinning of twist had developed and Thierry-Mieg claimed that French spinners "make better sewing cottons than the English and get a higher price for them than they do in foreign markets". The weaving branch of the cotton industry had also made progress in the 1850's. Many new establishments with mechanical looms were set up particularly in the valleys of the Vosges where both cheap labour and water power were available. The weaving and dyeing of cotton cloths had expanded at Sainte-Marie-aux-Mines and Ribeauville which had 10,000 power looms in 1860. In the printing branch of the cotton industry several old established firms in Alsace had closed down in 1850 and no new firms had been founded. But other printworks had expanded and there was no decline in total output. The printing of cotton fabrics was done partly by hand and partly by rollers. The Alsace firms specialized in printing high-quality luxury cloths.

In some of the French cotton districts—particularly in Normandy —there was considerable apprehension concerning competition from Lancashire when the Cobden Treaty came into operation. But before any serious expansion of imports of English cotton piece-goods took place another and more serious problem confronted the French cotton manufacturers. The outbreak of civil war in the United States was followed by the blockade of the southern ports and about nine-tenths of France's supply of raw cotton were cut off. There was however no immediate shortage of cotton since in recent years there had been heavy American cotton crops and French manufacturers had made more cotton goods than they could sell. The raw cotton and the piece-goods already in store enabled the French to postpone the evil day when there would not be enough raw material to keep the factories going. The crisis hit Normandy first. Previous over-production, the shortage and high price of raw cotton, coupled with increased competition from Lancashire, forced many factories in the Rouen district to close their doors. By the end of 1862 over 100,000 operatives were out of work or on short time. The more fortunate workers still had contacts with the villages in which they had been born and they were able to go back to the land. The others went on poor relief or found employment on the public works organized by the local authorities. Pessard of the *Temps* newspaper and Forcade of the *Revue des Deux Mondes* drew public attention to the distress in Normandy and eventually a relief fund of over 1,000,000 francs was raised to assist the unemployed operatives.

Alsace did not suffer so severely as Normandy. It was far from Le Havre and normally kept large stocks of the raw material in hand. More Egyptian cotton was spun in Alsace than in Normandy and the Alsace mills were not so dependent upon American cotton. Moreover the Alsace spinners produced fine cottons which were sold to customers who could afford to pay higher prices. It was not until the spring of 1863 that the output of Mulhouse had declined to seventy-five per cent of normal production. Some mills worked short time but few closed down.

The French Government made strenuous efforts to find new regions in which cotton could be grown. A decree of April 1860 offered bounties for cotton grown in Algeria, a higher payment being made if the cotton were exported. French and English companies were set up to foster cotton production in Algeria. Output increased to over a million kilogrammes in 1866 but subsequently declined when the bounty was withdrawn. During the period of the American civil war France secured cotton from India and Egypt.

It was some time before the French cotton industry recovered from the dislocation caused by the American civil war. Evidence given before an official inquiry of 1870 shows that various factors had combined to check the further expansion of the cotton industry. There was competition from other textiles. The shortage of cotton goods in the early 1860's caused people to buy woollen or linen cloths and it was some time before these lost markets were regained. There was increased competition between the major French cotton districts. At one time Alsace had made fine cloths and Normandy had made coarse cloths. Now Mulhouse was turning out cloths which competed with the products of Rouen and the completion of the railway network meant that cotton piece-goods from the factories of Alsace could be sent quickly to any part of France. The introduction of Napoleon III's liberal commercial policy meant that the French cotton industry had to face competition from English, German, and Swiss manufacturers. In the late 1860's there were considerable fluctuations in the price of raw cotton. Between January and December 1867 for example the price of American cotton at Le Havre fell from 345 francs a bale to 190 francs a bale. Some manufacturers gambled on cotton "futures" in the hope of recovering their trading losses. *Tulles* and *rouenneries* were no longer in demand and some conservative owners of small mills were slow to change over to the production of more profitable lines. There were sections of the cotton industry which were still very backward from a technical point of view. In lower Normandy many old-fashioned waterframes and handlooms continued to be operated as late as the 1870's.

The manufacture of woollen and worsted cloth took place in many parts of France. Reims and Sedan, the former specializing in the production of combed wool and the latter in the production of carded wool, were two of the most important centres of the woollen industry. Roubaix, Tourcoing, Rouen and Mulhouse had woollen factories as well as cotton mills. And clothworks were also to be found in small workshops in towns and villages in other districts. Large factories, in which up-to-date machines driven by steam engines, had been installed, existed side by side with small workshops. Whereas the cotton industry of France was smaller than that of

England, the woollen and worsted industries of the two countries were of about the same size. Between 1861 and 1870 the French woollen industry consumed 1,280 million tons of the raw material while the English industry consumed 1,290 million tons.

Before 1850 much of the raw material came from the home clip though some wool was imported from England and Belgium. At the time of the Second Empire, however, when the quality of French wool declined, new sources of supply were found in the Levant, Morocco, the La Plata region and Australia. Import duties on foreign wools were reduced in 1856 and were abolished in 1860.

In the larger establishments modern machines driven by steam engines were introduced. Mule-jennies were used in many spinning mills but only a few self-actors were installed. In the weaving branch of the industry power looms replaced handlooms. In a factory in Roubaix, for example, power looms made by Dobson and Barlow of Bolton were set to work in 1857. There were between 600 and 700 power looms in Elbeuf and Lisieux in 1870.

Reference may be made to two changes which occurred at this time. The first was in the worsted branch of the industry and followed the construction of mechanical combs by Heilmann, Hübner, Lister and Holden. Hitherto the spinners had combed their own wool. Now firms were established which specialized in the mechanical combing of wool on a commission basis. Lister and Holden set up woolcombing factories at St. Denis (near Paris) in 1849 and at Croix (near Roubaix) and Reims in 1852. When Isaac Holden visited Mulhouse in 1856 he was hailed as the "first comber in Europe". Meanwhile Allert-Rousseau and Amédee-Prouvost had set up mechanical woolcombing factories in Roubaix while the firm of Schlumberger was using the Heilmann combing machine in Alsace. In 1871 Roubaix had thirteen woolcombing establishments and Reims had ten. It was estimated that the French woolcombing firms were handling forty-eight million kilogrammes of wool a year at the time of the fall of the Second Empire.

The second change was also one of business organization. This was the "Motte system" introduced by Alfred Motte of Roubaix in the 1850's. He established a group of woollen and cotton factories which were each under autonomous management but were under his financial control. Each establishment specialized in one aspect of the manufacture of cloth—such as spinning or weaving or dyeing—while together the whole group of factories covered the entire range of processes.

On the whole the French woollen-worsted industry was able to compete on equal terms with the English woollen industry. The

French woollen and worsted manufacturers made few complaints concerning Napoleon III's liberal commercial policy and at the industrial inquiry of 1870 their representatives favoured the continuation of the Cobden Treaty.

Linen cloth was manufactured in many parts of France. Fine cambrics—a luxury export trade—were made at Cambrai while the coarser linens—made into sails and sacks—were produced in the provinces of Anjou and Maine. Even in the middle of the nineteenth century there were relatively few large factories in the towns—in Lille, Tourcoing and Lisieux for example—and a considerable proportion of the output of the industry came from small workshops run by part-time rural craftsmen. Competition from the more efficient Irish and Belgian industries and competition from other French textiles had checked the expansion of the linen industry in the 1840's. Some progress was made in the 1850's when the number of mechanical spindles rose from 330,000 to 525,000. Mechanical weaving, however, was still in its infancy. At the time of the Cotton Famine the linen industry enjoyed a brief period of prosperity.

The silk industry, too, was confronted by certain difficulties in the 1860's. They were, to some extent, of a rather different character from those which other French textiles had to face. Unlike some of the leaders of the cotton and linen industry the silk manufacturers of Lyons did not fear new competition in the home market as a result of Napoleon III's liberal commercial policy. On the contrary they hoped to extend their sales abroad since Britain had abolished all duties on silks and other countries in western Europe had lowered their tariffs. Again, the introduction of power-driven machinery—which had become essential in other textile industries—did not appear to be a matter of urgency in the manufacture of silk because the nature of the raw material rendered it inadvisable to use such machines. On the other hand the silk manufacturers and the silk merchants had to adjust themselves to new conditions in the 1860's. Their supplies of raw silk produced in France declined in volume and increased in price when epidemics killed off many silkworms. More raw silk from the Far East had to be used. Much of it was sent to London and not to Marseilles which had formerly handled the import of silk from the Near East. London challenged Lyons as the main centre for the distribution of raw silk to other European countries. Moreover the raw material from the Far East was relatively cheap and was used by France's competitors to make silks that could reach a wider market than the luxury products of Lyons. There was some fall in the demand for high-quality French silks and an increase in the opportunities to sell cheaper silks. As a result of the American civil war and the prohibitive American tariff the French were no longer able to sell expensive silks in the United States. To some extent, however, new markets were opened up in Germany and other continental countries which lowered their duties on silks after 1860. The opening of the Suez Canal in 1869 made it easier to supply the merchants and manufacturers of Lyons with raw silk from the Far East.

*The Industrial Workers.* The great expansion of the French economy during the industrial boom of 1852-7 brought prosperity to financiers, contractors and factory owners. The workers, however, did not gain a fair share of the wealth that they had helped to create. There was no lack of employment during the boom, money wages rose and hours of work generally declined. But prices were rising more rapidly and the rapid growth of industrial and mining towns led to a worsening of the already deplorable housing conditions.

In the 1860's the position of some of the workers deteriorated. There was unemployment in Normandy during the Cotton Famine and some workers suffered when firms collapsed during the crises of 1863-4 and 1867. Housing conditions were as bad as ever. On the other hand there was a tendency for real wages to improve in the 1860's.

There was much discontent among the industrial workers and this led to strikes and riots. Napoleon III depended upon the good will of the great industrialists and—until he repented at the eleventh hour—he adopted a policy of repression. Trade unions were illegal and strikes were forbidden. There were some progressive employers who tried to improve the lot of the workers. In Mulhouse they gave financial support to a society established in 1853 to build cottages which workers could purchase on the instalment system. In ten years over 600 cottages were built. A grant from the Government enabled baths, wash-houses, a school and a communal kitchen and bakery to be erected. By 1866 this *cité ouvriere* had found imitators not only in Alsace but also in Baden and Switzerland.

The efforts of a few philanthropists touched only the fringes of the social problem in France. The Government did little to remove the grievances of the workers. Minor concessions could not arrest the rising tide of resentment against the régime. In 1853 an inspector was appointed to enforce the factory laws in the Nord Department. In 1864 the word *coalition* was deleted from three articles of the penal code. This meant that a strike was no longer automatically illegal. The authorities, however, still had ample powers to deal with strikers who disturbed the peace. Police and soldiers continued to be used to stop demonstrations and to put down strikes.

In 1868 the Government declared that although the laws prohibiting the formation of associations (*syndicats*) would not be repealed, associations of workers would in future be tolerated in the same way that associations of employers had been tolerated for many years. Workers would no longer be prosecuted merely for forming and for joining an association. This was obviously an unsatisfactory arrangement. Workers' associations existed only on sufferance and they could at any time be dissolved by any new government which was prepared to revoke the undertaking given in 1868. Another reform of 1868 repealed Article 1781 of the civil code by which a court of law was bound to accept without question the word of an employer concerning the wages which he was paying to his workers. At the same time greater freedom was given to hold public meetings without giving previous notice to the police.

The modest concessions of 1864 and 1868 did not appease the workers. Various types of working-class associations (*syndicats*) were in existence—friendly societies, savings groups, co-operative societies (retail shops), producers' co-operative workshops and trade unions. In some regions groups of such associations were linked in "chambers" and by 1870 there was in Paris a Federation of Workers' Syndicate Chambers which had its offices in the same building as the headquarters of the French branch of the International Working Men's Association.

No political party of any consequence was established to represent the workers. There were various left-wing groups of Republicans, Socialists and anarchists—such as the followers of Proudhon, Blanqui, Louis Blanc and Karl Marx—but they did not form a united front. Some looked back to the June days of 1848 and dreamed of a new rising against their oppressors. Others hoped to attain their ends through the ballot box rather than from behind barricades of paving stones.

In 1862 200 French workers were sent, at the expense of the Government, to visit the industrial exhibition in London. Like the German delegates they made contact with Socialist exiles in England and two years later some of them played their part in forming the International Working Men's Association (the first International). Although the French section of the International at first secured little support from the workers—its membership was probably only about 600 in 1867—the Government brought its leaders to trial in 1868 and they were sent to prison. In the same year another left-wing group—the Proudhonists led by Tolain—were hopelessly discredited when their "labour-bank" failed.

The Socialist movement, however, recovered and by 1870 the

Paris branch of the International claimed to have 70,000 adherents. The authorities struck again in the summer of that year and thirty-eight of the International's leading members were charged with founding a dangerous society. Chalian, one of the defendants, summed up the grievances of the French workers in his address to the court. He declared that the proletariat was "sick of resignation, victimisation by parasites, condemnation to hopeless toil, and trifling concessions in lieu of genuine liberty". "We suffer from crises, unemployment, wage-cuts, and speed-up and you can offer us only the *laissez-faire* doctrine of the economists. When we demand better conditions you meet us with force. When you refrain from using force you insult us and call us looters and levellers. Looters and levellers indeed! Those are the epithets you hurl at those who pay taxes for higher education but cannot read themselves—who are taxed to pay for land expropriations and are themselves flung out of their homes by stock-jobbers and speculators to be dumped on the confines of the great cities in foul hovels which have no space, no air and no light—who have to die fighting their own comrades when they attack the property of those idlers who enjoy the odious privilege of living without having to work."

The bitter discontent of many French workers in the late 1860's—particularly during and after the slump of 1867—led to an outbreak of demonstrations and strikes. Two examples may be given. In March 1867 the weavers in the Roubaix cotton factories were faced with a reduction in wages and were told that they would have to operate two looms instead of one. They rose in revolt, attacked several factories, destroyed machinery, and broke the windows of their employers' homes. In January 1870 there was a great strike at the Le Creusot steelworks in sympathy with a group of men who had been locked out. It was led by Alphonse Assi. The strike was particularly embarrassing to the Emperor since Eugène Schneider, the head of the steelworks, had succeeded Rouher as président of the *corps législatif*. The Government sent 3,000 soldiers to Le Creusot "to maintain law and order". The ground was being prepared for the violence that accompanied the rise and fall of the Paris Commune when the armies of Napoleon III were defeated in the Franco-Prussian war.

## (iv) 1871-1914

### RECOVERY AND RELAPSE, 1871–82

After the Franco-Prussian war France lost Alsace-Loraine and was faced with an increased national debt, a large budget deficit, and an indemnity of 5,000 million francs. German troops occupied twenty-one departments as a pledge that the indemnity would be paid. The destruction brought about by two sieges had paralysed Paris, the hub of the French economy. The investment of the city by the Prussians had been bad enough but the siege by the Government troops when the capital was held by the revolutionary Commune was far worse. A serious insurrection in Algeria added to the anxieties of the Government. At a time when unity in the face of a national disaster was essential the political parties quarrelled bitterly among themselves. The position of Thiers, the head of the executive, was an unenviable one.

Giffen estimated that the cost of the war to France amounted to £695 million. This included direct military expenditure, requisitions levied by the occupying troops, the indemnity and the losses incurred by giving up Alsace-Lorraine. The loss of these provinces had serious effects upon the French economy. The textile industries of Mulhouse had been the most advanced in France while the iron-ore deposits of Lorraine attained a new importance when the Gilchrist Thomas process of making basic steel from phosphoric ores was invented. In Lorraine the French lost twenty-five blast furnaces with an annual output of over 200,000 tons of pig-iron. The French Eastern Railway lost an important part of its revenues when the lines of Alsace-Lorraine were transferred to Germany. Paris was virtually out of action as a business centre for several months since numerous public buildings, workshops, and houses had been destroyed. About 50,000 workers disappeared from the capital. Some fell at the barricades, some were shot or transported after the fall of the Commune, and some fled abroad to save their lives. French exiles made tapestries at Windsor and shoes in Northampton, while building contractors in Brussels were glad to employ skilled French workers who had formerly worked on the various building projects in Paris for which Haussmann was responsible.

Thiers paid off the last instalment of the indemnity in September 1873 and so liberated his country from foreign occupation. The money was raised by the Bank of France and by public loans and the problems of transferring it to Germany without weakening the franc was successfully solved. To increase the revenues various excise duties and other indirect taxes were imposed in 1871 and 1872. The efforts to combine a return to Protection with the raising of new revenues from import duties failed. A law of July 1872 imposed import duties upon several raw materials and "compensatory" duties upon goods manufactured from those materials. Various countries complained that the new tariff infringed the commercial treaties which France had signed in the 1860's.

Shortly after Thiers resigned from office the tariff of 1872 was repealed and a new commercial treaty with Britain (July 1873) reaffirmed the terms of the Cobden Treaty. The problem of raising taxes to repay what had been borrowed to discharge the indemnity remained, and Magne's budget of 1873 imposed new taxes.

The ability of the French to shoulder a heavy burden of additional taxation was a significant factor in promoting the recovery of the country after the war against Germany. The Tariff Commission of 1892 asserted that the national debt amounted to 35·75 francs per head of the population whereas those of Britain and Germany amounted to only 16·25 francs and 7·50 francs respectively. The Commission also estimated that national taxation imposed upon every Frenchman an annual burden of 92 francs whereas a German paid only 67 francs.

The economic revival after the Franco-Prussian war was assisted by the transfer of some plants from the annexed territories and by the development of new industrial regions in France. The firm of Dupont gave up its works at Ars-sur-Moselle and opened the Pompey furnaces in French Lorraine and the firm of de Wendel established a plant to make basic steel at Joeuf (on the River Orne) on the French side of the frontier. It was realized that the Germans had not annexed the whole of the Lorraine ironfield. The deposits of French Lorraine remained in French hands and when those of the Briey region were exploited there was a great expansion of the heavy industries of the district. It was in French Lorraine that one of the first French trusts was established. In 1876 four ironmasters set up the *Comptoir Métallurgique de Longwy* as a marketing agency. This grew into an organization which controlled not merely the sale but also the output of Lorraine pig-iron. The cotton industry on the western slopes of the Vosges was considerably expanded when some Alsace manufacturers migrated to France and built up a new commercial and industrial organization around Épinal and Thâon. Thus the new steelworks of French Lorraine and the new cotton mills of the Vosges to some extent replaced the lost industries of Alsace-Lorraine.

The recovery of the iron and coal industries was stimulated by the boom of 1870–3. There was a great demand for rails to build new railways in many parts of the world. As soon as a normal output of pig-iron and steel could be resumed when hostilities were over the French plants secured large orders and this, in turn, stimulated the demand for coal. The output of pig-iron rose from a mere 860,000 tons in 1871 to 1·2 million tons in 1872. Despite the slump in the mid-1870's, when production was stagnant the iron and steel industries made progress. By 1880 output had increased to 1·7 million tons. Coal output rose from 13·2 million tons in 1867 (when the average price was 11 francs 62 centimes a ton) to 17·5 million tons in 1873 (when the price was 16 francs 61 centimes a ton). The production of the Loire coal-field reached the record figure of 3·9 million tons in 1873.

A few statistics may be given to illustrate the economic revival after the war against Germany. According to Mulhall the average annual foreign trade of France—exports and imports added together—rose from £220 million per annum in the 1860's to £297 million per annum in the 1870's. The growth of the textile industry may be judged by the increase in the consumption of raw cotton from 760,000 tons a year in the 1860's to 950,000 tons a year in the 1870's. The consumption of raw wool rose in the same period from 128,000 tons a year to 176,000 tons a year. The output of beet sugar rose from 188,000 tons a year in 1860–9 to 370,000 tons a year in 1870–9. The steam tonnage of the mercantile marine rose from 170,000 tons in 1870 to 278,000 tons in 1880. Just as the exhibition of 1867 had celebrated the rebuilding of Paris and the progress of manufactures under the Second Empire so the exhibition of 1878 was organized to show the world that the Third Republic had taken her place among the great industrial nations of the world. In December 1880 investors enthusiastically took up shares in the Panama Canal Company to the value of 300 million francs and it seemed as if—under the leadership of the veteran Ferdinand de Lesseps—French economic influence would be established in Central America. In 1881 the establishment of a protectorate over Tunis opened a new era of colonial expansion.

English observers were astonished at the rapidity and the magnitude of France's economic recovery from the effects of the Franco-Prussian war. Goschen declared in 1876 that "the financial history of France during the last four years is indeed full of the most instructive lessons. Her immense recuperative power has risen superior to every disaster, and her budgets have been as creditable to her statesmen and to her patriotism as they have been conspicuous by the elasticity and growth of her resources. The nation which has paid an indemnity of £200,000,000 has, since the payment, been financially and commercially more successful than the nation that received it; a problem which deserves to be probed to the bottom by statesmen and economists . . .The dwindled contents of the Bank of France have now once more reached an almost fabulous sum, and though banknotes are legal tender, France has absorbed more than £33,000,000 of silver during the last four years." In 1878 Stephen Bourne observed that "France is of all the European nations the one of most growing prosperity. We saw her wealth in the ease with which she provided for the German indemnity and in the rapidity with which she is recovering from disasters enough to have paralysed and destroyed nations even stronger than she . . . At present and indeed for some time past she seems to be accumulating bullion largely; she is sharing in the profits from discounting our mercantile bills; and, notwithstanding that she does import more than she exports, manifests a steady growth in wealth and power."

Yet France had still many economic problems to solve. The organizers of the exhibition of 1878 were rather optimistic in regarding France's recovery as complete. In that year several of the smaller French railway companies failed and it was clear that a reorganization and extension of both the railway and canal networks was long overdue. In the same year the grain harvest failed yet the price of cereals was exceptionally low. Many vineyards were devastated by phylloxera and there was a sharp fall in the output of wine. In the same year Bontoux established a bank called the *Société de l'Union Générale* which was supported by Royalists and clericals. Taking advantage of the confidence inspired by France's rapid recovery after the war against Germany, Bontoux succeeded in securing large sums of money from investors who hoped to get rich quickly. By November 1881 deposits amounted to 130 million francs and the share capital was raised to 150 million francs. The *Union Générale* and an associated Austrian land-bank were engaged in activities very similar to those of the *Crédit Mobilier* in the 1850's. Bontoux helped to found a large number of public utilities, banks, mining enterprises and manufacturing companies in France, Austria-Hungary and Serbia. But he over-reached himself more quickly than the Pereires had done in the 1860's. In November 1881 Neuwirth and Tomaszczuk asked some searching questions about the Austrian Land Bank in the Austrian legislature. In January 1882 the Bank of Lyons and the Loire (a subsidiary of the *Union Générale*) closed its doors. There was a financial crisis in Lyons and the *Crédit Lyonnais* lost forty million francs. The Bank of France placed 100 million francs at the disposal of a group of Lyons finance houses to allay the crisis. On the Paris bourse there was panic selling of "Bontoux shares". The shares of the *Union Générale* and of various institutions that it had helped to establish fell rapidly in value. The *Union Générale* was unable to meet its payments on January 29. When the creditors of the bank met in April they found that the *Union*

*Générale*'s assets amounted to only 112 million francs but its debts amounted to 247 million francs. But when the shareholders had paid for their shares in full it was possible to pay all the debts of the bank. The shareholders had lost their money. The outbuist of speculation in France associated with the meteoric rise and fall of Bontoux (1878–82) revealed some of the weaknesses of French business and financial organization. These troubles came at a time of falling prices and of unemployment. There was much social unrest. Many workers went on strike such as the silkweavers of Lyons, the builders of Paris, the textile workers of Lille and Roubaix, and the coal-miners of Commentry. In 1882–3 there were 163 strikes in France, a substantially larger number than in previous years.

## THE FREYCINET PLAN

The great improvement of France's system of communications in the last quarter of the nineteenth century owed much to the skill and energy of Freycinet. An engineer by profession, he took charge of the War Department under Gambetta in 1870. He was appointed Minister of Public Works in 1877 and subsequently held office on several occasions as prime minister until he fell from office owing to the Panama scandal in 1893.

In the 1870's it became clear that many of the small railways recently built with Government assistance by the local authorities and by private companies were never likely to pay their way. Eventually a law was passed in 1878 giving authority to the Government to purchase 2,615 km. of these lines—some not yet completed —and to place them provisionally under Freycinet's administration. This was the origin of a nationalized network of railways in France.

Freycinet considered that the completion of a small network of secondary lines should be regarded as part of a much larger problem. He believed that the communications of France—particularly the railways and the canals—should be modernized so as to provide the country with a really efficient transport system. This "national equipment", as he called it, would promote the expansion of French industry and agriculture.

Freycinet proposed that a "third network" of lines should be added to the "old" and "new" railway systems.[1] His plan envisaged the construction of 10,000 km. of new lines at an estimated cost of 3,000 million francs. After being discussed by the Chambers,

[1] For the "old" (first) and the "new" (second) railway networks see above, p. 139.

Freycinet's proposals were accepted with some modifications. Provision was made for the State to build 8,848 km. of railways. The Government pushed ahead vigorously with the construction of these lines but no decision was reached as to who would ultimately operate them.

The collapse of the *Union Générale* and the financial crisis of 1882 threw Freycinet's plans into the melting pot again. It was impossible for the Government to continue borrowing on a large scale to finance railway construction. Investors held back and the Government had to admit that it could not complete Freycinet's ambitious scheme. The six main railway companies, which had been financially embarrassed when Freycinet's plan was first put forward, had enjoyed a few years of prosperity and were now in a position to help the State. The financial relations between the Government and the railways—as laid down in the conventions of 1858 —were revised in 1883 by new agreements.

Under the new conventions of 1883 the companies agreed to take over 11,485 km. of railways. This included most of Freycinet's "third network", the construction of which had as yet by no means been completed. The State agreed to subsidize the new lines by paying all construction costs in excess of a basic payment by the companies. The former distinction between the "old" (or first) and the "new" (or second) networks disappeared and the companies now secured a State guarantee of interest on their shares which covered all the lines that they operated. The slump that followed the failure of the *Union Générale* caused railway revenues to fall so that for some time the financial burden assumed by the State under the new conventions was heavier than the original estimate. By the end of 1903 the railway companies owed the State well over 1,000 million francs in respect of payments received to guarantee a minimum rate of interest to shareholders. Agreement was also reached on an exchange of lines between the State Railways and the Paris–Orleans Railway which gave the Government a small but fairly compact network of nearly 3,000 km. of lines situated between Tours, Nantes and Bordeaux. Leroy-Beaulieu stated that the management of this nationalized railway was "generally considered to be of a mediocre and unprogressive character". "From the financial point of view the results given by the old state railways have always been bad." In 1909 the nationalized railways were greatly extended when the State took over the Western Railway Company which owed the Government 396 million francs, a debt greater than the estimated value of the rolling stock. But these lines did not prosper under new management. Leroy-Beaulieu declared that between 1909 and 1911 working expenses rose from 152·8 million francs to 207·3 million francs while gross receipts only increased from 219·3 million francs to 231·4 million francs. On the State railways the "exploitation coefficient"—the relation of expenditure to receipts—was higher than that of any of the great private companies. "The main trouble, it would seem, was that by careful planning France had built up a fine and evenly spread network of railways all over the country, but the amount of passenger and freight traffic available was not, over very large areas, sufficient to yield an adequate revenue."

Freycinet was also responsible for an ambitious scheme to modernize France's network of waterways. He planned to improve 4,000 km. of rivers and 3,650 km. of canals as well as to build 1,382 km. of new canals. He was responsible for the preparation of a law in 1879 which embodied this plan and contained provisions for the future nationalization of the waterways. Navigation on the main rivers and canals was to be administered by the State. When the Government could afford to do so it would take over canals from private companies after paying them compensation. By 1909 all the privately owned major canals had been nationalized except the Sambre–Oise Canal and the waterways owned by the City of Paris. Under the law of 1879 waterways of secondary importance might be leased to companies for a limited period. Freycinet's plan provided that the main waterways should conform to uniform standards —depth 2 metres, length of locks 38·5 metres, width of locks 5·2 metres, and bridge clearance 3·7 metres. Such waterways could carry *péniches* (Flemish barges) which were 38·5 metres in length and had a capacity of 300 tons.

In 1903 a new law, prepared by Baudin (Minister of Public Works), authorized further improvements and new works on the waterways to be undertaken when the Freycinet plan had been completed. In the thirty years 1879–1909 more was done to improve and to extend the French waterways than in any similar period in the past. Over 3,300 km. of waterways were improved and 650 km. of new canals were constructed. Between 1880 and 1906 the freight carried by the French waterways showed an increase of ninety per cent.

THE MÉLINE TARIFF, 1892

It has been seen that, immediately after the Franco-Prussian war, Thiers made an attempt to increase import duties partly to raise additional revenue and partly to give greater protection to French industry. But countries with which France had signed commercial treaties protested and the tariff of 1872 was quickly repealed. When the trade agreements expired France regained her freedom of action in tariff matters. There was a renewal of the controversy between the Free Traders (led by Léon Say) and the Protectionists (led by Méline). Tirard's general tariff of 1881 was a reverse for the Protectionists since farm products and most raw materials remained on the free list while import duties on manufactured goods were generally only about twenty-five per cent higher than the duties charged upon goods coming from countries with which France had trade agreements. New commercial treaties were negotiated in 1881–3. Most-favoured-nation treatment was accorded to Britain (without signing a treaty) and to Germany (in accordance with Article 11 of the Treaty of Frankfurt).[1]

In the 1880's the propaganda of the Protectionists was intensified. Many landowners and farmers were in difficulties owing to the slump in agriculture when the prices of farm products fell sharply. The vineyards were decimated by phylloxera so that wine growers and wine merchants were now actually faced with competition in the home market. Those who reared silkworms faced hard times when the silkworms were attacked by disease. Arable farmers had to meet unwelcome competition from the wheat fields of North America, the Ukraine and Hungary. Average wheat prices were much lower in 1881–90 than they had been in 1871–80. The agrarian interest (represented by the *Société des Agriculteurs*) supported the return to high Protection. The Protectionists found a champion in Méline who led a successful agitation in favour of the establishment of a Ministry of Agriculture and was himself at its head as a member of Ferry's cabinet (1883–5). He was able to secure the imposition of import duties on some farm products. In 1881 the import of American pork was prohibited. The surtax on foreign sugar was increased in 1884 so as to give further assistance to the growers of suger beet in the north-eastern departments. After the general election of 1885 the position of the Protectionists was strengthened and the Corn Laws were revived. Import duties were imposed upon rye, barley and oats for the first time since 1861. Between 1885 and 1887 the import duty on flour was increased from 1 franc 20 centimes per 100 kilogrammes to 8 francs. Méline had little difficulty in securing the support of the majority of the industrialists for his fiscal policy. Many manufacturers were now facing stiff competition at home but they found that access to the German, Austrian, Italian and Russian markets was restricted by the high tariffs of those countries.

Méline was the chairman and *rapporteur* of the Tariff Commission which drafted a new tariff in 1892. The majority of the members

[1] For Article 11 of the Treaty of Frankfurt (1871) see above, p. 49.

were Protectionists and their report summarized clearly the arguments in favour of imposing high duties on imports and of granting bounties to certain exports. The Commission stated that French manufacturers suffered from exceptional disabilities. France lacked the resources of coal and iron-ore with which some of her rivals were richly endowed and therefore the cost of producing manufactured goods was higher in France than in some other industrial countries. France had no great merchant navy and her industries were not concentrated in a few major regions. It was claimed that French manufacturers were more highly taxed than those of other countries and that conscription interfered with the vocational training of the skilled workers of the future. The social legislation under consideration—the bills which proposed to limit the number of hours worked in factories and mines and to make employers responsible for compensating operatives injured at work—would also add to the production costs of the industrialists. The Tariff Commission considered that high import duties should be imposed to "compensate" manufacturers for these disabilities and to place them in a position which would enable them to compete with their rivals on more equal terms.

The Méline Tariff Law of 1892 laid down two tariffs. The higher was called the "general tariff" and the lower the "minimum tariff". The Tariff Commission stated that the former was the "common tariff applicable in principle to everybody" while the latter was "a tariff of favour which would be conceded to the nations which would accord to us corresponding advantages and . . . would treat us on the level of the most-favoured-nation". In future any state which entered into negotiations with France for a commercial treaty would know exactly what were the lowest rates of duty on its exports that could be secured.

The tariff of 1892 made few changes in the Corn Laws but most other farm products (sheep, cattle, meat, vegetables, fruits and dairy products) were now protected by import duties of twenty-five per cent *ad valorem*. Raw cotton, wool, silk, flax and hides remained on the free list so as to avoid raising the prices which the textile and leather industries paid for their raw materials. Manufactured and semi-manufactured goods were now subject to high import duties. The largest increases were those on textile yarns and cloths. The Méline tariff was much higher than the German conventional tariff established by the Caprivi commercial treaties. A system of bounties and subsidies was introduced to encourage shipping, shipbuilding, flax growing, the raising of silkworms and the manufacture of silk. At the same time a change occurred in French fiscal policy with regard to her colonies and—at any rate for some of the overseas possessions—a policy of "tariff assimilation" was adopted.[1]

Between 1892 and 1914 French import duties tended to increase and France returned to the old system of high Protection that had been in force before the signing of the Cobden Treaty in 1860. Farmers, manufacturers, shippers and those who traded with the colonies all enjoyed protection from foreign competition. Up to a point the French achieved their object and attained a considerable measure of self-sufficiency behind a high tariff wall. But there were some disadvantages in reducing imports as much as possible. France became involved in "tariff wars"—with Italy (1889–98) and Switzerland (1893–5), for example—which harmed the French economy. France did not have a mercantile marine which could compare with those of Britain or Germany. She developed neither a great shipbuilding industry nor those branches of manufacture which are concerned with the handling and processing of imported foodstuffs. A country which excludes frozen foods from its ports is unlikely to develop that branch of the engineering industry which builds refrigeration plants. The French consumer paid more for his food and his manufactured articles than he would have done if import duties had been reduced. William Smart, writing in 1904, declared that "since the days of Colbert, France has set before herself the object of being self-sufficient as regards agriculture and manufacture. It is the nemesis of Protection that her very prosperity makes the realisation of this ideal impossible; she has a surplus and exports it; and, in spite of all her planning, the imports which pay for those exports compete with her home producers and prevent the self-sufficiency."

## FRENCH INDUSTRY IN THE EARLY TWENTIETH CENTURY

Between the introduction of the Méline tariff and the outbreak of the First World War the progress of French industry was steady if unspectacular. Iron and steel made a remarkable recovery after the loss of Lorraine but shipbuilding made little progress and the new chemical and electrical industries showed no signs of expanding in the same way as those in Germany. The steam power used in industry rose from 336,000 h.p. in 1870 to nearly 1·8 million h.p. in 1900.

In the early 1890's confidence in the soundness of the economy— already shaken by the Bontoux scandal—received a new shock when the affairs of the Panama Canal Company were revealed to the public.

[1] For the policy of colonial tariff assimilation see below, pp. 192–3.

The company had been in the hands of its creditors since 1888 and in 1891 the serious irregularities in its management at last became known. Several politicians and journalists had improperly secured large sums of money from de Lesseps and his associates. In 1892 five leading members of the company were found guilty of embezzlement. On appeal, however, the conviction of de Lesseps and his son was quashed on technical grounds.

When confidence had been restored again rising prices, better communications, a high tariff and the growth of new industrial regions in French Lorraine and the Vosges enabled France to recover from the effects of the Great Depression. Although the small family firm was still the typical unit of production some larger firms —such as Schneider of Le Creusot—were expanding rapidly. A certain number of cartels were established though not on the same scale as in Germany. In 1910 the mines in France's largest coal-field in the Department of the Nord and Pas de Calais were controlled by a cartel. At the same time there were nine cartels in the iron, steel and engineering industries. Moreover certain industries were becoming more concentrated from a geographical point of view.

Increased industrial activity coincided with a modest expansion of exports from 3,393 million francs a year in 1883–91 to 3,623 million francs a year in 1893–1901. The strength of the French economy was reflected in the growth of its overseas investments which amounted to 45,000 million francs in 1914. Over a quarter of this sum had been lent to Russia. But the prosperity of the Third Republic, like that of the Second Empire, was not fully shared by the factory workers and in the early years of the twentieth century there was serious industrial unrest in France.

A brief survey of her main industries will indicate the progress made by France as a manufacturing country in the late nineteenth and early twentieth centuries. In 1913 her annual production of coal amounted to only 40 million tons which was insignificant in comparison with the output of Britain (287 million tons) and Germany (190 million tons of coal and 87 million tons of lignite). France did not produce enough coal to satisfy her requirements and 22 million tons were imported in 1913. Coal was not only scarce in France but it was also expensive and this increased the costs of French manufactures. On the eve of the first World War the northern coal-field (in the Departments of the Nord and Pas de Calais) had become by far the most important in France. It had an annual output of over 27 million tons. The Loire (or Saint Étienne) coal-field came next with an annual output of 4 million tons. Three other coal-fields on the edge of the central highlands—Le Creusot-Blanzy, Alais (Bessèges-

Grand' Combe) and Decazeville-Carmaux—each produced about two million tons a year.

Significant changes occurred in the French iron and steel industries after 1871. France had ample supplies of iron-ore. Although a number of small ironfields were now exhausted the vast *minette* deposits of the Briey district were exploited from the 1880's onwards. The iron and steel industry did not expand sufficiently to use all the available iron-ore. In 1913 France produced 21·9 million tons of iron-ore and imported 1·4 million tons. Her consumption of iron-ore, however, was only 13·2 million tons so that 10 million tons were available for export.

After 1870 many small ironworks closed down and the production of pig-iron was concentrated on the ironfield of French Lorraine and at certain ports at which both iron-ore and coal could be imported. Steelworks, engineering plants and armament works were more widely dispersed than blast furnaces. In 1913 France had 164 blast furnaces (of which 35 were idle) and the industry produced. 5·2 million tons of pig-iron and ferro-alloys and 4·6 million tons of steel ingots and castings.

The most important iron and steel regions were French Lorraine and the northern districts. The former produced pig-iron and steel, the latter wrought iron and cast iron. When Germany annexed Lorraine in 1871 France retained fourteen blast furnaces in the Longwy district. In the 1880's and 1890's new *minette* deposits were exploited in the Briey region and now that the Gilchrist Thomas process was available the phosphoric ores of Longwy and Briey could be used to manufacture steel. Iron-ore from Briey was used not only in local steelworks but also elsewhere in France and in Belgium and Germany. By the early twentieth century the pig-iron and the basic steel made by the Thomas process from the *minette* ores of French Lorraine dominated the metallurgical industries of France. On the eve of the first World War French Lorraine had twenty plants which produced either pig-iron or both pig-iron and basic steel. Ten of them had retained their independence while ten had become parts of larger French, Belgian or German concerns. At that time French Lorraine (Longwy, Briey and Nancy) produced nearly 3·5 million tons of pig-iron and nearly 2·3 million tons of steel.

In the industrial region of northern France the local supplies of iron-ore—in the Ardennes—were being worked out by the 1870's. In 1914 only four blast furnaces survived in the Maubeuge district and they secured their raw material from French Lorraine. In the Departments of the Nord and Pas de Calais the ironworks and steelworks used either *minette* from French Lorraine or other types of iron-ore from Spain and North Africa. The output of pig-iron in northern France (Nord, Pas de Calais and Ardennes) rose from 577,000 tons in 1910 to 935,000 tons in 1913. Steel ouput in 1913 amounted to 900,000 tons. The production of wrought iron and cast iron was particularly important in this region. Over one-third of the pig-iron produced in the northern districts was made by the *Société de Denain et Anzin*. The Bessemer process was generally used in northern France while the Gilchrist Thomas process was used in French Lorraine.

At Le Creusot the local reserves of both coal and iron-ore were declining. In the 1880's some of the blast furnaces were closed though a few survived by using imported iron-ore. The firm of Schneider acquired an interest in steelworks in French Lorraine and concentrated upon the production of armaments and locomotives in the Le Creusot plants. The Schneider concern expanded rapidly. In 1914, in addition to the original works at Le Creusot, the firm had an iron-ore mine at Droitaumont in the Briey basin, engineering and naval construction works at Chalon-sur-Saône, armament and electrical works at Champagne-sur-Seine, and artillery works at Le Havre and Harfleur. Schneider controlled various subsidiary firms such as the *Société d'Outillage Mécanique et d'Usinage d'Artilleries*, the *Société de Moteurs à gaz et d'Industrie Mécanique*, the *Société d'Optique et de Mécanique de Haute Précision*, as well as a coal-mine and an iron-ore mine in Belgium. After 1905 Schneider also had an interest in the Putilov armament works in St. Petersburg. At Saint Étienne, too, the output of pig-iron declined after 1880. The manufacturers therefore acquired blast furnaces in French Lorraine and in the Nord Department and specialized in engineering and in the production of high quality steels. The Terre Noire plant at Saint Étienne was particularly successful in producing new types of steel. In the 1870's Gautier made mild steel in these works by using ferro-manganese in which the proportion of manganese was seventy-five per cent or more. Later the Terre Noire metallurgists successfully employed silicon and manganese in the production of steel castings.

The cotton industry in 1906 employed 167,200 operatives in 731 factories. The consumption of raw cotton amounted to 945,000 bales in 1911. Self-actors and ring-frames had now largely replaced mule-jennies while power looms had taken the place of handlooms. In the Nord Department, the centre of fine spinning, the number of spindles increased from 1·7 million at the end of the 1880's to 3 million in 1914. Not much of the yarn spun in Lille and neighbouring towns was woven on the spot for there were only between 5,000 and

6,000 power looms in the district. The yarn was sent to other regions to be made into lace, embroidery, and hosiery. The Eastern region (the Vosges) had made remarkable progress since 1871. In this district there were 3 million spindles and over 65,000 power looms in 1914. Hydro-electric power was used to a much greater extent than in other French cotton districts. The old-established cotton industry of Normandy did not show any signs of expansion in the last quarter of the nineteenth century. In 1914 it had 1·7 million spindles and 36,000 power looms. The Rhône-Loire cotton region was a purely weaving district. After 1870 the power loom was introduced into Roanne but some handlooms still survived in the surrounding villages in 1914. It was a cotton enclave in a region traditionally associated with the silk industry. There were two important federations of employers' associations in the cotton industry—the *Union Textile* (1900) and the *Syndicat General* (1901).

The manufacture of woollen and worsted cloths and of dress materials were important branches of the French textile industry. In 1913 the raw wool handled by the spinners amounted to 264,000 tons. Expansion was less rapid than in Germany or the United States but in the production of fine cloths and well-designed materials the French maintained their lead. Nearly a third of France's annual output of dress materials was exported. The industry was not nearly so scattered as it had been in the middle of the nineteenth century. Roubaix, Tourcoing and Reims were important centres of mechanical combing and the spinning and weaving of worsteds. On the other hand the small family workshops of Elbeuf, Vienne, Fourmies, Le Cateau, and St. Quentin were declining. The relatively high cost of both coal and machinery made it difficult for the smaller workshops to compete with the larger factories and hindered the expansion of the export trade. In fact the average annual value of France's exports of woollen piece-goods declined between 1899 and 1910—at a time when Germany's exports of woollens were expanding rapidly.

Various changes occurred in the manufacture of silk after 1870. The French industry was now dependent upon foreign countries both for its raw materials and for its markets. In the early twentieth century the silk manufacturers secured a high proportion of their raw silk from the Far East. A disease among the silkworms in the middle of the nineteenth century had drastically reduced the ouput of cocoons in the Rhône valley and in 1910 the production of raw silk in France amounted to a mere 500 tons which was only five per cent of the total consumption. At this time China and Japan together had an annual output of 17,000 tons. The prosperity of the French silk industry had long depended upon its ability to sell large quantities of silks abroad. In this connexion certain difficulties had to be overcome in the latter part of the nineteenth century. It was pointed out that "since the sewing machine has come into general use, the fashions of ladies' dresses have become more elaborate and more changeable so that there has been much less demand for the fine and costly but lasting cloths which used to be the glory of the French looms, silks of an inferior and less durable quality, and mixed fabrics having the appearance of silk, have been more sought after; and since the looms of Germany and Switzerland were more speedily adapted to meet the wants of this new taste, the French industry suffered greatly in competition". The rapidity with which fashions could change may be illustrated by the sudden fall in favour of "watered silk". In 1894 the Lyons industry produced fabrics of this type worth eight million francs. Yet in the following year output had to be reduced to one million francs. Again in 1912 there was a sharp decline in the sale of silk muslins. The French silk industry tried to meet this situation by ceasing to concentrate upon luxury fabrics and by manufacturing cheaper silks for a wider circle of customers. Unfortunately the high tariffs of the United States, Germany, Austria-Hungary and Russia greatly reduced the volume of French exports of silks to those countries. The British market, however, remained open and this saved the situation. More French silks were sold in Britain than in France itself. The manufacture of silks at Lyons and of ribbons at Saint Étienne was still largely in the hands of small workshops. The introduction of electric power into the homes and workshops of certain silkweavers enabled some of the small producers to resist competition from the bigger establishments. Lyons remained the centre of the world's trade in raw silk. It resisted the challenge of Milan in the early twentieth century as successfully as it had once resisted the challenge of London.

The shipbuilding, chemical and electrical industries did not expand as rapidly as might have been expected at the time of the Third Republic. In 1913 the gross tonnage of the French mercantile marine was 2·2 million—steamships and motor vessels accounting for 1·8 million—as compared with Great Britain's 18·7 million tons, Germany's 5 million tons and Norway's 2·4 million tons. The survival of a substantial fleet of sailing vessels was due partly to the high bounties offered after 1892 to those who constructed such ships and partly to the fact that sailing ships could still be profitably employed in the Mediterranean coasting trades. Various adverse factors checked the growth of shipbuilding—the high cost of imported materials which were heavily taxed, the great distance of ports suited to shipbuilding from supplies of iron, steel and coal, and the fact that French overseas trade included so few bulky articles for export and therefore did not require a large fleet of tramp steamers. The bounties offered for the building of steamships could hardly be regarded as adequate "compensation" for these drawbacks. The shipbuilding industry, however, appears to have been making some progress in the years immediately before the first World War since the tonnage of merchant ships and naval vessels built in France rose from 138,000 tons in 1909 to nearly 252,000 tons in 1913. Shipbuilding was concentrated in fifteen yards, the most important being in the estuaries of the Loire (St. Nazaire and Nantes) and the Seine (Le Havre, Granville, Harfleur, Le Trait and Grand Quevilly).

France had once led the world in chemical knowledge and in the application of that knowledge to industrial purposes. But after 1871 it was the Germans who went ahead in this industry. The French failed to adapt their system of vocational education so as to train chemists in the middle ranks of industry. Moreover, they lacked the vast supplies of coal-tar which the Germans possessed and had no potash deposits similar to those which the Germans were able to exploit at Stassfurt and Wittelsheim. It it true that in 1913 France produced rather more superphosphates than Germany—1,980 tons as against 1,850 tons—but her output of sulphuric acid products was only 1,480,000 tons as compared with Germany's 2,700,000 tons and her output of nitrogen products was a mere 18,000 tons compared with Germany's 121,000 tons. France's production of coal-tar dyes (2,000 tons) was trifling compared with Germany's 127,000 tons. The manufacture of medicines and perfumes were important branches of the chemical industry in France. Exports of these products were valued at 53·5 million francs in 1913. France was also slow to develop the various branches of the electrical industry. By 1913 "the capital invested in the French electrical industries was not much more than a third of that invested in the corresponding German industries".

France's economic progress was reflected in the growth of her national wealth. One estimate suggested that wealth of the French people rose from 151 thousand million francs just before the Franco-Prussian war to 212 thousand million francs in the early years of the twentieth century. It seems probable that—in terms of wealth per head of population—France was as rich a country as Germany in 1914. But, owing to her smaller population, the total national wealth of France was less than that of Germany. The Frenchman's standard of living was rising between 1870 and 1914 for the consumption per head of meat, sugar, coffee, tobacco and alcohol was increasing. Levasseur considered that in the early twentieth century the national income was being less unequally distributed than before and that the position of those with low incomes was improving. Kuczynski's index of real wages (1900=100) shows an increase from 87 in 1870 to 100 in 1900.

## THE SOCIAL QUESTION

The working-class movement in France could make little progress after the collapse of the Commune. The horrors of the last days of the Commune—when Paris was in flames and hostages were shot— had left bitter memories. The upper and middle classes were terrified at the prospect of a new rising of the workers and supported the repressive measures of the Government. In a circular note of June 7, 1871, to French envoys abroad Jules Favre claimed that the International Working Men's Association must bear the major responsibility for the establishment of the Commune and suggested that all European states should unite to put down the Association. The National Assembly passed a law on March 14, 1872, which banned the International in France and when Thiers resigned as President he claimed that Socialism had been stamped out in France.

Socialism had been driven underground for a time but the trade-union movement soon showed signs of revival. It appears that as early as 1878 there were over 130 trade unions in Paris and in the following year their representatives organized a conference which accepted Louis Blanc's ideas concerning the establishment of co-operative workshops. In 1878 a working man was a candidate at the municipal elections in Paris claiming to represent a *Parti Ouvrier*. A conference of working-class representatives held at Marseilles in 1878 stated that its policy was to secure "the nationalization of the means of production".

In 1880 the Government at last declared an amnesty for those who had taken part in the Commune. The exiled supporters of the Commune were able to return to France and many of them were actively engaged in Socialist propaganda. There were several Socialist groups in France—the Labour Party led by Jules Guesde which adopted a Marxist programme, the Revolutionary Socialists led by Blanqui, and the Republican Socialist Alliance which supported industrial co-operative societies. In 1881 Brousse left Guesde's party to form the Federation of Socialist Workers; in 1882 Allemane seceded the Brousse faction to form a new "revolutionary" party; while in 1885 Malou formed yet another Socialist group called the Independent Socialists. Any possibility of securing some influence over French politics was frustrated by these internecine quarrels.

Although the Socialists were divided and the trade unions were weak the revival of working-class agitation—particularly the strikes of the early 1880's—alarmed the Government. Since repression appeared to have failed Jules Ferry's government decided to bid for the support of the workers for the Third Republic by pursuing a policy of conciliation. A law of 1884 legalized the establishment of organizations (*syndicats*) formed to defend the "economic, industrial, commercial, and agricultural interests" of their members and trade unions were specifically mentioned as associations which now enjoyed the protection of the law. Trade unions were allowed to take legal proceedings and were permitted to run employment agencies. They were, however, not allowed to acquire real estate except halls for meetings, and classrooms and libraries for vocational studies. Trade unions of government employees were not permitted.

The law of 1884 legalized not only trade unions but any industrial or agrarian organization formed to promote the interests of its members. Thus benefit clubs, savings banks, and co-operative societies were given a status which they had not previously enjoyed. Indeed Waldeck-Rousseau, the Minister of the Interior in Ferry's government, issued a circular urging Prefects to foster in their departments the establishment of friendly societies and similar working-class organizations. Perhaps the most striking example of the expansion of new societies under the law of 1884 was the growth of producers' co-operative associations among farmers and small holders. One of the most successful examples of co-partnership in French industry was that of Godin iron foundry at Guise. The scheme came into full operation in about 1880. Godin divided his workers into four classes—*auxiliaires, participants, sociétaires* and *associés*. The first group (*auxiliaires*) were new or casual workers. They enjoyed factory welfare services but did not share in the profits. The second group (*participants*) received a share in the profits in proportion to the amount of their wages. The third group (*sociétaires*) received a share in the profits fifty per cent greater than the *participants*. The highest class (*associés*) received a share of the profits which was twice as great as that of the *participants*. The *associés* met annually to determine the policy to be pursued by the society. Since the workers' share of the profits was paid in capital only, the ownership of the plant was gradually transferred from Godin's hands to those of the workers. By 1894 the process was complete.

The legalization of various types of associations in 1884 was followed by an expansion of the trade-union movement. Membership of existing unions increased and new unions were established. By the 1890's unions all over the country were linked in two national organizations—the Federation of Labour Exchanges (1892) and the General Confederation of Labour (1895). The latter was founded at Limoges at a meeting of some 700 trade union delegates. Twenty years later 3,000 unions, with a membership of 357,000, were affiliated to it. The two most powerful and militant unions supporting the General Confederation of Labour were the builders (100,000 members) and the metal workers (25,000 members). Since there were 5,260 trade unions and 977,000 trade unionists in France in 1910 it is clear that the General Confederation of Labour by no means included all the trade unionists in France. It was a much less representative body than the Trades Union Congress in England. Many French trade unions were supported by only a few of the workers who were eligible to join. Subscriptions were often small and it was rare for any attempt to be made to build up a strike fund. In 1908 for example strike pay was paid in only 36 out of about 1,000 strikes. In ten strikes food was distributed to the strikers. This situation encouraged extremists who tried to injure the employers by fomenting sabotage in the factories instead of using the weapon of the strike.

The second way in which trade unions co-operated was through the employment exchanges. There were several types of employment agencies in France. The majority were licensed registry offices (*bureaux de placement autorisés*) while others were run by journeymen-gilds, by friendly societies, by philanthropic agencies and by municipalities. Other employment exchanges, known as *bourses du travail*, were operated—with some help from public funds—by "trade syndicates". A few of these were run by associations of employers but most of them were run by associations of workers. In certain towns employment exchanges operated by associations of workers developed far wider functions than the finding of jobs for men who were out of work. They were virtually associations of local trade-union branches and they became a focus of trade-union activities. In 1892 a federation of labour exchanges was established. The movement ran into difficulties when the Government dissolved the council of the important Paris labour exchange and when the federation quarrelled with the General Confederation of Labour. But it survived as a means of providing a link between trade unions in various localities.

The policy of conciliating the workers so as to gain their support for the Republic—a policy initiated by the legalizing of workers' associations—was carried a step further in the 1890's. Some of the social reforms which the leaders of the workers were demanding through the trade unions and through the various Socialist parties were adopted by the Government and were passed into law. The identity card (*livret*) to which workers had so long objected was abolished in 1890. The same year saw the establishment of inspectors of mines. In 1891 the *Office du travail* and the *Conseil supérieur du travail* were set up. Two factory laws were passed in 1892–3 which at last gave factory operatives and miners the legal protection which workers in other industrial countries enjoyed. A law of 1892 restricted the working hours of women and children in factories, mines and quarries. No children under 13 years of age could be employed unless they passed an educational test. Children aged from 13 to 16 were not allowed to work in a factory for more than 10 hours a day. Youths aged between 16 and 18 might not work for more than 12 hours a day. The labour of girls of this age was limited to 11 hours a day. Women, too, were not allowed to work for over 11 hours a day in a factory. Night work was prohibited for young people (boys under 18 and girls under 21). Women and girls were forbidden to work underground in mines. Unfortunately the law made provision for the temporary relaxation of some of these regulations by administrative orders. A law of 1893 protected all factory workers—and not merely women and children—and dealt with the health of the workers and the prevention of accidents. Detailed regulations were to be drawn up on the advice of the Consultative Committee on Arts and Manufactures. A law of December 1892 provided for the establishment of new councils to which industrial disputes might be submitted for settlement by conciliation or arbitration. A law of July 1892 granted free medical aid to those "without means of subsistence". In 1873 the Government decreed that foreigners engaged upon public works should be limited to ten per cent of the total labour force so employed. These reforms, however, fell far short of the comprehensive schemes which Bismarck had recently introduced in Germany and they did not satisfy the aspirations of the French industrial workers.

When the future of the Republic was threatened at the time of the Dreyfus affair the Socialists, led by Jaurès, rallied to its defence and formed a coalition with the left-wing Radicals. In 1899 Waldeck-Rousseau appointed Millerand, who was a Socialist, to be Minister of Commerce. Once more there were violent dissensions among the Socialists which Jaurès was unable to heal until the party congress held at Rouen in 1905. The right wing of the party was prepared to work through local councils and the legislature to secure reforms for the workers. In 1906 Briand entered the cabinet and in 1910 he became the first Socialist in Europe to hold office as a prime minister. At the same time Socialists were playing their part in local administration. "In 1907 there were 149 mayors, 219 deputy mayors, and

2,160 municipal councillors in France who belonged to the Socialist party." Socialist and Radical participation in the Government, and the growth of trade-union membership from 492,000 in 1900 to 1,026,000 in 1914, helped to bring about certain reforms in the early twentieth century—a reduction of hours in factories (1900), an eight-hour day for miners (1905), a weekly day of rest (1906), the abolition of the truck system (1910), the introduction of a voluntary old-age pension scheme (1910), and the codification of the factory laws (1910). The left-wing Socialists, however, were not prepared to co-operate with the Radicals or other bourgeois political parties. They firmly believed in the class struggle and favoured "direct action" to secure their aims. These Socialists were behind the Syndicalist movement which played so important a part in the history of the French working classes in the ten years before the outbreak of the first World War.

The Syndicalists, inspired by the ideas of the Marxist writer Georges Sorel—whose *Réflexions sur la Violence* appeared in 1909 —held that the working classes could best achieve their aims by a general strike and that the necessary preliminary moves should include "direct action" in the factories such as boycotts and sabotage. They damaged machinery, employed go-slow tactics, and obstructed the regularity of railway and postal services. The General Confederation of Labour fell under their control and there was serious labour unrest in both urban and rural France between 1904 and 1914. In 1904 there were over 1,000 strikes—nearly double the number of the previous year. One of the most serious was a great strike in the vineyards of southern France. In 1906 there were so many strikes—438,000 workers were affected—that an outbreak of revolutionary violence seemed likely. In Paris there was such alarm that some people fled to England for safety and the Government concentrated troops on the capital. In 1908 several workers were killed when the police intervened in a strike of builders near Paris. In the spring of 1909 the General Confederation of Labour was largely responsible for organizing a general strike of Post Office employees which inflicted considerable inconvenience on the public. The Government hesitated at first but eventually took a firm line with the strikers and dismissed 600 of them. This brought the strike to an end. In the following year an even more serious strike occurred. There was unrest on the southern railway lines in May 1910. In October the Northern Railway was affected and the National Federation of Railwaymen declared a general strike on all the French lines. The men demanded a weekly day of rest (already granted in other industries) and a minimum wage of five francs per day. Briand, the Socialist prime minister, ordered the arrest of five of the ringleaders (under a railway law of 1845) and called the strikers up to serve in the army reserve. The railways were operated by the military authorities and the strike quickly collapsed. The strikers on the State Railway were dismissed. The long neglect of the social question in France had so exasperated the more militant trade unionists and Socialists that the decade 1904–14 was one of the most disturbed in the turbulent history of the Third Republic.

## FRANCE'S TRADE WITH HER COLONIES

In the seventeenth and eighteenth centuries the French had built up a great colonial empire in India, Canada and the West Indies. Trading stations at the mouth of the River Senegal in West Africa enabled the French to keep their plantations in San Domingo, Martinique and Guadeloupe supplied with negro slaves while Mauritius, Bourbon (Réunion) and the Seychelles were stepping stones on the route to India. Girault states that "in the eighteenth century the commerce with the colonies represented two-thirds of the external commerce of France". Colonial trade in those days was largely in the hands of privileged companies. Foreign merchants and foreign ships were excluded from the overseas territories. Even after the loss of the American and Indian possessions in 1763 the French still held some valuable sugar islands in the West Indies. In 1789 the overseas possessions sent to the mother country produce worth 185 million livres and French trade with San Domingo alone was valued at nearly 200 million livres.

During the Revolutionary and Napoleonic wars the French lost San Domingo, Mauritius and the Seychelles while Louisiana was sold to the United States of America. In 1815 France retained only her "old colonies"—Guadeloupe and Martinique in the West Indies (Antilles), St. Pierre and Miquelon off the south-east coast of New-foundland, Cayenne (French Guiana) in South America, a few trading posts in West Africa (such as St. Louis and Goree Island), Réunion in the Indian Ocean, and a few small districts in India (such as Pondicherry and Chandernagore). From an economic point of view Guadeloupe and Martinique (which produced sugar) and St. Pierre and Miquelon (visited by cod-fishing fleets) were the only colonial possessions of any value at that time. In 1829 the trade of the French West Indies accounted for seventy per cent of the total commerce of all the French colonies.

By 1900 France had acquired vast new territories in Africa, Asia and the Pacific. She had become the second largest colonial power in the world. Her colonial population (over 56 millions) was much greater than her home population (nearly 39 millions).

Napoleon's brief Egyptian campaign had fired the imagination of the French public in the early years of the nineteenth century and had pointed the way to new colonial activities in Africa. Egypt itself was the scene of brilliant triumphs and dramatic failures for the French. The great Emperor's grandiose plans to found a new colony on the route to India were frustrated by Nelson's victory at Aboukir Bay. In 1839 an imposing French naval force was assembled in the Levant to support the claims of Mehemet Ali in Syria but Louis Philippe gave way when Britain, Russia, Austria and Prussia combined to support the Sultan against his unruly Egyptian vassal.

Thirty years later the Suez Canal—a project carried through by de Lesseps in face of determined opposition—was opened by the Empress Eugènie but in 1875 the British Government purchased from the bankrupt Khedive 176,602 of the 400,000 ordinary shares of the Suez Canal Company. In 1876 Goschen and Joubert advised Ismail Pasha on methods of improving Egypt's finances. At the same time a Public Debt Commission was set up by France, Austria, and Italy. In the following year Cromer was appointed to this Commission by the British Government. In 1879, when Ismail Pasha was replaced by Tewfik Pasha as Khedive, Anglo-French "dual control" of Egyptian affairs was strengthened, but when Arabi Pasha seized Alexandria in 1882 the French left the British to put down the rising.

In the Sudan Marchand's march from the Congo to the upper waters of the White Nile might have added the Southern Sudan to France's colonial empire and so prevented a junction between the Sudan and Uganda. But the French were too late. Kitchener had just defeated the Dervishes and—on instruction from the British Government—he demanded the withdrawal of Marchand's force from Fashoda (Kodok). France and Britain were on the brink of war but at the last moment the French gave way. In 1904 when the "entente cordiale" was established France acknowledged Britain's leading position in Egypt in return for British support for her own claims in Morocco.

France had greater success in the west, the north and the centre of Africa. As early as the 1820's the French began to explore the interior of the Senegal region. René Callié undertook a hazardous journey from Sierra Leone to Timbuktu and Tangiers (1829). Baron Roget, Governor of Senegal between 1822 and 1827, set up posts in the hinterland to trade with the natives and encouraged the formation of companies to establish cotton and indigo plantations. By these means he hoped to develop a new economy to replace the slave trade. The bad climate, the poor soil and the scarcity of labour led to the failure of the plantation companies. They lost about a million francs. On the other hand commerce with the natives—particularly the gum trade—made some progress and Senegal's exports rose in value from under 1·6 million francs in 1821 to 5 million francs in 1837.

In the 1830's, however, the north African coast offered greater opportunities for French colonization than West Africa. Algeria was much closer to France than Senegal. The climate and soil of the valleys of the "Tell" region—between the Mediterranean and the Lower Atlas mountains—were much better suited to white settlement than the unhealthy forests of West Africa. Opposition from other Powers was not to be expected since the Algerian ports had long harboured the notorious Barbary pirates whose depredations were a constant menace to Mediterranean shipping.

When a French consul was insulted in 1827 Charles X caused preparations to be made for a punitive expedition against Algeria. These took three years to complete. In June 1830 troops were landed and the port of Algiers fell on July 5. A few weeks later Charles X had to abdicate, but Louis Philippe's accession made no difference to France's expansionist policy in North Africa. Oran was seized early in 1831 and Bône in 1832. When the French advanced into the interior strong resistance was encountered from Abd-el-Kader. The elder Dumas in his description of a journey in France's new colony (*Tangier to Tunis*) gave a lively description of Algeria as he saw it in 1846. He met some of the explorers and pioneer settlers who were already penetrating into the interior. It was not until 1847 that the campaigns of Clausel and Bugeaud were crowned with success. Abd-el-Kader surrendered and was exiled. In 1848 the Bey of Constantine—the last independent ruler in Algeria—was defeated. But the Kabyles still had to be put down and several expeditions were sent against them before they were subdued in 1857.

The Second Republic was important in French colonial history since slavery was abolished in 1848. The first emancipation at the time of the French Revolution had been revoked by Napoleon. Only a comparatively small number of slaves were affected by the emancipation of 1848, most of them being employed on plantations in Martinique, Guadeloupe and Senegal. After the slaves had gained their freedom a system of share-cropping (*métayage*) developed on the sugar plantations of the French West Indies. A number of the former slaves rented small holdings and—instead of paying their rent in cash—handed over to their landlord a proportion of their harvest each year.

The Second Empire was a period of steady if unspectacular progress in colonial affairs. The French position in Algeria was strengthened by successful military operations against the Kabyles. In Senegal General Faidherbe (governor in 1854–61 and 1863–5)—"a man of great enterprise and intelligence"—realized that Dakar on the mainland had a better harbour than the island of Goree. A jetty was built at Dakar in 1863. In the hinterland Faidherbe waged war on the Tukulov leader El Hadj Omar who was eventually killed by the Fulani in 1864. Faidherbe annexed the Wati district between the River Senegal and the River Gambia.

Meanwhile the French were also establishing their authority along some 200 miles of the coast of West Africa south of Libreville which had been founded in 1849 as a colony for emancipated slaves. Attempts to penetrate into the hinterland by way of the Como and the Mouni failed, but in 1857–9 Paul du Chaillou showed that the Ogowé was the key to the interior. In 1860 naval officers signed several treaties with native chiefs on the lower reaches of the River Ogowé. In Napoleon III's reign French interests in the Far East were extended by the seizure of three provinces in Indo-China. In East Africa the French annexed Obok and Amabo in Somaliland.

The Second Empire—by a series of enactments culminating in a consolidating measure of July 9, 1868—abolished the old colonial tariff system (the *pacte colonial*) and introduced a more liberal fiscal policy in conformity with the Free Trade principles embodied in the Anglo-French commercial treaty of 1860. The first article of the decree of 1868 provided that "products of all kinds and of any origin may be imported under any flag into the various overseas French possessions, where the Navigation Act of September 21st, 1792, is still in force. Products exported from these territories may be sent to any destination and under any flag."

The Third Republic saw both a great extension of France's colonial possessions and a change in France's tariff policy concerning overseas territories. The Protectionist reaction in France in the 1870's and 1880's led to a reversal of Napoleon III's fiscal policy. A law of January 11, 1892, tried to "assimilate" a number of the colonial tariffs with that of the mother country. The ultimate object of this policy appears to have been the establishment of a customs union between France and her colonies which would be surrounded by a high tariff wall to keep foreigners out. In practice, however, fiscal considerations sometimes prevented the Government from admitting colonial products into France free of import duty, though substantial preferences were granted. According to Girault the term "tariff assimilation" was "nothing but a deceptive euphemism". It was really a policy by which the "colonial consumer was openly sacrificed to the producer of the imperial state". "The legislators of 1892 were hypnotised by statistics which they did not take the trouble to analyse, and sought to produce a diminution in the trade of the colonies with France." In fact it proved to be impossible to carry out a policy of tariff assimilation to its logical conclusion. Some territories such as Tunis, Morocco, and most of the West African colonies had autonomous tariffs. In certain other territories the policy of the Open Door was pursued. Colonies lying in the conventional Congo basin came under the provisions of the Berlin Congo Act and an agreement of 1899 provided that French and British merchants and goods should enjoy equality of treatment in an area of West Africa which included Dahomey and the Ivory Coast.

France's defeat in the Franco-Prussian war coincided with a major insurrection in Algeria. Soon afterwards a wave of colonial chauvinism swept aside the opposition of those who believed that imperial expansion would be costly in men and money and would involve France in disputes with other countries. The colonial enthusiasts found a champion in Jules Ferry who sought to revive France's self-esteem and to re-establish France as a Great Power by a policy of expansion overseas. Bismarck encouraged Ferry in the hope that colonial adventures would distract France's attention from plans of revenge against Germany.

French imperialists dreamed of uniting French possessions on the coasts of Africa—Algiers, St. Louis, Dakar, Libreville and Jibuti—in a huge empire that would extend over all northern and central Africa from the Atlantic to the Mediterranean and the Red Sea. These grandiose schemes were not realized. Britain secured control over Nigeria and the Sudan; Belgium gained the Congo; Germany established herself in the Cameroons; while the Italians seized Tripoli. Nevertheless France secured immense territories in West Africa, Equatorial Africa, Tunis and Morocco. In addition France still held her "old colonies" in the West Indies, South America and India as well as Madagascar, Indo-China and various islands in the Pacific of which Tahiti was the most important. In twenty years—between 1880 and 1900—France added 3,000,000 square miles of territory to her overseas empire and increased her colonial population by nearly 50,000,000. In 1914 the area of France's colonial possessions was estimated at 3·7 million square miles and the colonial population was about 56 millions.

In 1912 the value of her colonial trade represented over ten per cent of France's external commerce as compared with only six per cent in 1866. In this respect France was in a very different position from Germany whose colonial trade was less than one per cent of her total overseas trade. France had a favourable balance of commodity trade with her colonies and protectorates since she sold rather more goods to her overseas possessions than she purchased from them. The largest imports from the colonies were cereals, oxen and sheep (from North Africa), ground-nuts, copra and phosphates. But France did not obtain from her overseas possessions any appreciable quantities of rubber, cotton, coffee or cocoa. French exports to her colonies and protectorates included cotton piece-goods, engineering products, and wines. One-third of all France's exports of cotton goods were sent to the overseas possessions—particularly to Algeria, Madagascar and Indo-China—and this "explains the eagerness with which French manufacturers seek to reserve for themselves the colonial market". Indeed the leaders of the French cotton industry were among the most powerful champions of the policy of "tariff assimilation" with the colonies. Colonial commerce was of great significance to certain French ports—particularly Marseilles and Bordeaux—and to the mercantile marine. Marseilles had a colonial trade valued at nearly 820 million francs in 1910.

The reasons for the economic expansion of the French colonies are not far to seek. The area of France's overseas possessions increased by leaps and bounds. So did the size of the native and white populations. Algeria, for example, had a population of 5·5 millions in 1911, of whom nearly 800,000 were of European origin. Public and private investment in the overseas possessions contributed to their progress. The state and colonial authorities undertook many great public works such as harbours, roads, and railways. Private entrepreneurs and joint-stock companies established plantations and opened up mines for the extraction of mineral ores and phosphates. Protectionists claimed that the policy of "tariff assimilation" had contributed to the economic development of the overseas possessions. There seems little doubt that this was true of Algeria but it is less certain that tariff assimilation was equally advantageous to other colonies.

Algeria was the most important French colony from an economic point of view. The foreign trade of this territory had developed in the early period of French rule and by 1850 its exports were valued at 72·6 million francs and imports at 10·2 million francs. Whereas in 1840 Algeria's chief exports had been animal products (hides, wool and tallow), in 1850 they were olive oil and cereals. Efforts were made to induce white settlers to establish farms and plantations in the new colony. Considerable difficulties were experienced in securing land for European settlers and the policy of the French authorities in seizing certain public and communal lands and forests was of questionable legality. The traditional agrarian economy of the Arabs was disrupted by the land policy of the invaders. The pioneer white settlers found that the climate of Algeria was marred by periodic droughts and floods. They suffered from malaria while their cattle were attacked by wild beasts and their crops were ravaged by beetles and locusts.

Nevertheless by 1864 there were over a quarter of a million white settlers in Algeria and nearly sixty per cent of them were of French origin. This was a much larger number of free migrants than those going to Australia in the period before gold was discovered there. There were about 100,000 white planters and farmers in Algeria in the 1860's and they cultivated over half a million hectares of land. In the early 1860's there was an increase in the land under cotton owing to the shortage of cotton in France at the time of the American civil war. It may be doubted, however, whether the economic advantages gained from Algeria were an adequate compensation for the cost of conquering the territory and maintaining law and order there. In 1870 Lord Clarendon referred to Algeria as a "costly and unproductive colony" which required a permanent garrison of 60,000 men.

After the suppression of an insurrection in 1871 there was a period of reconstruction. Railways were built with financial assistance from the State and new plantations were established. By 1914 Algeria had a railway network which was over 2,500 km. in length. All the lines were nationalized in 1905. Public and private investment fostered the expansion of the Algerian economy. In 1912 the value of Algeria's imports and exports had risen to 1,200 million francs.

At that time over four-fifths of Algeria's exports went to France. The mother country purchased a high proportion of the output of Algeria's vineyards, farms and plantations. Wine was now Algeria's most important export. It was often mixed with French wine and the mixture was an improvement upon both original wines. Agricultural products—cereals, sheep, fruit and olive oil—were sent to France and to neighbouring north African territories. Fish caught by Italian fishermen off the coast of Algeria were exported to Italy. A considerable proportion of Algeria's raw materials and fertilizers were exported to foreign countries and not to France. Phosphates were sent to Germany and Spain, iron-ore to Britain and zinc-ore to Belgium. Algeria's imports were to a great extent consumed by the European population. They included foods and drinks (such as coffee), coal and manufactured products (particularly cloth and mechanical appliances). Nine-tenths of Algeria's imports came from France. From the French point of view Algeria had developed a prosperous economy by 1914 but many of the natives of the colony had lost heavily by the French occupation because their lands had been ruthlessly expropriated and they had to pay exorbitant taxes.

When Tunis came under French control in 1881 the value of its external trade was estimated to be 38 million francs. By 1904 the external commerce of the protectorate had increased to 160 million francs. This was about a quarter of Algeria's external trade. The economy of Tunis was changing in the early years of the twentieth century owing to the expansion of the mining industry and the construction of public works. A railway network was constructed almost entirely from the resources of the colony itself. The main railways were operated by the Bône-Gelma Company (1,500 km.) and the Gafsa Company (360 km.). Between 1894 and 1914 there was an increase in the export of phosphates and mineral ores and the territory was less dependent upon the French market than it had been when it became a French protectorate. Phosphates, valued at nearly 48 million francs in 1912, represented about one-third of the exports of Tunis. Next in importance came mineral ores. Iron-ore was sent to Britain and Holland, lead to Belgium, Italy and Spain, and zinc to Belgium, France, and Algeria. Agriculture was fostered in various ways—for example by establishing a colonial agricultural school in 1898. The most important farm products to be exported were cattle, sheep and grain and these were sent both to France and to neighbouring Mediterranean territories.

When Morocco became a French protectorate in 1912 the value of her exports was 66 million francs of which nearly one-third went to France. The most important exports were hides, wool, fruit and vegetables. Imports, valued at 134 million francs, came mainly from France (44 per cent) and Britain (32 per cent). They included cotton piece-goods, sugar, tea, wines and alcohol. Economic expansion was slow in the brief period between the establishment of the protectorate and the outbreak of the first World War. Lyautey, the Resident General, found that his hands were tied by international agreements affecting the territory. One result of this was that in 1914 Morocco had only a few narrow gauge railways used exclusively by the military authorities. But during the war of 1914–18 Lyautey for practical purposes had a free hand and substantial progress was made in the construction of essential public works. Morocco's trade rose to over 700 million francs in 1919. And Lyautey's new harbour at Casablanca handled 800,000 tons of merchandise in 1919 as compared with only 130,000 tons in 1911. The discovery of phosphate deposits in 1921 gave Morocco an important new export.

Serious difficulties hampered the development of French West Africa. Europeans had to contend with an exceptionally trying climate and with tropical diseases. The native population was small in relation to the size of the territory. Only the Guinea Coast and the Upper Volta region had a population sufficiently dense for the economic needs of the colony. Some parts of the territory were of great potential value from an economic point of view but there were also arid regions and deserts. Communications between the coast and isolated fertile regions in the hinterland were unsatisfactory. The River Senegal was navigable as far as Kayes for only two and a half months in the year and the delta of the Niger was not in French territory. Only the construction of railways could bring about an expansion of the economy. Roume, the Governor General who has been described as "the economic founder of West Africa", emphasized the need for railways when he declared in 1906 that "the resources of science and capital permit us now to open these countries hitherto hermetically sealed by nature, by improving the few natural sea-outlets, by correcting the defects of the river routes wherever possible, and above all by creating artificial routes—the railways".

In Senegal a railway was built between 1882 and 1885 along the coast to join the ports of Dakar and St. Louis (264 km.). Baltzer declared that this early line was "a striking example of the beneficial effects of a railway upon an underdeveloped country". The rapid expansion of the production of ground-nuts in the Cayor and Baol districts was due almost entirely to this railway. A line was planned to run from Thiès (on the Dakar–St. Louis line) to Kayes on the River Senegal. In 1910 the sections between Thiès and Guinguincó (140 km.) and between Kayes and Ambidedi (44 km.) were open to traffic. A line was built from Kayes to Bahamo and Kulikovo (555 km.) to link the Senegal and the Niger. Construction began in 1881 and was not completed until 1904. In French Guinea a railway from Conakry on the coast to Kurussa on the Niger (589 km.) was opened in 1911. On the Ivory Coast the French built a line from the port of Abidjean to Buake which was opened in 1912. In Dahomey railways joined Kotonu and Save (262 km.) as well as Porto Novo and Saheti (38·5 km.).

The impetus given to the economy by the construction of railways was soon seen in the expansion of French West Africa's external trade. This grew in value from 78·7 million francs in 1895 to 253·2 million francs in 1912. French West Africa produced large quantities of ground-nuts and rubber. Most of the ground-nuts were grown in Senegal and the bulk of the crop was sent to the mother country. Ground-nuts represented a third of the exports of French West Africa. The value of the nuts exported in 1910 was over 50 million francs. There was a fall in output in 1911 and 1912 owing to lack of rain and the ravages of pests. There was also a decline in rubber exports from 37 million francs in 1910 to 25 million francs in 1912. This was due to a fall in the world price of rubber owing to the expansion of output from Malaya. Much of the rubber of French West Africa came from the Guinea Coast and about half of the exports were sent to the mother country. Other exports which deserve mention were palm oil (from Dahomey), wood (from the Ivory Coast) and oxen (from Upper Senegal).

French West Africa imported manufactured goods. The most important were cotton piece-goods and Lancashire had the lion's share of this trade until—just before the outbreak of the first World War—France placed a virtually prohibitive duty on the importation of cotton goods into the colony. Girault observes that, under a relatively liberal fiscal régime, "The external trade of western Africa has developed with a rapidity much greater than that of the other colonies and their capacity for buying has increased." It may be added that most of the external trade of French West Africa was carried in foreign vessels.

French Equatorial Africa[1] has been described as "a huge coastal forest, an intermediate series of agricultural plateaux, and a pastoral steppe zone, gradually merging into the northern desert". The resources of the forests—timber, ivory, rubber and palm products— were the first to be exploited. In the early years of the twentieth century the external trade of the colony made little progress. Gabon exported ivory, rubber, coffee and cocoa and imported manufactured products such as textiles. The Middle Congo, Ubangi-Shari and the Chad Territory exported ivory, rubber and copper while cotton goods were among the most important imports.

The failure of the economy of this vast region to develop more quickly was due partly to gross mismanagement on the part of the great privileged companies and partly to the failure of the Government to open up the country by constructing public works. Goods coming from the interior by the River Congo route could go no farther than Brazzaville (by Stanley Pool) which was 400 km. from

[1] French Equatorial Africa included the Chad Territory, Ubangi-Shari, the Middle Congo and Gabon. The population was estimated at 5 millions prior to the transfer of the New Cameroons to Germany in 1911. The area of the New Cameroons was 280,000 sq. km.

the sea. Fortunately for the French the first railway to be built in the neighbouring Belgian Congo ran from the port of Matadi to Leopoldville which lay immediately opposite Brazzaville on the other side of the River Congo. The line was opened in 1898 and for many years the economic development of "the Cinderella of the French Empire" was largely dependent upon the efficient working of this Belgian railway.

In the 1890's the French Government, anxious to exploit quickly the natural resources of Equatorial Africa, embarked upon a policy of granting monopoly concessions to great companies. The first concessions were granted in 1893 but they aroused considerable opposition and were withdrawn two years later. In 1899 a decree declared that *terrès vacantes et sans maître* belonged to the State. The Government now indulged in "an orgy of concessions". About 327,000 square miles of land were allocated to some forty companies with a registered capital of nearly 60 million francs. The companies were granted a monopoly over forest produce for thirty years in return for a small annual rent and fifteen per cent of the profits. The companies introduced a system of forced labour and the natives were grossly maltreated.

Eventually public opinion in France was aroused and the veteran de Brazza was sent to the colony to investigate complaints against the companies. He died at Dakar on the return journey and the Government suppressed his report, but in a book entitled *Le Congo français* his colleague Félicien Challaye gave an account of the state of affairs in the colony which was a serious indictment of the policy pursued by the companies. He stated that they "made the natives work for a trifle, using threats or even violence to secure their services. The Government, without rendering a single service, crushes the natives with taxes and forced labour. Instead of being drawn towards the Europeans, as formerly, the natives doubt them and flee as far as possible. The routes habitually used by Europeans are almost denuded of villages, whereas formerly the natives used to cluster there. Regions described by the first explorers as inhabited and fertile have become deserts."

English merchants, such as John Holt of Liverpool, protested that they were being squeezed out by the privileged companies. The British Foreign Office supported these complaints and invoked the Open Door provision of the Berlin Congo Act. At first the French Government ignored these protests but in 1906 the English traders received some compensation. By this time it was clear that many of the land companies were having little success in opening up the colony since nine of them were out of business and twenty-nine were in debt. Only ten were making a profit. In 1910 the French Government made new agreements with some of the companies by which they gave up their rights over large tracts of land in return for complete ownership over smaller areas. The "robber economy" of the companies had greatly harmed the colony's economy. Frankel observes that "in the French Congo large rubber resources were completely exhausted and replanting was almost wholly neglected".[1]

Madagascar was another French colony which hardly made the economic progress that might have been expected in the early years of the twentieth century. The island had an area of 590,000 square km. and a population of 2·7 millions. It became a French colony in 1896 and the policy of "tariff assimilation" was soon applied. Every effort was made to exclude English goods from Madagascar. The result was that the pattern of Madagascar's external commerce was radically changed between 1898 and 1912. Prior to 1898 Madagascar had sent more of her products to non-French than to French markets but in 1912 two-thirds of the island's exports went to the mother country. The chief exports were hides, gold, vanilla and raffia. Nine-tenths of Madagascar's imports came from France in 1912. Britain had been virtually ousted from the import trade. Above all Lancashire cotton goods had been practically eliminated from the Madagascar market. Imports consisted of textiles, wines, brandy and engineering products. There was some reluctance on the part of the government to spend money on public works. It took about seven years to build Madagascar's first railway from Tananarivo to Brickaville. But when the whole of this 266 km. line was opened on January 1, 1909, Madagascar's external trade soon began to show welcome signs of rapid expansion. It doubled in four years. The railway was extended to Tamatave in 1913.

Indo-China[2] was a very important French colony from an economic point of view. Its area was 665,000 square km. and its population was about 17 millions. Its external commerce represented nearly one-half of the external commerce of all the French overseas possessions. It was an "assimilated"colony and since 1887 the French general tariff had been applied to Indo-China. Between 1889 and 1912 the external commerce of the colony increased in value from 78 million francs to 533 million francs. These figures may not be

---

[1] For the concession system in the French Congo see E. D. Morel, "France and her Congo" in the *Contemporary Review*, December 1911. For similar scandals in the Belgian Congo see E. D. Morel, *Red Rubber* (1906).

[2] Cochin-China (1862), Cambodia (1863), Tonkin (1873 to 1885), and Annam (1884). The coaling station of Kwang-Chow was leased by France from China in 1898.

entirely reliable since in 1900 the customs authorities made substantial increases in the official prices at which they valued certain imports. But there can be no doubt that the external trade of Indo-China increased rapidly in the early years of the twentieth century.

The construction of public works promoted economic expansion. In 1898 Indo-China was authorized to borrow 200 million francs for railway construction. All materials purchased with this money—if not available locally—had to be bought in France and had to be shipped in French vessels. Hanoi became a railway centre of considerable importance. From that city lines were constructed to Kuangsi (1902), to Vinh (1905), to the harbour of Haifong at the delta of the Red River (1906) and to Hunnansen in China (1910). From Saigon lines were built to Mytho (1885) and to Phantiet (1909). By 1914 the colony had over 1,700 km. of railways. The growth of the European population—20,000 in 1914—also stimulated the demand for French goods in Indo-China.

When examining Indo-China's external commerce a distinction should be made between two types of trade—first the trade between Indo-China and Europe and, secondly, the trade between Indo-China and other parts of the Far East. Indo-China exported or re-exported to Hong Kong or Singapore fish, shrimps, tortoise shell, cinnamon bark, cotton, silk, straw mats, silver and coal. From Hong Kong and Singapore these products—valued at 86·7 million francs in 1911—were distributed to various parts of the Far East but some of them no doubt found their way to Europe by this circuitous route. Indo-China's exports to Europe nearly all went to France (56·8 million francs). They included hides, fish-oil, copra, pepper, tea, rubber and zinc-ore. Indo-China's imports from Europe came mainly from France and included foods and drinks (tinned milk, wine, beer, rye, sugar) and manufactured products (machinery, textiles, motor cars, paper). Tobacco was imported from Algeria while petrol came from the United States. Among the more important imports from Hong Kong and Singapore were rye, nuts, vermicelli, and sugar. Opium came from India and petrol was imported from the Dutch East Indies.

# CHAPTER V

# THE INDUSTRIAL REVOLUTION IN RUSSIA

## (i) Introduction

IN the last quarter of the nineteenth century Russia was still a predominantly agricultural country. Most Russians lived in villages or small towns and not in large cities. They gained a livelihood from farming, forestry or fishing rather than from industry or commerce. But Russia was beginning to be industrialized. Her vast territories sprawling across two continents contained immense natural wealth. She had vast resources of coal, iron-ore, oil and timber. Her grain harvests enabled Russia to export over six million tons of cereals a year in the early twentieth century. Flax and cotton were grown and were worked up by both factory and cottage industries. There were many old-established craft manufactures the products of which were sold at various fairs. With a large and growing population Russia had a substantial home market and a big potential labour force for her factories.

Industrialization was actively supported by all the resources of an autocratic monarchy. One Russian writer remarked that "nothing could be less spontaneous than the development of our manufacturing industries". Subsidies, loans, premiums, land grants, tax reductions, exemptions from military service and other privileges were available to enterprising entrepreneurs. Prohibitive tariffs kept foreign competitors at bay. In 1877 it was decided to assess import duties on a gold basis—and not on the basis of the paper rouble. This substantially increased the protection given to Russian manufacturers. Rosa Luxemburg considered that this was "a special landmark in the absolutist government's new policy of forcing the growth of capitalism". The Russian Government spared no expense when pressing forward with the construction of railways and other public works which would open up the country and facilitate industrial expansion. The State—as owner, investor, manager, or controller—dominated important economic activities such as the railways, the banks, the sugar industry, the timber trade and sale of vodka.

Since industrialization started later in the Czar's dominions than in other manufacturing countries of Europe the Russians were able to secure capital, machinery, and expert advice on a scale which had hardly been possible when France and Germany were passing through the early phases of their industrial revolutions. In 1914 Russia was the greatest borrower in Europe. Count Witte stated in his memoirs that when he was Minister of Finance the national debt rose by 1,900 million roubles. He claimed that all this money was spent on "productive purposes" such as railway construction and the establishment of a sound currency. He added that throughout his administration he had defended borrowing from abroad and that in his opinion "no country has ever developed without foreign capital". It has been estimated that direct foreign investment in Russian industry amounted to 2,242 million roubles in 1917.

English capital, machinery, and skilled labour helped to establish the Russian cotton industry. In the middle of the eighteenth century two English entrepreneurs, named Chamberlin and Cozzens, were granted a monopoly of cotton weaving by the Government and nearly a hundred years later it was English machinery and English credit which enabled Knoop to set up modern cotton spinning mills in Russia. Thornton operated a large woollen mill on the River Neva. John Hughes established ironworks and engineering plants in the Donetz region. Belgian and French investors and engineers opened up coal-mines in the Donetz basin. French capital was behind the Gdatsevski company which mined iron-ore at Krivoi-Rog. The Swedish brothers Robert and Ludvig Nobel opened up the rich oil fields of Baku. Foreign investments accounted for perhaps one-half of the capital invested in Russian companies in 1910. Certain industrial enterprises were constructed on a huge scale and there was sometimes hardly any intermediate stage between small workshops and large factories. In the early years of the twentieth century over one-third of Russia's industrial workers were to be found in establishments each employing over 500 men. Particularly after the slump in the early twentieth century some of these large enterprises were associated in cartels such as the Engineering Trust and the Donetz Coal Trust.

There were however many obstacles which checked the advance of modern industry in Russia. The railway network was inadequate, the rivers and harbours were frozen in the winter, and many roads lacked a firm surface. Russia had only a small mercantile marine and she lacked a warm-water port. Much of her overseas trade was carried in foreign vessels and passed through foreign ports.

The persistence of serfdom in the first half of the nineteenth century was one of the main reasons for the continued backwardness of Russia as an industrial country. In 1815 the economist Storch—Nicholas I's tutor—observed that the failure to abolish serfdom was the principal cause of Russia's inability to develop modern manufactures. He declared that "the superiority of free labour over serf labour is even more apparent in industry than in agriculture".

Only after the serfs had been freed was it possible for a class of wage-earning factory workers to develop. Only with the help of foreign experts could these operatives of peasant origin be trained to use the new machines imported from abroad. Only the fiscal policy of Protection and generous State aid to entrepreneurs made possible the development of the industrial sector of the economy. Foreign capital too had to be attracted to Russia to assist in the expansion of manufactures. The construction of a network of railways and the opening up of new sources of raw materials beyond the Urals promoted industrialization. It was not until the last decade of the nineteenth century that real progress was made in overcoming the many obstacles that formerly hindered Russia's progress as a manufacturing country. Only then—owing largely to Count Witte's energetic policy—did Russia at last take her place among the great manufacturing nations of the world.

Even after the serfs had been emancipated it proved to be difficult to recruit industrial labour in Russia. Although the rural population was increasing and there was a land hunger in parts of European Russia the peasants were nevertheless reluctant to migrate to the towns and to work in factories. Industrial employment was uncongenial to them and factory discipline was irksome. Sometimes poverty forced workers into the factories but they were often only temporary workers who returned to their villages as soon as they had saved a little money. And when labour was available the Russian mineowner or factory owner often had to face the expense of housing and feeding his workers. Industrial workers were not only difficult to secure in Russia, but they were inefficient when compared with the workers of western Europe. In 1893 in the Urals 142,000 men were employed in the iron-ore mines and foundries. It was estimated that in Belgium only 11,000 men would be needed to produce the same amount of iron ore, pig iron and steel.

In Russia manufactured articles produced in the factories had to compete with goods made in rural workshops. In Britain and Germany the factories forced many domestic workers out of business but in Russia domestic industry for some time flourished side by side with factory industry. Indeed the factories were actually responsible for the creation or revival of rural crafts because peasants who had learned the rudiments of an industrial skill in a factory sometimes used that skill at home when they returned to their villages. Some owners of great estates encouraged their tenants to practise rural crafts so as to earn money to pay the rent. In the nineteenth century, particularly after the emancipation of the serfs, there was a considerable expansion of *kustar* industry owing to the migration of craftsmen from one region to another. In the 1890's the Government took various steps to encourage the development of domestic industries. Geographical specialization—a well-known characteristic of factory industry—occurred in certain branches of domestic industry as well. In the 1870's a group of villages in Vladimir province specialized in painting icons; nineteen villages near Nizhny-Novgorod turned out axes; eighty villages near Pavlovo made cutlery; while some 200 hamlets in the Uloma district produced nails. In Nizhny-Novgorod province the peasants produced a large number of enamelled wooden spoons for export to the Far East. While some branches of domestic manufacture held their own—and even expanded—in face of factory competition, others eventually succumbed. In the cotton industry for example the number of factory workers rose from 94,500 to 242,000 between 1866 and 1895 while the number of domestic workers declined from 66,000 to 20,000.

Another obstacle to industrialization was the inefficiency of many Russian factory owners and managers. They lacked the stimulus of foreign competition since they enjoyed a monopoly or semi-monopoly of the home market. Many of the most successful industries were those in which foreign capital, managers and skilled workers were to be found. The Russian industrialists depended too much upon State assistance and were reluctant to stand upon their own feet.

The backward state of industry, the isolation of the country, the lack of educational facilities, and the conservatism of masters and men made it difficult to introduce foreign machines or to benefit from the skill of Russian inventors. Thus Zvorykin's discoveries in 1892 concerning the mechanics of cutting metals were ignored by Russian engineers. Nearly fifty years elapsed before Zvorykin's theories were rediscovered by scientists in western Europe and were used by western engineers.

## (ii) Industrial Expansion

### PETER THE GREAT

Peter the Great (1682–1725) has been described as the father of Russian manufacturing industry. He wished to westernize Russia and to expand its territories. A great army and navy were necessary to achieve these aims and Peter's many campaigns could be supported only by expanding the manufacturing side of the economy.

It has however been pointed out that substantial commercial and manufacturing enterprises had existed in Russia a century or more before Peter ascended the throne. These enterprises had been operated by the feudal nobility (who had used the labour of their own serfs) or by foreign entrepreneurs (who enjoyed special privileges). The Stroganov family had manufactured salt on a large scale while Morozov operated potash plants, iron foundries, distilleries, brick-kilns and linen works. Among the foreigners Vinius (a Dutchman) and Koet (a Swede) deserve mention. The former had established ironworks near Tula (1632) while the latter had set up glassworks near Moscow (1634).

Although it cannot be claimed that Peter the Great originated large-scale manufacturing enterprises in Russia it is true that he gave a powerful impetus to industrialization. Stalin has described Peter's policy as "a peculiar attempt to jump out of the framework of backwardness". Kirilov, writing in 1727, asserted that 233 industrial establishments had been established in Peter the Great's reign. Lyashchenko considers that Kirilov's figures were "obviously quite low for some branches (of industry) while they include . . . some enterprises of a non-manufacturing type". The State factories, mines and foundries established at this time included over twenty ironworks in the Ekaterinburg district of the Urals, armament plants at Tula and elsewhere, a sailcloth factory at Moscow, saltpetre plants in Kazan, a glass factory at St. Petersburg, silkworks in the Akhtuba region, and various establishments for the manufacture of woollen and cotton cloths. The size of some of these enterprises may be judged from the number of serfs allocated to them. Nine mines at Perm had 25,000 serfs while the Moscow sailcloth factory had over 1,000 workers. Large numbers of serfs felled trees in State forests for the building of naval vessels. Serfs drafted from the land to work in mines, foundries and factories were not always very efficient workers and Peter the Great tried to attract foreign artisans to Russia to improve standards of workmanship.

Peter the Great not only founded a number of industrial enterprises himself but he gave every encouragement to private entrepreneurs to establish new factories. Russian and foreign merchants came forward as founders of factories but very few nobles responded to the Czar's appeals. Although some of Peter's industrial establishments did not long survive his death it would be wrong to dismiss his economic policy as a failure. Mavor rightly observes that Peter "showed his people in what the material wealth of Russia consisted, and he showed them how it might be exploited".

In the eighteenth century there were many factories in Russia and some of them employed a considerable number of workers. Power-driven machinery of course was not introduced until much later and the work was done by hand with tools or quite simple equipment. Certain factories consisted of several large buildings, some of which were workshops while others provided living accommodation for the operatives. Others were no more than a number of small workshops or adjacent attics under common management. Tugan-Baronovsky considered that many of Peter's factories were large establishments but Tarlé and Kulischer argued that the majority of them were quite small concerns which employed only a few workers on the spot and used the labour of craftsmen who worked in their own homes. From the point of view of management and organization it is necessary to differentiate between nationalized concerns, merchants' "possessional factories", nobles' factories, serfs' factories and small domestic workshops (*kustar*).

## FACTORIES IN THE EIGHTEENTH CENTURY

After Peter the Great's death some of the industrial enterprises which he had established disappeared and others were given or sold or leased to private persons. In 1730 an official inquiry concerning factories founded in Peter's reign revealed that a number of them had already closed down. In 1744 the Government closed thirty-four industrial establishments because the quality of their products was unsatisfactory. But there was still a public sector of the economy and many serfs were employed in State mines, armament works and forests. Catherine the Great, who ruled from 1762 to 1796, gave a new impetus to the expansion of manufactures. During her reign the number of "large enterprises" rose from just under 1,000 to over 2,000.

In addition to fully nationalized enterprises there were "possessional" factories run jointly by the State and by private merchants. Some of these works had originally been set up by private entrepreneurs while others were State factories which had been transferred to private persons. An edict of 1721 allowed these factories to acquire entire villages and to use the labour of serfs living in them. Such serfs were attached to the factory and not to an individual owner. If the works changed hands so did the serfs.

Merchants' "possessional" factories were controlled by the bureaucracy. The quality, quantity, price and sale of the goods made in these workshops were regulated by government officials. This was one reason why "possessional" factories failed to expand. Another was the low standard of workmanship associated with the forced labour of peasants. It is not surprising that the Government complained in 1740 of the poor quality of the cloth supplied for the manufacture of army uniforms. Moreover the system of buying peasants for factory work introduced by the edict of 1721 was open to serious abuses. An official inquiry of 1740 stated that some "possessional" workshops were "fraudulent factories" since their output was negligible and the managers were using the serf labour for purposes other than industrial production.

Moreover the merchants' "possessional" factories had to face the hostility of the nobles who operated large workshops both on their own estates and in the towns. The nobles wished to monopolize serf labour and declared that the country's agrarian economy was being undermined by the purchase of villages to enable merchants to employ serfs in "possessional" factories. The Government vaccillated between the rival claims of the nobles and the merchants. Eventually the nobles got their way and an edict of 1762 prohibited the purchase of peasant villages which had been allowed since 1721. The "possessional" workshops declined after 1762 largely because of the difficulty of securing free labourers for the factories.

The factories of the nobles developed in the late eighteenth and early nineteenth centuries. The nobles used their peasants as factory operatives and moved their serfs from farm work to industrial employment to suit their own convenience. Cloth factories, distilleries, sawmills and even foundries situated on great landed properties used raw materials from the nobles' own farms, forests and mines. Although the nobles had many advantages over the merchants from the point of view of operating industrial establishments they could not get over the inevitable difficulties associated with the employment of serfs. The quality of forced labour was poor and the nobles found that their industrial serfs could often be employed only "on rough and simple processes such as the manufacture of coarse cloth made for soldiers' uniforms".

In view of the oppressed condition of the peasants before Emancipation the existence of factories owned by serfs is rather surprising. Despite the immense obstacles which they had to overcome there were serfs in Russia whose industrial careers would have rejoiced the heart of Samuel Smiles. In Ivanovo, one of Russia's leading textile centres, two serfs named Garelin and Grachev were engaged in linen weaving from the 1750's onwards. They subsequently turned their attention to calico printing. The number of workers employed

THE INDUSTRIAL REVOLUTION IN RUSSIA

by Grachev increased from 22 to 121 between 1789 and 1797. Grachev is said to have been the first peasant in Ivanovo to have purchased his freedom from Count Sheremetyev. This was in 1795 and it cost Grachev 130,000 roubles. "By 1807 the Grachev firm had grown to major standing. Its factories comprised four stone buildings (one of them three stories high) and many wooden structures among which were seven dormitories to house the workers."

Savva Morozov was a serf who set up a small workshop for the manufacture of silk and lace at Zuyevo (Bogorodsk district) in 1801. He was a weaver and his wife was an expert at colouring. In 1820 their enterprise had twenty looms and employed forty operatives. Morozov purchased his own freedom and that of his family—except for one son. This son had to wait for some years before his owner accepted a "fabulous sum" to set him free. In 1825 Morozov gave up manufacturing silks and opened a factory in Moscow to manufacture a mixed woollen-cotton cloth. He also imported cotton yarns on a large scale and sold them to other manufacturers.

The three brothers Kondratyev—Fedor, Kirill and Egor—built up a substantial silk business in Moscow. They began on a modest scale in the 1760's in the village of Grebnovo (Bogorodsk district) and were helped by their master General Bibikov. Few of the Kondratyevs succeeded in buying their freedom. Kirill Kondratyev and his son I. M. Kondratyev were the leading entrepreneurs of the family after the Napoleonic wars. They used only hired labour and employed no foreign craftsmen. By 1841 the Kondratyevs had 700 looms and employed 1,500 operatives.

The progress made by Russian industry in the eighteenth century may be seen from Heinrich Storch's account of the industries of the capital in the 1790's which appears in his *Picture of St. Petersburg* (1801). Storch stated that the quality of the curtains and carpets made at the State tapestry works was equal to that of the Gobelins in France. The imperial porcelain and faience factories also turned out products of high quality. The nationalized bronze factory "merits honourable mention on account of the neatness and taste of its execution". St. Petersburg had about 100 private manufactories in the 1790's which made sugar, tobacco, paper, leather goods, glassware, jewellery, silks, cottons and woollens.

Although factories were of considerable importance in the eighteenth century the output of small village workshops—the *kustar* industry—was also of significance in the Russian economy. Many peasants plied a craft—such as woodworking or clothmaking—in the winter when work in the fields was impossible. At first this was simply the manufacturing aspect of a self-sufficient economy. Later some of the goods made at home by peasant craftsmen were sold to raise the money needed to pay *obrok* to the landlord. This was a cash payment made by certain peasants in lieu of working for their landlord. Some domestic workshops developed in the nineteenth century because the peasants were using at home skills acquired by working in a factory. Some craftsmen worked in *artels* which were originally "temporary itinerant associations of workmen who during the summer lived together, fed together, worked together, and periodically divided among themselves the profit". Eventually *artels* of a more permanent character were formed some of which came under the control of capitalist contractors.

*Cotton Industry.* The first branch of manufacture in which modern industry was introduced on a large scale was the cotton industry. One of the main centres for the production of cotton goods was Ivanovo[1] in the province of Vladimir. Various factors favoured the development of the manufacture of cotton. Labour was available since linen weaving was an old-established craft in the district and the town was conveniently situated from the point of view of sending its products by water to Nizhny-Novgorod. In the second half of the eighteenth century a number of workshops specializing in the colouring of linen were set up by the serfs and in 1792 calendering machines were introduced by Grachev. In the early years of the nineteenth century the cotton industry developed in Moscow and St. Petersburg. In 1808 Moscow had its first spinning machines. The fire of Moscow in 1812 halted the advance of the cotton industry there but stimulated the production of cotton in Ivanovo. The calico printers of Ivanovo later looked back upon the decade 1812–22 as a golden age of prosperity when quick profits were gained and great fortunes were made. Two factors subsequently promoted the expansion of the cotton industry. The first was the Russian tariff of 1822 which placed a high duty upon British cotton piece-goods and so gave Russian manufacturers a virtual monopoly of the home market. The value of British finished cotton goods sent to Russia declined from £700,000 in 1820 to £59,000 in 1838. The second—and more important—development was the introduction into Russia of Lancashire cotton yarns which were much superior in quality to Asiatic yarns. Moreover the price of English cotton yarn was steadily declining at this time owing to the introduction of more efficient machinery into the Lancashire mills. The firm of Kiselev Brothers of Shuya, for example, paid only between 63 and 68 roubles per pud (of 36 lb.) for their English yarn in 1845 as compared with 106 to 112 roubles in 1822. Between 1820 and 1838 the English cotton twist

[1] In 1871 the name of Ivanovo was changed to Ivanovo-Voznesensk.

sent to Russia rose considerably in value. In 1843 there were forty cotton mills in Russia in which 350,000 spindles were at work.

For many years Ivanovo concentrated on the finishing processes. In the 1830's roller printing machines were introduced into the larger establishments. The cloth used by the calico printers had been woven (from Lancashire yarn) in village workshops. It was not until 1846 that the first mechanical loom was installed in Russia. This was in a factory in Shuya. Even in 1860 only three cotton weaving sheds in the province of Vladimir used power looms. Many of the calico printers were serfs of Count Sheremetyev, the owner of the lands upon which the "Manchester of Russia" had developed.

After the Napoleonic wars the Moscow and Lodz cotton industries also developed. When Moscow recovered from the fire of 1812 the cotton industry revived. Savva Morozov opened his first cotton weaving establishment in Moscow in 1825. Two years later Ludwig Geyer set up a cotton factory at Lodz in Poland. Other German entrepreneurs followed his example and an important cotton industry developed at Lodz.

The introduction of mechanical spinning was largely the work of Ludwig Knoop. As early as 1793 a spinning machine had been set up at Schlüsselburg and mechanical spinning made some progress in the early nineteenth century although progress was checked at the time of the French invasion of 1812. But in the 1840's a high proportion of the cotton yarn woven in Russia still came from abroad and not from local mills. Knoop was born in Bremen in 1821 and when fourteen years of age was apprenticed to a merchant in his native city. Next he went to Manchester where he served as a clerk in the offices of C. B. de Jersey & Co. (shippers and general merchants) who exported Lancashire cotton yarns to Russia. Knoop not only learned the commercial side of the business but also gained practical experience of spinning in a Rochdale mill. In 1839 Knoop, at the age of eighteen, went to Russia as assistant to C.B. de Jersey's representative in Moscow.

C. W. Morozov, a member of the well-known cotton firm of that name, asked Knoop to set up on his behalf an up-to-date cotton spinning mill with English machinery. At first the difficulties appeared to be insurmountable. Until 1843 the export of machinery from England was prohibited (except under licence) and the possibility of a young man like Knoop securing credit from English engineering firms seemed somewhat remote. But Knoop succeeded in building a mill for Morozov at Nikolskoye near Moscow. Knoop's younger brother, who was now working in Manchester, gave him every possible help. The firm of C. B. de Jersey & Co. gave him credit. Ludwig Knoop's success brought him many orders from Moscow and Ivanovo merchants who wanted to have spinning mills erected. When he died in 1894 he had built 122 cotton factories.

Knoop's position in the Russian cotton industry was unique since he monopolized the English machines, technical skill and financial support without which spinning mills could not be erected. Knoop worked in close association with a small group of Lancashire firms. His former employers (C.B. de Jersey) arranged for the preparation of blue prints and the selection of building contractors. Platt Brothers of Oldham supplied and installed the machines—and they sold cotton machinery to no one else in Russia. Hick, Hargreaves & Co. (Bolton) and John Musgrove & Sons supplied steam engines to drive the machinery. Mather & Platt of Salford supplied electrical installations.

These firms gave credit to Knoop and he gave credit to his Russian clients. By accepting their bills of exchange Knoop acted as a banker for cotton firms at a time when modern banking facilities had not been fully developed in Russia. Knoop secured for the new mills competent English managers, foremen, technicians and spinners. He imported into Russia the raw material which his clients required. He generally retained a financial interest in factories which he built by holding a mortgage on the property or by retaining a block of the firm's shares.

Knoop was also a cotton spinner on his own account. In 1860 he established a large mill at Kränholm near Narva (Esthonia). Power was derived from a waterfall in the River Narva. Spinning machines and power looms were imported from England and for many years the factory was in charge of a manager from Blackburn. Raw cotton and coal were imported from England. The undertaking was the biggest and one of the most up-to-date cotton factories in Russia. It had over 40,000 spindles and 2,000 power looms in the 1890's, Kränholm was "a piece of England on Russian soil". It may be added that English influence in the Russian cotton industry survived until the first World War. In 1912 a football team, raised by the English managing director of a cotton mill at Zuyevo, was playing in the Moscow League.

Knoop's activities led to a substantial increase in the amount of raw cotton imported by Russia. Imports rose from 2,250,000 lb. in 1821–5 to 93,400,000 lb. in 1856–60. In 1860 Russia had fifty-seven spinning mills employing nearly 42,000 operatives. The industry was firmly enough established to withstand the crisis caused by the Cotton Famine at the time of the American civil war. It was unfortunate that the raw material should have been in short supply just when the emancipation of the serfs had "put on the market an unlimited supply of cheap labour". Russian spinning firms had some raw cotton to hand when the American civil war broke out and additional supplies were obtained from Turkestan and Persia. After the Cotton Famine the Russian Government encouraged the expansion of cotton culture in Turkestan. In the Fergana district American varieties of cotton were successfully grown in the irrigated lands of the Syr Darya valley. The building of the Trans-Caspian Railway enabled cotton from Turkestan to reach Moscow and Ivanovo more quickly than before. On the eve of the first World War the cotton fields of Turkestan and Trans-Caucasia supplied the Russian factories with over 500 million lb. of raw cotton. The extent to which the Russian cotton industry expanded in the latter part of the nineteenth century may be seen from the fact that in 1891 Russia had six million cotton spindles which was more than any other country on the Continent. In 1906 the industry had 745 factories employing 388,000 operatives and turning out products valued at 589 million roubles.

*Linen.* Flax had long been grown in Russia on a large scale and in the 1880's the crop was over half the world crop. About one-third of the Russian crop was used at home and the rest was exported. Russian linens were of the coarse variety, the manufacture of sailcloth being of particular importance. The first modern factory was established in 1830 by the firm of C. Schoyz at Marimont near Warsaw and was later moved to Girardo. The earliest machines used in this establishment were those invented by Philippe de Girard who installed them himself. The Alexandrovsky linen mills near St. Petersburg were among the largest factories of their kind in the 1860's. Hemp was also grown in Russia and was used to manufacture ropes and sacks. Russia exported not only the raw materials but some manufactured linen and hempen products as well. But Russian hand-made linens could not compete successfully with the machine-made linens of Northern Ireland and Belgium and only the coarser Russian linens were successfully marketed abroad. A report on the London industrial exhibition of 1862 praised the high quality of the sailcloth shown by Baron Stieglitz's "famous establishment". "It is made both by hemp and flax material, in various qualities and of all numbers. The material is generally very good, the yarn well spun, carefully boiled or bleached, and the cloth well manufactured." In 1914 it was estimated that Russia produced 456,000 tons of flax and 217,000 tons of hemp a year. Modern linen factories had been established with the aid of foreign capital in the last quarter of the nineteenth century. The home market was virtually reserved to Russian manufacturers by a very high tariff.

*Wool Textiles.* Russia had far larger flocks of sheep than any other European country and the manufacture of cloth had been an industry of major importance since Peter the Great's reign. After the Napoleonic wars the output of the cloth workshops and factories increased rapidly so that by 1830 Russia had 390 woollen factories in which 67,000 workers were employed. The Polish rising of 1830 was followed by the transfer of a number of clothworks from Lodz to Russia and this improved the standards in the woollen industry. The manufacture of woollen cloths continued to expand and was stimulated in the middle of the nineteenth century by army orders during the Crimean war. Subsequently excellent progress was made except during the recession of 1880–87. Early in the twentieth century the woollen industry—with 700,000 spindles, 4,500 looms and 150,000 operatives—had an annual output valued at 160 million roubles. Moscow, St. Petersburg and Lodz were the most important centres of production. The Government helped the industry by imposing high duties on imported woollens and by ordering over 1·5 million yarns of coarse cloth every year for the army. The Russian factories still imported some fine wools (such as merino wool) and yarns. The value of these purchases from abroad was 37·3 million roubles in 1903. Despite the high tariff the importation of woollen piece goods rose from 3·5 million roubles a year in 1891–3 to 9·1 million roubles in 1903. The worsted branch of the industry was relatively new and had developed only after about 1880. It was largely in the hands of German and Austrian manufacturers who set up factories in the Lodz district.

*Iron.* The iron industry in Russia developed in the seventeenth century first at Tula and later in the Urals. In 1632 the Dutch merchant André Vinius secured a concession to establish ironworks near Tula where iron-ore, timber, and water power were available. Tula later became famous for its State small arms factory and for its many cutlery workshops. It was a blacksmith from Tula named Nikita Demidov who, in Peter the Great's reign, established a number of ironworks in the Ekaterinburg mining region of the Urals. Large supplies of timber (for charcoal) were at hand and waterwheels, erected on the main streams, worked the bellows and the hammers. In the summer the pig-iron was sent by water to Nizhny-Novgorod. The new mining enterprises in the Urals were placed under the general supervision of an expert from Saxony named Henning.

In the eighteenth century the iron industry of the Urals was one of the most important in Europe. Output of pig-iron was estimated at about 130,000 tons in 1790 at a time when Britain was producing only 68,000 tons. Heckscher points out that "for a short period towards the end of the eighteenth century, England even bought more iron from Russia than from Sweden, although total Swedish exports remained larger than the Russian". In the first half of the nineteenth century however the inventions which revolutionized the English iron and steel industry were not introduced into Russia. Several attempts were made to introduce coke smelting, puddling and rolling, the hot blast and later the converter and the open-hearth furnace but they all failed. Coking coal was not available in the Urals and it was almost impossible to teach serfs how to use new machines. Technical backwardness—which Samuel Bentham had noted on his travels in the 1780's—was still a characteristic of the mining industry of the Urals over a hundred years later.

In 1870 Russia produced only 350,000 tons of pig-iron. The industry in the Urals was still very backward and virtually nothing had been done to develop Russia's other ironfields. Iron had been discovered in the Donetz region towards the end of the eighteenth century. In 1797 furnaces were set up at Lugansk to smelt ore with coal brought from Lisichansk some fifty miles away. But little progress was made in the Donetz region at that time. The iron-ore had a low metallic content and contained impurities. Moreover the coal in the Donetz basin was difficult to mine as many of the seams were only eighteen inches thick. The rich iron-ore deposits of Krivoi-Rog (225 miles to the west of the Donetz region) had been examined by Le Play in 1837 but he had reported that they were too remote to be profitably exploited.

The establishment of a great modern iron industry in the Ukraine was largely the work of John Hughes and A. N. Pol. Hughes (born in 1814) had received his early training as a "practical mechanic" in the Cyfarthfa Iron Works. Eventually he migrated to London where he became manager at the works of the Millwall Iron and Shipbuilding Company. He invented a new type of armour-plating known as "Millwall Shield". In 1869 he formed the New Russia Company to establish an ironworks in the Donetz basin. He made an agreement with the Russian Government which granted him free land, a loan, a premium on the pig-iron he produced, an order from the State railways for rails, and a concession to build a railway from his works to Mariupol on the Sea of Azov. Hughes selected an excellent site for his works on the banks of the River Kalmius close to the rich seams of coal. He drew his iron-ore first from Mariupol and later from Krivoi-Rog. His first blast furnace was fired in January 1872.

To begin with Hughes employed skilled Welsh miners, furnacemen, and puddlers. John John of Dowlais who went to Russia in 1875 was Hughes's right-hand man for some years. Hughes died in 1889 and his four sons carried on the management of the plant. When Schulze-Gävernitz visited the works of the New Russia Company in 1893 four furnaces were in operation and another two were being erected. Some 6,000 men were employed and this number was soon increased to 8,000. The town of Hughesovka (or Yuzovka)[1] had grown up round Hughes's plant. The New Russia Company on several occasions declared a dividend of 100 per cent. At the same time that Hughes set up his first furnace the brothers Pastukhov established new ironworks at Sulinsk. They used anthracite to smelt their iron ore. After the establishment of these two plants by Hughes and Pastukhov no further progress was made in the Donetz basin until 1886.

In 1884 and 1887 the Russian Government substantially increased the import duty on iron products such as rails. In 1886 it was announced that no reduction in iron duties would be made in the next twelve years. This assurance attracted foreign capital to the Donetz basin. Mainly owing to the untiring efforts of A. N. Pol a railway was opened in 1886 which made it possible for high-grade iron-ore to be sent from Krivoi-Rog to the Donetz region. There was a great boom in the Donetz basin following the firing in 1887 of blast furnaces at the Alexandrovsky and Dneprovsky works. Thirteen great ironworks were set up in ten years, land values rocketed sky high, new townships sprang up overnight. Up-to-date equipment was installed in the new engineering plant. In 1896 for example the Alexandrovsky Company spent 1·3 million roubles on new equipment. Numerous small engineering works were established at this time in addition to the giant concerns. Over 100 such plants were reported to be in existence in the Alexandrovsky district in 1895.

The great new ironworks and engineering plants in the Ukraine were largely financed by foreign capital and relied upon big Government orders for rails and railway equipment. In 1901 Russia's pig-iron output amounted to 2·8 million tons of which nearly 1·5 million tons came from the Donetz basin. Russia now made more pig-iron than France and held fourth place among the iron-producing countries of the world. Lyashchenko observes that "the development of the iron and steel industry during the five-year period 1895–1900 resulted in a general doubling of production in the country as a whole, and an increase of between three and four times for the

[1] Now Stalino.

metallurgy of the south, as a result of which the south finally forced out of existence the old iron industry of the Urals".

*Engineering.* The origins of the Russian engineering industry may be traced back to the eighteenth century. It is stated that in 1717 Desaguliers set up a Newcomen engine in St. Petersburg to work a pump operating the fountains in the palace gardens. Subsequently the invention of Watt's steam engine aroused great interest in Russian official circles. Catherine II[1] persuaded Charles Gascoyne to settle in Russia and he was responsible for establishing an iron foundry at Olonets. In 1797 the Russian Government asked Boulton and Watt to supply the machinery to operate a mint. Russian mechanics were sent to Birmingham to learn how to use this machinery. One of them—named Deryabin—later became Director of Mints, Mines and Saltworks in Russia. Meanwhile an iron-founder named Charles Baird had established a private plant at St. Petersburg to construct steam engines (1790) and Gascoyne had set up State engineering works near St. Petersburg which later developed into the great establishments at Cronstadt and Izhora which supplied the varied needs of the army and navy. In 1805 the Alexandrovsky work were set up at St. Petersburg to make textile machinery. The were in charge of an Englishman named Wilson who had already established workshops in Moscow for the manufacture of agricultural implements. In 1825 the famous Alexandrovsky Crown Casting and Engineering Works were established in St. Petersburg. In 1838 the Swedish industrialist Immanuel Nobel set up an engineering plant in St. Petersburg and received some government orders for mines for the army and navy. His business prospered during the Crimean war but subsequently government orders fell off and in 1859 Immanuel Nobel abandoned the factory to his creditors and returned to Sweden. Machine building in Russia before 1850 "was chiefly developed and perfected at the Crown manufactories or where it was aided by subsidies and orders from the government".

It was not until the 1880's that the Russian engineering industry made substantial progress. By the end of the nineteenth century the industry was turning out looms and self-actor mules as well as machines for flour mills, sugar refineries and distilleries. Russia's railway workshops were capable of making 700 locomotives and 25,000 waggons a year. Cutlery was manufactured in small workshops at Tula and elsewhere. In 1897 Russia had 682 engineering plants in which 120,000 workers were employed. In 1902 an engineering cartel

[1] The oft-repeated story that Catherine II visited the Soho engineering plant is a myth. See S. J. Tomkireff, "The Empress Cathrine and Mathew Boulton" (*Times Literary Supplement*, December 22, 1950).

called *Prodameta* was established. It included thirty metallurgical enterprises making sheet iron, tyres, axles and other products—but not pig-iron. Many of the companies in the cartel were under French control and in 1910 a representative of the *Banque de l'Union Parisienne* was elected chairman of the cartel.

*Coal.* The expansion of the coal industry in Russia was slow. In western Europe the decline of the forests had encouraged the exploitation of all available resources of coal but Russia's timber supplies were so considerable that wood continued to be used on a large scale for heating, for power and for smelting iron. At the end of the nineteenth century it was estimated that 174 million tons of wood a year were being consumed as fuel by factories and private households. Moreover communications in Russia were poor and it was difficult to move so heavy and bulky a commodity as coal.

Russia's output of coal rose from 156,000 tons in 1855 to 29·1 million tons in 1913. The main deposits lay in the Donetz basin, the Moscow region, the Urals, Poland and Siberia. Peter the Great had been shown a piece of coal from the Donetz basin and had declared that this mineral would be useful to his descendants. Some coal was worked in the area in 1789 but it was about a hundred years later before mining on a large scale was undertaken. Then mining companies supported by Belgian and French capital were founded and by 1901 output had increased to eleven million tons. In 1904 eighteen firms in the Donetz basin joined a trust (called *Produgol*) which controlled sixty per cent of Russia's output. Much of the Donetz coal was coked and was used for smelting iron. The anthracite deposits of the region were neglected in the early twentieth century. The coalfield in Poland—an extension of the coalfield of Upper Silesia—produced four million tons of coal in 1901. In the Urals about three-quarters of the coal was used by the railways. When the Trans-Siberian Railway was built in the 1890's it became possible to exploit some of Siberia's vast deposits of coal. The most important were in the great Kuznetz coalfield in which coal was mined from 1898 onwards.

*Oil.* The petroleum industry "affords perhaps the most remarkable instance in Russia of the rapid rise of a new trade to a position of world-wide importance". The exploitation of the Baku oil wells began in the 1860's on a small scale with primitive equipment. The oil was obtained from shallow wells dug by hand and was carried away in leather bottles. It was then transported in skins or barrels which were loaded on carts or camels. In 1873 the Swedish industrialist Robert Nobel visited Baku and realized the potentialities of the oilfield. With his brother Ludvig he founded a company to exploit oil by improved methods. Steam engines were used to bore new wells. Refineries were set up in the "Black Town" district of Baku to distil the crude oil. In 1883 Messrs Nobel erected a factory to make the sulphuric acid which they used in their oil refineries. After various products had been distilled—kerosene, paraffin, lubricating oils and so forth—the residue (*ostatki*) was used as a coal substitute to drive locomotives and marine engines. In 1890 Messrs Nobel produced nearly 18 million puds of various petroleum products. At that time most of the steamers on the Caspian and the Volga used *ostatki* fuel.

Other oil prospectors followed the Nobel brothers and from the 1880's onwards the output of crude oil rapidly increased. The production of Russia's oil wells (mainly at Baku and Grozny) rose from 88,000 barrels (of 42 gallons) in 1868 to nearly 73 million barrels in 1916. The completion in 1883 of the construction of the Trans-Caucasian Railway from Baku to Tiflis and Batum and the building of the North Caucasus Railway facilitated the transport of oil. In 1871 the Astrakhan merchants Artemjeff, Ragosin and Schipoff began to transport crude oil and *ostatki* on the Caspian Sea and the River Volga in the holds of wooden sailing barques. But oil was lost since it penetrated the planks of the ships and there were a number of fires. To improve the transport of carrying oil by water Messrs Nobel ordered a vessel called the *Zoroaster* from the Lindholmen-Motala shipbuilding yard in Sweden. This oil-burning vessel was launched in 1878 and plied on the Caspian. It could carry about 250 tons of kerosene in 21 vertical iron cylinder tanks. Subsequently the tanks were removed and the kerosone was carried in the hold. In the early 1880's Messrs Nobel had a dozen tank-steamers plying regularly between Baku and Astrakhan. The round trip took six days. The largest of these vessels had a capacity of about 800 tons and their holds were lined with cement. Oil products were taken up the River Volga in Messrs Nobel's shallow-draught barges. Messrs Nobel were also the first firm to use tank-waggons instead of barrels to convey oil products by rail. In 1889 the company built a pipe line from Mikhailovo to Kvirila. Subsequently a pipe line from the Caspian to the Black Sea was laid alongside the Trans-Caucasian Railway. By 1914 the Russian oil industry had, to a considerable extent, fallen under the domination of four competing firms in which foreign shareholders had a controlling interest. Heavy royalties were levied by the Government on the output of crude oil. The development of the industry was marred by unsatisfactory labour relations. The condition of the workers in the oilfield was far from satisfactory. Strikes, violence, and arson were by no means uncommon.

*Sugar*. In the nineteenth century the refining of home-grown beet sugar expanded owing to the introduction of technical improvements in the factories. After about 1880 it was possible not only to meet the demands of the Russian consumer but also to develop a considerable export trade as well. In 1901 Russia had 1·3 million acres of land under sugar-beet cultivation. There were 277 refineries with an output of 880,000 tons a year. A trust (*normirovka*) controlled nearly the whole output of the industry. After 1895 the manufacture of sugar was subject to strict State regulation. The Government decided how much sugar should be sold in the home market, how much should be sold abroad, and how much should be put in reserve. The price in the home market was fixed by the State.

*Timber*. Russia's vast timber resources were the basis of a great export trade—valued at nearly 57 million roubles in 1901—and also provided the raw materials for various industries. At the beginning of the twentieth century Russia had over 1,300 sawmills and over 300 furniture factories. To a considerable extent, however, the woodworking industry was still in the hands of village craftsmen. Woodpulp was used to make paper and cardboard. The value of the products of the paper trade were valued at over 45 million roubles in 1897.

*The Industrial Economy*. Although by 1914 Russia had not become industrialized to the same extent as Germany or the United States there were clear signs that the manufacturing side of the economy was expanding rapidly. Important concentrations of industry were to be found in the Donetz basin, in St. Petersburg, at Baku and in the provinces of Moscow, Vladimir and Nizhny - Novgorod. Though the Russian *kustar* industries survived to a much greater extent than the craft industries of western Europe the large-scale factory industries were growing at the expense of the village workshops. The number of steam engines installed in Russian industrial plants was increasing year by year. The capacity of the steam engines in the factories rose from 114,977 horsepower in 1878 to 345,209 horsepower in 1892. Joint-stock companies, trusts and combines were becoming more and more important. The urban population of European Russia was nearly doubled between 1863 and 1897 while the rural population was increased by just under fifty per cent. Moreover the large industrial and commercial centres were expanding more rapidly than the smaller towns. In eleven years (1885-97) about 2·5 million persons migrated from the countryside to the towns.

If the Russian economy was still backward in some respects it was also true that vigorous State action, foreign capital and foreign machinery had given Russia a powerful impetus on the road to industrialization. In his great work on *The Development of Capitalism in Russia* (1899) Lenin wrote: "As to whether the development of capitalism in Russia is slow or rapid, it all depends on what we compare this development with. If we compare the pre-capitalized epoch in Russia with the capitalist . . . the development of social economy under capitalism must be considered extremely rapid. If, however, we compare the present rapidity of development with that which could be achieved with the modern level of technique and culture as it is in general, the present rate of development of capitalism in Russia really must be considered slow."

The development of modern manufactures in Russia by no means proceeded at a uniform pace in Russia in the nineteenth century. Whether one examines the economy as a whole or particular branches of industry, sudden forward movements are to be found. The expansion of calico printing at Ivanovo after 1812, the growth of Knoop's cotton mills in the 1850's and 1860's, the sudden rise of the iron industry in the Donetz basin and of the oil industry in Baku, the railway boom of the 1880's, and the remarkable increase in industrial output between 1906 and 1914 arc examples of "the essential bumpiness and jerkiness" of the process of industrialization in Russia.

### (iii) Communications

The provision of an efficient system of communications in Russia was essential if modern industries were to develop. Long before the rise of great industries or the building of railways there had been a considerable volume of traffic on the caravan routes and on the great rivers. Foreign travellers were astonished at the extent of the business transacted at the Russian fairs where goods were displayed which had obviously been transported for many hundreds of miles.

*Fairs.* Freiherr von Haxthausen visited the Nizhny-Novgorod fair in 1843. He described the bazaar built of stone which had over 2,500 stalls. Here a great variety of foodstuffs and manufactured products were offered for sale—tea, tobacco, cottons, woollens, silks, furniture, clocks and many more. Haxthausen saw other sections of the fair situated by the River Oka (where the products of the iron industry were displayed) and the River Volga (where some 40,000 chests of tea were stored). A street running to the bridge over the River Oka was devoted to retail trade. A large number of stalls were erected and peasants came long distances to buy sheepskins, fur caps, and a great variety of articles of domestic manufacture.

In addition to the transport of goods over long distances to the fairs there was also—in European Russia—an exchange of grain and timber products between the black-earth regions of the south and the forest region of the centre. The grain was moved to the north by roads and inland waterways while the products of the woodworking industry were moved to the south.

*Roads*. The highways and rivers were quite inadequate to carry this traffic. Mackenzie Wallace, who lived in Russia between 1870 and 1876, stated that roads "are nearly all of the unmade natural kind and are so conservative in their nature that they have at the present day the same appearance that they had many years ago. The only perceptible change that takes place in them during a series of generations is that the ruts shift their position." He explained that "in many regions it is difficult, or practically impossible, to procure in sufficient quantity stone of any kind and especially hard stone fit for roadmaking. Besides this, when roads are made, the severity of the climate renders it difficult to keep them in good repair." And the bridges were so unsafe that "the cautious driver will generally prefer to take to the water, if there is a ford within reasonable distance". In the winter sleighs could travel smoothly over the frozen snow but in the spring and autumn many roads were so deep in mud that it was impossible to use them.

*Rivers*. Russia had many long waterways. In European Russia the rivers rise in the centre of the country and flow to the Baltic, the White Sea, the Black Sea and the Caspian. Unfortunately their sources are generally not in mountains but in lakes or swamps and so the rivers are often slow-moving. The water level is very irregular. There are floods in the spring when the snows melt while in the summer navigation may be difficult because the water-level is so low. Rivers and seaports are frozen in the winter and cannot be used. Mackenzie Wallace, describing the Russia of the 1870's, stated that the River Don "is extremely shallow and the sandbanks are continually shifting, so that many times in the course of the day the steamer runs aground". Geoffrey Drage, writing at the beginning of the twentieth century, observed that Odessa harbour had "many grave defects". There had been numerous complaints "of the delay caused by the lack of proper facilities for the handling of grain and other cargoes".

*Railways*. Russia's railways were unevenly distributed over the country. In 1914 the network was largely concentrated in the area between the Baltic and the Black Sea and between the Vistula and the Volga. East of the great arc of the Volga only a few lines—such as the Trans-Caspian, the Orenburg–Tashkent, and the Trans-Siberian railways—served the vast regions between the Volga and the Urals and beyond to central Asia and the Pacific.

Strategic, political and economic factors all influenced the routes chosen for the main lines. Some lines in both European and Asiatic Russia were built purely for strategic reasons to enable reserves to be sent to distant frontiers in the event of war. The railways beyond the Caucasus and east of the Caspian were built to enable the central government to control remote "colonial" regions. Lyashchenko suggests that a number of the lines in European Russia were constructed to link districts which produced grain with urban regions in which the grain was consumed. And subsequently these lines were extended to ports, such as Odessa, from which cereals were exported.

The first railway in Russia, which was constructed by a private company, was a short line from St. Petersburg to the Czar's summer palace at Tsarskoe-Selo. This line was begun in 1836 and was opened in 1838. A little later the Government built State lines between Warsaw and Cracow and between St. Petersburg and Moscow. Both were opened in 1851. An American company was allowed to take over the Alexandrovsky Crown Casting and Engineering Works at St. Petersburg so as to build rolling stock for the railways. This company constructed 200 locomotives, 250 passenger coaches and 2,700 goods waggons.

During the Crimean war Russia's military operations were hampered because there was no railway between Moscow and the Black Sea. After the war the Great Russian Railway Company (1857) received a concession to operate the Nicholas (St. Petersburg–Moscow) Railway, to complete the St. Petersburg–Warsaw railway with an extension to the frontier of Prussia and to construct lines from Moscow to Nizhny-Novgorod, from Moscow to Odessa and from Archangel to Libau. Much of the capital was raised abroad. The shareholders included Baring Brothers (London), Hope & Co. (Amsterdam), Mendelssohn & Co. (Berlin), the Pereire brothers (Paris), B. L. Fould and Fould-Oppenheim (Paris) and Hottinguer & Co. (Paris). Nine of the nineteen directors were foreigners. French companies constructed the bridges required on the new lines and supplied locomotives and rolling stock. The Great Russian Railway Company has been described as "by far the largest enterprise of its nature which had been undertaken in Europe to that date". In 1861, however, the Russian Government revoked the concession for two of the lines not yet completed and increased the number of Russian directors. The first Russian railway boom came a few years later. In ten years (1868–78) iron rails to the value of 150 million roubles were imported and the Government gave a subsidy to John Hughes to enable him to erect blast furnaces and engineering works for the manufacture of rails.

In the early 1870's lines radiated from Moscow to St. Petersburg, Warsaw, Nizhny-Novgorod, Kiev, Kharkov, Odessa and Rostov on Don. The centre of the country was linked with western Europe, the Baltic and the Black Sea. East of the Volga a line ran from Samara to Orenburg; south of the Caucasus a railway linked Poti and Tiflis; while the mines of the Urals were served by lines from Ekaterinburg to Perm and Berezniaki.

Most of these lines were operated by joint-stock companies which had received government assistance in various ways. The State generally guaranteed the interest on their shares and sometimes lent money to the railways or held blocks of their shares. A government committee reported in 1876 that many lines were being mismanaged and were a drain upon the national finances. The State itself owned about 730 miles of railways in 1870 and shortly afterwards it virtually assumed control over the Great Russian Railway Company.

Soon afterwards the Government decided to build a State line to link the high-grade Krivoi-Rog iron-ore deposits with the coal-measures of the Donetz basin. But the project was postponed owing to the outbreak of the Russo-Turkish war. In this campaign the Odessa Railway Company transported Russian troops to the front. Sergius Witte (the future Finance Minister) was manager of the line at that time.

After the Russo-Turkish war several lines were built and operated by the State. They included the Ekaterinoslav, the Trans-Caucasian, and the Trans-Caspian lines. The Ekaterinoslav railway, opened in 1886, linked Krivoi-Rog and the Donetz basin. The Trans-Caucasian railway (1883) stimulated the development of the Baku oil wells. The construction of the first section of the Trans-Caspian railway (1886) promoted the pacification and economic expansion of recently conquered territories in central Asia. This line ran from Krasnovodsk to Merv (487 miles). Between 1886 and 1888 the line was extended nearly 400 miles to Samarkand. Between 1870 and 1887 the length of Russia's railways was increased from 7,100 miles to 18,380 miles. By 1886 the State was operating 2,250 miles of nationalized lines. Moreover several amalgamations of private lines—such as the South Western Railway Company—took place at this time. Count Witte in his memoirs called the early 1880's "the golden age of private railway construction. It witnessed the growth of huge fortunes in the hands of several railroad kings" Railway construction in this period gave a vigorous impetus to the industrial economy. Gerschenkron considers that Russia's "greatest industrial upswing came when—from the middle of the 1880's on—the railroad building of the State assumed unprecedented proportions and became the main lever of the rapid industrialization policy". In 1887, for example, new blast furnaces were fired at the Alexandrovsk and Dneprovsky works in the Ukraine in order to meet the greatly increased demand for rails.

Between 1893 and 1903 Count Witte, Minister of Finance, showed great energy in pushing ahead with schemes for constructing new railways. About one-third of Russia's railway network was constructed in this period. The Trans-Caspian Railway was completed, and the Trans-Siberian Railway was built. The section of the Trans-Caspian Railway which ran from Samarkand to Tashkent and Andijan (335 miles) was constructed between 1896 and 1899. The length of the whole railway—including the Merv-Kushk branch line to the frontier of Afghanistan—was 1,374 miles. Although originally built for military and political purposes this line fostered the economic development of Turkestan. Raw cotton, wool and silk from Turkestan were now sent to the textile manufacturing districts of European Russia by rail instead of by caravan.

The building of the Trans-Siberian Railway began in 1891. Construction commenced at Chelyabinsk on the eastern side of the Urals. Chelyabinsk was the terminus of a main line to Samara, Moscow and St. Petersburg and of a railway which served the mining district of Ekaterinburg. From Chelyabinsk the Trans-Siberian Railway ran to Omsk, Irkutsk and Stretnesk on the River Shilka. At Kaidalovo (near Stretnesk) the line was joined by the Chinese Eastern Railway which ran through the Chinese province of Manchuria to Harbin. From Harbin one branch ran to the Russian port of Vladivostok and another ran to Port Arthur which had been leased by Russia in 1894. The Trans-Siberian Railway reached Omsk in December 1895 and Sretensk in 1901 while the first section of the line through Manchuria—built by Russian engineers with Chinese labour—was completed in 1902. The section of the Trans-Siberian Railway which ran round the southern end of Lake Baikal was opened in 1905.

The Russo-Japanese war broke out in 1905 and Port Arthur fell into Japanese hands. Russia lost her privileged position in Manchuria. So the Russians built a new railway in their own territory from Sretensk along the Amur valley to the Khabarovsk-

Vladivostok railway. This line was completed in 1916. Only then was the great railway from the Baltic to the Pacific completely under Russian control.

Another important Russian railway constructed in the early twentieth century was the Orenburg–Tashkent line (1904) which linked the Trans-Caspian and the Trans-Siberian railways.

Between 1890 and 1913 many lines were nationalized and the length of the railway network was increased by 19,500 miles. But in relation to the area and the population of Russia the railway network was still smaller than those of Britain, Germany or the United States. The great lines beyond the Urals had been expensive to build but did not immediately attract sufficient traffic to make a profit. Lines had been built to satisfy future rather than existing needs. Count Witte claimed that he had put forward various proposals to construct lines which would have fostered the economic expansion of the country but his suggestions had met with strenuous opposition from the Minister of War who wanted to build strategic lines for military purposes. And such lines were sometimes approved by the Government despite Witte's recommendations to the contrary.

In 1912 a committee of the third Duma criticized both the construction and the running of nationalized and private railways. Examples were given of financial irregularities, wastefulness and inefficiency. Just before the first World War the management of the Russian railways was improving. Between 1908 and 1912 the revenue from the nationalized lines rose from 512 million roubles to 742 million roubles although there was only a small increase in running expenses.

Even in the railway age vast quantities of goods were still conveyed by road. In 1894, for example, over 1·5 million tons of grain reached the Baltic ports by road.

### (iv) Finance and Capital

Towards the end of the nineteenth century, when great efforts were being made to graft modern industries upon a traditionally agrarian country, Russia faced several serious economic problems. The rural economy was breaking down since many of the landed gentry could not adjust the management of their estates to the new situation brought about by the emancipation of the serfs. The rural population was growing so rapidly that the peasants were continually trying to secure more land. At the same time the Government was borrowing large sums of money from abroad to foster industrialization in various ways and the national debt steadily increased.

*Gold Standard.* The existence of a depreciated and fluctuating currency seriously hampered economic progress. Between 1843 and 1856 a silver standard had been in operation and the paper rouble had maintained its value[1]. Three and a half paper roubles could be exchanged for one silver rouble. But convertibility ceased after the Crimean war and the value of the paper rouble fluctuated on the foreign exchanges. A budget deficit, a rise in the national debt, a failure of the harvest, or an excess of imports over exports might lead to a loss of confidence in the Russian currency and this would cause the rouble to decline in value on foreign exchanges. There was, for example, a sharp fall in the value of the paper rouble in 1882. The activities of speculators aggravated these fluctuations of the exchange rate. In London the value of the rouble in February, September and December 1888 was 1s. 7d., 2s. 7d., and 1s. 9d.

By the 1880's it was becoming clear that a solution to the problem could be found only in a return to convertibility and the establishment of a stable silver or gold rouble. Strong arguments could be advanced in favour of the latter. First, there had been a marked depreciation in the value of silver in the 1870's. Secondly, both Britain and Germany had a gold standard and the volume of Russia's trade with those two countries was far greater than her trade with any other states.

Vishnegradsky (Minister of Finance, 1887–92) exercised strict economy in Government spending and balanced the budget. He raised the gold stocks in the Treasury from 55 to 236 million roubles and slightly reduced the volume of paper money in circulation. Count Witte (Minister of Finance, 1893–1903) established the gold standard. First he stopped the speculation in paper roubles on the Berlin exchange. In January 1893 he forbade Russian bankers to sell paper roubles to foreign firms and in the following March an export duty was placed on paper roubles. Then he instructed the Berlin banking house of Mendelssohn to buy paper roubles on behalf of the Russian Government. In October 1894 the speculators who had agreed to deliver paper roubles to Mendelssohn at the rate of 2·2 marks per rouble discovered that no roubles were available. They appealed to Witte to allow paper roubles to be sent to Germany so that they could fulfil their obligations to Mendelssohn. Witte

[1] An Imperial Edict of July 1, 1839—printed in Tooke and Newmarch *A History of Prices*, Vol. IV (edition of 1928), pp. 454–7—provided for the conversion of bank *assignats* to notes payable on demand in silver roubles. The new arrangement came into operation in 1843.

allowed three million notes to be transferred to Berlin but the speculators had to pay 2·34 marks per rouble for them. They lost 14 pfennigs on every paper rouble which they sold to Mendelssohn. The speculators had burned their fingers badly and they now left the Russian paper rouble severely alone. After 1894 Count Witte was able to keep the value of the paper rouble steady on the foreign exchanges. In 1895 transactions in gold and paper roubles were allowed at the ratio of 1·5 paper roubles to one gold rouble.

In 1897 Russia adopted the gold standard. The gold rouble was devalued so as to equal the paper rouble in value. New gold coins of ten, seven and a half and five roubles were minted. Convertibility between gold coins and bank notes was now possible.

*Foreign Loans.* Count Witte's attempt to establish Russia's national finances on a sound basis were less successful than his work in stabilizing the currency. In his memoirs Witte claimed that when he was Finance Minister he always balanced the budget. It is true that increased taxation and other measures greatly improved the state of the national finances in the 1890's. But Witte's surpluses were sometimes secured by a skilful adjustment of the ordinary and extraordinary budgets or by regarding borrowed money as income. In 1902, for example, Witte admitted that his "free balance" for that year included the proceeds of a loan of 127 million roubles.

The national debt increased rapidly after the Crimean war, numerous government loans being raised to finance railway construction. Between 1870 and 1887 much German capital was invested in Russian State loans and industrial securities. In 1884 the Prussian Overseas Trading Corporation (*Seehandlung*) received subscriptions for a large Russian loan. Two years later however German bankers began to doubt whether their money was safe in Russia. A group of German banks failed to agree with the Russian Government on plans for a conversion scheme. In 1887 the *Kreuzzeitung* declared that German investors owned Russian securities to the value of 2,500 million roubles—perhaps an overestimate—and articles appeared in the German press casting doubts upon the solvency of the Russian State. German investors were strongly advised to sell their shares in Russian companies and many did so at a considerable sacrifice.

In November 1887 Bismarck instructed the Reichsbank not to accept Russian bonds as security for loans. French investors, encouraged by their Government, stepped into the breach. They subscribed to loans raised by the Russian Government, municipalities and railways and they also purchased shares of joint-stock companies. By 1914 the French had invested over 12,000 million francs in

Russian securities—mostly bonds issued or guaranteed by the Russian Government. Some of this money had been spent on arms purchased from Schneider and other French armament firms. French investments in joint-stock companies—though only a very small part of total French investments in Russia—represented about one-third of foreign investments in this type of security. Pasvolsky and Moulton estimate that in 1917 Czarist Russia's foreign indebtedness amounted to nearly 14,000 million roubles. This included government and municipal loans raised abroad before 1914, foreign loans raised during the first World War, and foreign corporate and debenture capital directly invested in Russian industry.

*Banks.* The development of banking and credit facilities was essential if an industrial economy were to be established in Russia. Since Peter the Great's reign there had been a public sector of the economy financed and managed by the Government. Witte had nationalized many railways and had brought the vodka trade under Government control. For over two hundred years the State had fostered industrialization by means of subsidies, loans and tax exemptions. But by 1900 the methods of the age of mercantilism were out of date and Russian entrepreneurs needed the support of credit banks of the type that had flourished in France and Germany for many years. Private enterprise was slow to establish institutions of this kind and the State itself became the leading banker and money-lender in Russia.

The most important Government financial institutions were the Imperial Bank of Russia, the Nobles Land Bank, the Peasants Land Bank, and the State Savings Bank. The Bank of Russia had been established in 1860. It had absorbed the Loan Bank, the Deposit Bank and the Boards of Public Utility. The Bank of Russia was not an independent institution but was subordinate to the Ministry of Finance. Its initial capital of 15 million roubles was increased to 25 million roubles in 1876 and to 50 million roubles in 1894. The deposits made by the Government were a far higher proportion— over two-thirds in 1899—of the total deposits than was customary in other central banks. After the adoption of the gold standard the Bank of Russia was authorized to issue notes on its own account and not merely on behalf of the Treasury.

The Bank of Russia gained the confidence of private banks and merchants and gradually "consolidated its position as the central reservoir of the internal money market". It had 982 branches in 1914. The Bank's loans to industry amounted to over 40 million roubles in 1901. Count Witte complained that much of this money was not lent to genuine industrialists but found its way into the pockets of "members of the court camarilla and their friends". By means of industrial loans the Bank of Russia secured for itself an increasing influence over the production of coal, iron and sugar.

Agriculture was assisted by the Nobles Land Bank and by the Peasants Bank. The former was established in 1885 and lent money on mortgage to the owners of large estates. It absorbed the Mutual Land Loan Society. The object of the Nobles Land Bank was to help landowners to keep their estates intact despite the financial difficulties caused by the fall in grain prices in the 1880's. Nevertheless the amount of land held by the gentry declined from 196 million acres in 1877 to 138 million acres in 1907.

The Peasants Land Bank was set up in 1882 with the twofold object of facilitating the transition from communal to individual farming and of enabling peasants—whose numbers were increasing rapidly—to increase the size of their holdings. The second object to some extent clashed with the policy of the Nobles Land Bank which hoped to arrest the decline of large estates owing to sales of land to the peasants. At first virtually all the loans granted by the Peasants Land Bank were made to village communes or to associations of peasants. Gradually however more and more loans were made to individual peasants. Critics of the Peasants Bank alleged that its operations caused a general rise in land values and favoured the prosperous *kulak* rather than the average peasant. The loans made to peasants were on a much smaller scale than those made to the landed gentry. In 1900 the total advances made by the Nobles Land Bank (and the Mutual Land Loan Society) amounted to over 660 million roubles compared with loans of 170 million roubles made by the Peasants Land Bank. Moreover the Peasants Bank charged between six and six and a half per cent for loans while the Nobles Bank charged only five per cent.

The earliest State savings banks were established under a law of 1862 but it was not until 1895 that new regulations simplified the opening of such banks and led to an increase in their numbers. There were 8,000 State savings banks (excluding savings groups in schools) in 1912. Various forms of life insurance were handled by these banks after 1905. The savings banks were more firmly established in the urban than in the rural districts. In 1914 seventy per cent of the savings books were held by people who lived in towns. Deposits were invested in Government loans, in railway loans, and in mortgage deeds held by the Nobles Land Bank. After 1910 twenty million roubles a year were advanced by the State savings banks which lent money to peasants and to co-operative societies.

There were also public banks called Social Credit Institutions

230

which were established by local authorities such as municipalities and county councils (*zemstvos*). Their main function was to discount bills but they also granted loans of the security of real estate in the urban districts. Other public financial institutions in this group were the municipal loan offices, village savings banks, Petty Credit Institutions and various local banks which catered for the needs of particular classes such as the landed gentry or the merchants.

There were forty-seven joint-stock banks in Russia on the eve of the first World War. Most of their operations consisted of discounting commercial bills. In view of the substantial loans granted to manufacturers by the Bank of Russia and other State institutions the joint-stock banks played a less important role than similar institutions in France and Germany in promoting new industrial enterprises.

## (v) The Industrial Workers

The social discontent in Russia which culminated in the risings of 1905 and the revolution of 1917 was due to the failure of the Czarist régime to solve the political and economic problems that faced agriculture and industry after the emancipation of the serfs. The great landed proprietors no longer owned any serfs but they retained their position as the most powerful social class in the country. Their economic position, however, was weakened. Although the serfs were freed on financial terms which were very favourable to their former owners, the years that followed the Edict of Emancipation brought no prosperity to the aristocracy. Many of the nobles realized that the management of their estates should be radically changed. The old subsistence economy was out of date and farming for the urban and the export markets should have taken its place. The change might have been made if the nobles had used wisely the large sums of money which they received in the period following emancipation. In thirty years they were paid 870 million roubles by the Government in the form of manumission loans and 174 million roubles by the former serfs as "premiums". By 1900 the landed gentry had borrowed over 660 million roubles from the Nobles Land Bank. At the same time they were raising short-term loans every year from the Bank of Russia and from private banks on the security of grain which had not yet been harvested. Some of this money was invested in the land and stimulated improvements in farming technique. But many of the nobles used funds raised in this way to pay off old debts or to maintain traditional living standards. Although there was some expansion in the volume of output on some of the great estates, productivity did not increase quickly enough to prevent a continual decline in the economic position of the aristocracy. The traditions and habits of many of the nobles made it extremely difficult for them to adjust themselves to a new situation and to manage their estates in a new way. And progressive landed proprietors who engaged competent estate managers frequently found that the innate conservatism of the peasants made it virtually impossible to change farming methods or to introduce new machines. An efficient German farm manager on a Russian estate told Mackenzie Wallace in the early 1870's: "The peasants have not been improved by liberty. They now work less and drink more than they did in the times of serfage, and if you say a word to them they'll go away and not work for you at all . . . They let their cattle wander into our fields and never lose an opportunity of stealing firewood from the forest." In thirty years (1877–1907) the amount of land held by the nobles declined by nearly thirty per cent. By 1914 many of the great estates were heavily mortgaged and their owners were up to their ears in debt.

The misfortunes of the landed gentry brought no comfort to the peasants who had troubles enough of their own. The Edict of Emancipation ended the status of serfdom but it did not turn the serf into a free man. Each former serf household was required to accept a plot of land and to pay for it. The peasants were often dissatisfied with the small holdings allocated to them since the land they received might be poor in quality or might lack access to water-courses, pasture or woodlands. Some redemption payments were not related to the value of the land but were assessed on the basis of annual *obrok* payments formerly made by certain serfs instead of working on the estate of the lord of the manor. High redemption charges might be made for relatively poor land because the peasant had formerly paid a high *obrok*—and the money came from the part-time industrial earnings of the peasant. Although they were no longer serfs the peasants were restricted in various ways by the household, by the village community (*mir*) and by the bureaucracy.

Peasants had to find money for redemption payments and for national and local taxes. At the same time the cost of living rose owing to the imposition of higher taxes upon a variety of products such as vodka, sugar, and matches. Moreover the rural population was increasing steadily so that more mouths had to be fed from the same land. It was imperative for the peasants to increase their incomes. This could have been achieved by increasing the productivity of the land. The size of the average Russian small holding was much larger than that farmed by the French peasant and if properly cultivated would have yielded increased crops. Changes which were urgently needed included the consolidation of strips, improved crop rotation, the use of better implements and machines, and the introduction of artificial fertilizers. But the peasants were often illiterate and backward; their farming technique was controlled by the village community; and they often lacked the stimulus of an adjacent urban market. Some enterprising peasants—particularly those who accumulated savings by part-time industrial work—gradually increased the size of their holdings. Some became full-time craftsmen instead of part-time craftsmen and so promoted the expansion of *kustar* industries which occurred after the emancipation of the serfs. Others gave up the struggle and either migrated to the factories in the towns or sought their fortunes on the farm lands of the Siberian steppes. Other sank into the position of share-croppers or agricultural labourers.

The grievances of the peasants led to serious outbreaks of violence. In 1902 granaries were looted in the Ukraine. In 1905 there was widespread unrest. Estates were robbed; manor houses were sacked; barns were burned; and timber was stolen. Peasants defaulted on rent and tax payments and refused to work on the great estates. In November an organization called the Peasants' Union held a congress in Moscow. Some speakers condemned violence and favoured demands for political reforms. Eventually the army aided by reactionary free corps (the Black Hundreds) restored order by the most brutal methods imaginable.

It was not only the peasants who revolted in 1905. The factory proletariat also staged demonstrations and embarked upon strikes which culminated in violence. For a long time the peasants had no working-class allies in the towns. From the 1880's however the rapid expansion of great industrial regions led to the growth of an urban proletariat. Peasants and farm labourers scattered in thousands of villages throughout the length and breadth of Russia were in no position to organize themselves against those whom they regarded as their oppressors. But the factory workers of the industrial regions were able to act in concert against their employers. No ban on trade unions or prohibition of public meetings could prevent miners or factory workers from striking in an attempt to secure better wages or shorters hours of work.

When factories with power-driven machines were set up in Russia the workers complained of long hours, low wages, the truck system and harsh discipline. In 1844 an outbreak of violence in a spinning mill near Moscow caused the Government to order an investigation into the conditions of work in the Moscow factories. It was found that over 2,000 children were employed in twenty-three cotton spinning mills. The factories worked round the clock and children were employed on night shifts. An edict of 1845 forbade night work for children under the age of twelve but it was a dead letter from the first. In the same year industrial strikes were forbidden by the Penal Code.

The growth of manufactures in the middle of the nineteenth century—particularly Knoop's cotton-spinning mills—was accompanied by some expansion of the labour force and an increase in the social evils associated with industrialization. In 1859 an official commission was appointed, with Stackelberg as chairman, to consider whether any regulation of factory work was desirable. The commission recommended that in both factories and workshops young persons (aged twelve to eighteen) should not be employed at night and should work for no more than ten hours a day. Factory inspectors should be appointed to enforce the law. It was also suggested that conciliation councils, modelled on the French *conseils des prud'hommes*, should be set up.

The emancipation of the serfs in 1861 made available a large reserve of cheap labour for the factories and this, in due course, stimulated industrial expansion. But there was no improvement in the condition of the miners and factory operatives. Karl Marx, writing in 1867, declared that in Russia "the horrors of the early days of the British factory system, are still in full bloom".

The reforms of Alexander II which followed the abolition of serfdom—the reoganization of the judicial system, local government and education—unfortunately did not include legislation to improve the condition of the factory workers. Nothing came of Stackelberg's proposals owing to the implacable hostility of the Moscow industrialists. The factories in the Moscow region drew their operatives from a relatively densely populated agricultural district. Their labour turnover was high and their workers were often incompetent, but they put up with these drawbacks because they paid very low wages. By exploiting cheap labour—including the labour of women and children—the Moscow industrialists could compete with the more efficient factories of St. Petersburg. The manufacturers of the St. Petersburg region, on the other hand, were in a different position. They had no large agricultural population from which to draw cheap labour. Their workers came from more distant regions. Consequently they had to pay higher wages. But they kept their workers for longer periods and they secured a more efficient service from their operatives. The St. Petersburg employers supported proposals for factory reform which might deprive their Moscow rivals of the advantages gained by employing very cheap labour.

In the 1870's many factory workers were grossly exploited by their employers and were not protected by the State in any way. Hours of work for men, women and children amounted to twelve or fourteen a day. Night shifts were common. The sanitary condition of many factories was disgraceful. Dust in the textile mills and noxious vapours in chemical works were injurious to health. It was rare for dangerous machinery to be fenced. Average wages were about 14 roubles a month for men, 10 for women and 7 for children. In the St. Petersburg region wages were higher. At the State munitions plant at Sestroretsk skilled men could earn between 25 and 100 roubles a month. In the Urals wages were exceptionally low but the miners and ironworkers of that region were generally also smallholders who enjoyed the use of arable land, meadows and woodlands either free or at a nominal rent. Wages in many Russian factories were reduced by arbitrary fines and sometimes also by forcing workers to shop at the employer's store where high prices were charged. It was not uncommon for workers to live in "factory barracks" provided by the employer. The sleeping arrangements were often extremely unsatisfactory since workers of all ages and both sexes might be herded together in one dormitory.

In the 1870's two movements began which had important consequences. The early Socialists—the Narodniks (or Popularists)—were actively engaged in propaganda against the existing régime. They were middle-class intellectuals who believed that since industrial capitalism had made little progress in the Czar's dominions a strictly Marxist policy would not be appropriate. They believed that a special brand of Russian Socialism could be achieved if the village community (*mir*) owned the land and if self-governing workshops (*artels*) were responsible for industrial production. The attempt of the Narodniks to spread their views among the peasants failed because so few villagers had the slightest idea as to what they were talking about. Eventually many of the Narodnik leaders were rounded up and exiled to Siberia. Some of the survivors formed a secret nihilist society which was responsible for the assassination of Alexander II in 1881. Soon afterwards the arguments of the Narodniks were undermined by the Socialist writer Plekhanov whose *Socialism and the Political Struggle* appeared in 1883.

The second movement of the 1870's was that of the industrial workers. They formed organizations such as the South Russian Workers' Union of Odessa (1875) and the Northern Union of Russian Workers of St. Petersburg (1878) to protect their interests but both these associations were soon broken up by the police. There was a demonstration of workers and students outside the Kazan cathedral in St. Petersburg in December 1876, a great strike of textile workers in St. Petersburg in 1878, and a strike at the Brothers

Khludov's cotton-spinning mill in Yegoryevsk in 1880. A speech by Peter Alexeyev—made at a trial of Moscow workers and students in 1877—was widely circulated in Russia. It described the hardships of factory life and declared that one day millions of workers would rise to overthrow the yoke of despotism.

In 1882, twenty-three years after Stackelberg's report on factory reform, an edict was issued prohibiting the employment of children under twelve years of age in factories. It was forbidden to employ young persons (aged twelve to fifteen) at night, on holidays, or on Sundays and their daily hours of work were limited to eight. Inspectors were appointed by the Ministry of Finance to enforce the law. The reports of the early factory inspectors—Yanzhul, Svyatlovsky, Davidov, and Peskov—brought to light the disgraceful conditions prevailing in many factories. They also showed that—since the inspectorate was far too small and many employers were hostile to the new law—it was extremely difficult to enforce the regulations.

In the early 1880's there was much labour unrest in Russia. There was for example a great strike in 1885 at Morozov's cotton factory at Orekhovo-Zuyevo. N. K. Bunge, Minister of Finance between 1881 and 1887, became alarmed at the situation that had arisen and he showed some sympathy towards the grievances of the factory workers. An official commission, presided over by V. K. Plehve, made recommendations as to how to remedy the worst abuses in the factories. These recommendations were embodied in the Factory Law of 1886 which increased the protection given to workers. At the same time the prohibition of the formation of trade unions was reaffirmed and the penalties for striking were increased. In some industrial districts Factory Councils were set up to maintain order in industrial establishments. They consisted of representatives of the local authorities, the judiciary and the factory inspectorate. The Moscow manufacturers who opposed the factory laws brought pressure to bear upon the authorities to modify the Factory Law of 1886. They were successful and an edict of 1890 permitted Factory Councils to waive certain provisions of the factory regulations for particular establishments or branches of industry. This meant that employers were sometimes able to secure a local dispensation to break the law.

According to Lenin there were about 6·5 million industrial wage-earners—men, women, and children—in Russia in the 1890's. They included 1·5 million workers in factories, mines, and railways; one million workers in the building trades; two million labourers (including lumbermen); and two million domestic craftsmen who were economically dependent upon capitalist employers. The factory laws of the 1880's were so imperfectly carried out that the grievances of the workers remained as serious as ever.[1] The famine of 1891–2 drove many villagers into the towns and this aggravated the problem of industrial unemployment. In the years 1894–8 there were many strikes in the large manufacturing centres. The workers demanded higher wages and shorter hours.

At this time Lenin helped to found the League of Struggle for the Liberation of the Working Classes (1895) which tried to spread Socialist doctrines among the mass of urban factory workers. The workers now began to demand not only factory reforms but also the right to hold meetings, the right to form trade unions, and the right to strike. The great strikes in St. Petersburg in May 1896 and in January 1897 alarmed the authorities and a Government commission was appointed to draft a new factory law. Its labours were embodied in an edict of June 2, 1897, which, for the first time, limited the hours worked by men—as distinct from children or young persons. The maximum length of the working day in the factory was now fixed at either eleven and a half hours or—if there were a night shift —at ten hours. Again the reactionary Moscow industrialists put pressure upon the Government to relax the law and on March 14, 1898, a circular from the Ministry of Finance "virtually repealed the law of June 2" by removing restrictions on overtime. Social unrest continued both in the towns and in the countryside. In the industrial centres of the Caucasus, for example, Joseph Dzhugaskvili (Stalin) was organizing strikes in 1900.

In 1898 the Russian Social Democratic Workers Party, led by Lenin, became the spearhead of a new revolutionary movement. Its policy was to establish a Socialist republic; to end the power of the landed gentry over their estates and of the factory owners over their industrial establishments; to nationalize the lands owned by the Czar and the Church; to return to the villagers the lands which their fathers had cultivated before the emancipation of the serfs; and to give back to the peasants the money which they had paid since 1861 to redeem their small holdings. The first newspaper of the Socialist party was published abroad in 1900 and was smuggled into Russia.

The economic depression 1900–03 led to unemployment and

[1] Yet J. Walkin when discussing Russian factory legislation in the 1880's claims that "the available evidence shows that workers were receiving compensation for accidents, child labour was declining, and in almost every case the purposes of the law were being achieved". "The bitter and persistent protests of the merchants and the industrialists against the legislation and the inspection alone attest to the fact that something significant was being achieved."

distress in many industrial centres. Over 100,000 workers were unemployed at some time during the slump. A strikers' demonstration at the Obukhov armaments factory at St. Petersburg on May 1, 1901, was put down by troops and some 800 workers were thrown into prison. In 1902 there was unrest among the workers in Batum as well as a strike of railway employees at Rostov on Don which was supported by local factory workers. The same year saw outbreaks of violence among the peasants in the Ukraine and in Trans-Caucasia. In 1903 there were many strikes in the industrial centres of southern Russia. Little success attended the efforts of the Government to set up working men's associations (such as the Moscow Engineers Mutual Aid Society, 1901) under its own control. When considering the unrest among the Russian factory workers and miners in the early years of the twentieth century it must be remembered—as B. D. Wolfe observes— that "this backward land with its hundreds of thousands of wooden villages now possessed if not the largest, yet the most highly concentrated working class in Europe". "In Germany, at the turn of the century, only 14 per cent of the factories had a (labour) force of more than 500 men, in Russia the corresponding figure was 34 per cent. Only 8 per cent of all German workers worked in factories employing over a thousand working men each. Twenty-four per cent, nearly a quarter, of all Russian industrial workers worked in factories of that size. These giant enterprises forced the new working class into close association. There rose an insatiable hunger for organization which the huge State machine sought in vain to direct or hold in check."

At a congress held in London in 1903 the Russian Socialist party split into the Bolsheviks (majority) led by Lenin and the Mensheviks (minority) led by Martov and Trotsky. There were disputes on procedural matters and rivalries concerning control over the party journal. But it soon became clear that the cleavage between the two groups was really on matters of doctrine. The Mensheviks accepted Marx's analysis of the future development—and inevitable collapse —of capitalism. They held that revolution in Russia would come only when a more advanced stage of industrialization had been reached and that the establishment of a socialist republic should be accomplished in two stages—first a "capitalist bourgeois revolution" (as in France in 1848) to end Czarist autocracy, and secondly, a "workers' revolution" to overthrow the capitalists. Lenin, on the other hand, was a revolutionary who had no intention of waiting for Russia to become fully industrialized. The Bolsheviks, under his leadership, believed that the Russian workers should seize the initiative as soon as possible and lead a mass movement of peasants in a nation-wide rising to overthrow the Czar, the nobles, and the industrialists at one and the same time.

In 1905 the "general rehearsal" of the Russian revolution—as Lenin later called it—took place. Demonstrations, strikes and outbreaks of violence occurred on a vast scale both in the towns and in the country. In January 1905 there was a strike at the Putilov works in St. Petersburg. When a demonstration of workers and their families led by Father Gapon marched on the Czar's winter palace the troops fired on the demonstrators and hundreds of them were shot down.[1] The day was remembered as "Bloody Sunday". In June the sailors on the cruiser *Potemkin* mutinied. The climax of the revolutionary movement came in October 1905 when Russia's defeat in the war against Japan led to a general strike of urban workers. In the last quarter of 1905 councils of workmen's deputies (called soviets) set up in a number of manufacturing towns. Generally they acted as strike committees but sometimes—as in Moscow—they exercised considerably wider powers. Trotsky established his reputation as a revolutionary leader when he presided over the soviet in St. Petersburg. In October 1905 the Czar issued a manifesto promising liberal reforms but when troops had been brought back from the Far East the Government ruthlessly put down the rebellious industrial workers and peasants.

When the army and the "Black Hundreds" had at last succeeded in suppressing demonstrations, strikes, risings, and soviets, the Russian industrialists took measures to prevent the revival of organized working-class activities. Strikes with economic—as distinct from political—objectives had been legalized in December 1905 and trade unions had been permitted in March 1906 but these concessions availed the workers little in view of the determined hostility of their employers.

For a few years the workers were in no position to resist the arbitrary actions of their employers. In April 1912, however, a strike occurred in the Lena goldfield in Siberia. The police fired on the strikers and there were some 500 casualties. This sparked off a new wave of unrest among the factory workers. In 1912–14 there were strikes and demonstrations in many of the great industrial centres. Some 1·5 million men went on strike in the first six months of 1914. Except for the introduction of State sickness insurance scheme in 1912 the Government remained a virtually passive spectator while the reactionary factory owners goaded their workers to new excesses.

---

[1] The number of casualties is not known. An inquiry conducted by members of the Russian Bar estimated that 150 had been killed and 200 injured. This is probably a conservative estimate.

A different policy, however, was adopted with regard to the peasants. P. A. Stolypin, the Czar's chief minister between July 1906 and his assassination in 1911, introduced important changes in the villages. He declared that he wanted to help "the sturdy individual proprietor who is called to play a part in the reconstruction of our Czardom on strong monarchical foundations". An edict of 1906 provided for the conversion to hereditary tenure of small holdings which had hitherto been periodically redistributed. Four years later another edict hastened the process. When hereditary tenure was introduced the entire holding was regarded as belonging to the head of the family and to the whole household. It is probable that by 1914 there were over 7·5 million hereditary peasant holdings in Russia. Moreover, under the supervision of the Land Organization Commission, the consolidation of strips into unified smallholdings had made considerable progress between 1906 and 1914. These rapid changes favoured the social and economic differentiation of the peasants. Many of the more prosperous peasants (the *kulaks*) were able to increase the size of their holdings. The rich peasants became richer while the poor peasants became poorer and sank to the level of a wage-earning village proletariat. In the circumstances it is not surprising that in 1917 the poor peasants made common cause with the factory workers to overthrow the autocratic régime of the Czars.

### (vi) Russia in Asia

Russia founded an empire in Asia and this had an important influence upon the economic development of the country. The empire consisted of territories immediately adjacent to European Russia so that the Russians had no oceans to cross to find new lands in which to settle or trade. Just as the original thirteen American states found opportunities for expansion beyond the Alleghenies so the Russians established vast dominions beyond the Urals. Siberia was Russia's Canada while central Asia was her India.

There were important differences between the two main parts of Russia's colonial territories. Siberia was a huge territory which had supported only a small population. The native inhabitants—mainly nomadic hunters and fishermen—offered relatively little organized resistance to Russian penetration. Central Asia, on the other hand, was a region inhabited by various peoples and divided into a number of states. Here the Russians met with strong opposition and there were many hard-fought campaigns before the territory was conquered.

Siberia, 5·5 million square miles in area, comprised three natural regions. In the south were steppes suitable both for cattle raising and arable farming. In the centre lay great forests and marshes. The north was a tundra zone where the subsoil was always frozen. Russian trappers and fur traders were the first to penetrate into the inhospitable regions of northern Siberia. R. H. Fisher observes that in the sixteenth century "Siberia's greatest resource was its abundant sables, among the finest furs in the world. They provided the incentive for Russia's conquest of Siberia; they also paid the costs of that conquest. In nearly every instance the presence in Siberia of the first Russian inhabitants—soldiers, traders, farmers, government officials and employees—was dictated directly or indirectly by the attractions and requirements of the sable trade."

The opening up of Siberia by the Russians began in the last quarter of the sixteenth century. The initiative was taken by the powerful Stroganov family which owned great estates in the Urals. The Stroganovs were feudal lords who owned silver and iron ore mines, manufactured salt and traded in furs. Their agents went far beyond the Urals to collect furs from the natives of Siberia. Many of the furs were sent to Germany where they were sold at the Leipzig fair.

By 1574 the Stroganovs were powerful enough to try to secure control over some of the territories east of the Urals in which their agents purchased furs. In that year the Stroganovs obtained from the Czar a charter which conveyed to them the northern half of the khanate of Sibir. The khan refused to cede these lands without a struggle. In September 1579 the famous Volga Cossack leader Yermak set out with some 800 men to conquer the khanate of Sibir. The precise connexion between this expedition and the Stroganov claim is not known. In 1581 Yermak captured the town of Sibir situated at the junction of the River Tobol and the River Irtysh. He sent the Czar a gift of valuable sable, black fox fur, and beaver pelts.

"The process by which Siberia was conquered is not peculiar to it. It repeats for the most part that by which a large part of the United States and most of Canada were explored and were subjected to European rule. The major difference lies in the practice by the Russian State of exacting formal tribute and furs from the Siberian natives. This had the effect of bringing about the political subjugation of a given area more quickly in Siberia than in North America. But otherwise both regions owe their opening and first exploitation to the fur trade."

Trading and brigandage played their part in the initial phase of the conquest of the lands beyond the Urals. Very soon, however, the Moscow Government embarked upon the systematic subjugation of Western Siberia. Between 1586 and 1618 a number of forts or blockhouses (*ostrogs*) were established at various strategic points. Some of them, such as Tobolsk and Tomsk, eventually became towns and were important as administrative and commercial centres. Military expeditions, based upon the forts, were sent into the surrounding districts to compel the natives to bring their furs to government posts for sale. A tribute called *Yasak*—normally the best ten out of every hundred unfinished pelts—was levied on the natives.

From Western Siberia the trappers and fur traders—soon followed by military expeditions—pressed on into Eastern Siberia and eventually to the Amur valley. Here the headlong eastward advance of the Russian traders and colonists received a decisive check. The Chinese, who claimed the Amur valley, put up a vigorous resistance and the Russian advance was halted in 1689. It was not until 1859 that China eventually ceded the province of Amur to the Russians.

When the furs of northern Siberia were depleted in the early eighteenth century the Russians became interested in the Northern Pacific as a new fur region. The great explorer Bering reported the existence of fur-bearing sea-mammals off Kamchatka. Before long about forty Russian companies were engaged in the Kamchatka fur trade. In 1799 the Russo-American Company was established.

The Russian colonists in Siberia intermarried with various Tartar and Mongolian tribes and a new "mixed race" developed. These "Siberians" were as different in race, culture, and outlook from European Russians as the Americans of the Middle West were different from the inhabitants of New England. Some of the native tribes, however, were not swallowed up into this new "race". The Yakuts and the Buriats, for example, retained their own languages and absorbed their conquerors. The native races were cruelly exploited by the Russians and the "Siberians". They were often robbed of their lands, their sables and their cattle and were reduced to penury.

In the seventeenth and eighteenth centuries new settlers came to Siberia from European Russia. To some extent there was an organized migration under Government auspices. Cossack settlements were formed to provide garrisons for the forts guarding the frontiers and for the posts on the great caravan routes. State serfs and their families were sent to Siberia to work in the iron-ore mines. The Russian Government used Siberia, as the English used Australia, as a dumping place for criminals. Convicts and vagabonds were deported to Siberia and were set to work in penal settlements such as salt-mines. Political exiles too were sent to Siberia. They were "compulsory settlers" and were allowed a certain amount of freedom. Some 680,000 criminals and political exiles were deported to Siberia between 1823 and 1881. It was only occasionally that these colonists proved to be satisfactory settlers. But the "Decembrist" exiles of 1825 introduced flax-growing and sheep-rearing into the Irkutsk province while the Poles who were deported after the risings of 1830 and 1863 brought improved farming techniques with them. Nevertheless most of the migrants to Siberia went there of their own accord and were not sent by the Government. Cossack adventurers bent upon plunder and hunters seeking a rich harvest of sables were followed by fugitive serfs, monks and religious dissenters who began to exploit the agricultural resources of the plains and river valleys. The Government encouraged both stock-raising and arable farming in the hope of making Siberia self-sufficient from the point of view of food supplies.

After the emancipation of the serfs emigration to Siberia increased. Many peasants had not received enough land to support their families and as the population of European Russia increased the situation became more serious. Emigration to Siberia appeared to offer a solution to the problem just as emigration to America had enabled Irish peasants to escape from an intolerable economic situation. The Government, far from encouraging emigration to Siberia, put obstacles in the way of the peasants who wished to leave European Russia. The authorities feared that an exodus of peasants from European Russia to Siberia would deprive the great landowners of agricultural labourers. In the 1880's however the Government decided that as it could not stop the eastward movement of the peasants something should be done to regulate migration. Several laws were passed which placed settlement under Government control. Migrants were given an allotment of forty and a half acres and were exempt from taxation for three years. Nearly twenty million acres were distributed in this way between 1885 and 1899. It was hoped that the bait of free land and other privileges would induce intending migrants to apply "through the proper channels" for permission to leave European Russia. But "unauthorized" migrations of entire villages continued and these settlers simply squatted on public lands and hoped that they would not be evicted. Between 1896 and 1913 about 4,759,000 people were officially recorded as having migrated from European Russia to Siberia. Most of the settlers at this time came from the Ukraine and the central agricultural provinces of European Russia and they settled in Western Siberia. The total population of Siberia on the eve of the first World War was probably between nine and nine and a half millions.

Although the fur trade survived in the 1890's it was now recognized that the economic wealth of Siberia lay in her farm products and minerals. In Western Siberia over twelve million acres were under cultivation at the beginning of the twentieth century, the most important prairie regions for growing grain being the Ishim steppe and the Altai district. These regions produced wheat, oats, rye, barley, potatoes, flax and tobacco. In central Siberia much less land was under cultivation but the black earth district of Minusinsk was a fertile region which produced wheat and potatoes. Siberia exported to European Russia and to foreign countries over a million tons of wheat a year. Cattle and horses were reared in large numbers on the steppes. In the 1890's a dairy industry suddenly sprang into existence owing to the enterprise of Danish and other foreign merchants. Exports of butter rose from 5·4 million lb. in 1898 to 90 million lb. in 1902. The value of butter exports in 1912 was 68 million roubles. The butter was sent by rail to various Baltic ports. From Copenhagen it was sent to London and Hamburg. Siberian butter was also forwarded to Port Arthur for export to China and Japan. Coal, iron, gold, silver and salt were mined in Siberia. Coal and iron came from the great deposits in the Kuznetz region.

The conquest of Siberia in the seventeenth century brought Russia into contact with the peoples of central Asia. They were Muslims: they were organized in tribal associations; and they belonged to two racial and linguistic groups. The oldest of the indigenous races was the Iranian group (the Tadzhiks being the most important) and the more recent arrivals were the Turkic group (which included the Uzbeks, the Kirgiz, the Kara-Kalpaks and the Turkmens). The forts on the southern frontier of Siberia were continually on their guard against raiding parties from Turkestan. Peter the Great's expeditions to Turkestan ended in disaster. In the middle years of the eighteenth century the Russian frontier was gradually pushed south to the River Emba. The conquest of Turkestan, however, was not achieved until the nineteenth century. A series of campaigns— which began when Count Perovsky built the fortress of Alexandrovsk on the eastern shores of Caspian—culminated in General Romanovsky's victory at Irgai in 1866. Turkestan was organized as a Russian province and in 1867 General Kauffman was appointed its first Governor. The khanates of Bokhara and Khiva were subdued between 1868 and 1876; the Turkmens of the Merv oasis were defeated at Geok Tepe in 1881; and the Pamir district was acquired in 1893.

Turkestan was a great arid plain surrounded by high mountains except in the north. The soil in the river valleys and on the foothills of the mountains was suitable for agriculture though irrigation was often necessary. Much of the soil of the great plains was unfit for farming. The land which could be cultivated was to a considerable extent already occupied so that—unless new lands were made available by irrigation—there were relatively few opportunities for the settlement of Russian colonists in Turkestan. The growing of cotton in Fergana and some other districts in central Asia was stimulated by the irrigating of more land, by the introduction of American varieties of cotton, by the construction of the Trans-Caspian Railway; and by the provision of credit to the peasant cultivators. The railway was built to serve military and administrative needs but it proved to be of considerable economic value since raw cotton could now reach the textile mills of European Russia much more quickly than before. Merchants and agents of the mill owners provided the cotton-growers with capital on a more generous scale than had formerly been available from village moneylenders. Loans to enable seed to be purchased and advances on the security of cotton still to be harvested enabled cultivators to use improved techniques and to extend their operations. But the new system brought many cotton growers under the domination of Russian capitalists. It was estimated that the value of Turkestan's agricultural produce was 350 roubles a year in the early twentieth century. The cotton crop probably accounted for one-half of this sum. The growing of cotton stimulated the development of processing industries such as ginning factories in which the fibre was cleaned. These establishments were generally financed by Russian capital. The export of raw silk to European Russia was also of some significance in the development of Turkestan's economy. Lyashchenko describes Turkestan in 1914 as an "agrarian-colonial appendage of the Mother Country", "The combined effect of the newly introduced capitalist forms of exploitation, the remnants of the native semi-patriarchal and semi-feudal customs, and local usurious practices and financial-agrarian exploitation weighed heavily upon the conditions of the labouring masses of the Turkestan nationalities." The Russians no doubt exploited their colonies in central Asia, but they established law and order and—although intolerant of dissent at home—the Czar did not interfere with the religious beliefs of his Muslim subjects beyond the Urals.

# APPENDIX

## MONEY, WEIGHTS AND MEASURES IN THE NINETEENTH CENTURY

### FRANCE
*Currency*
| | |
|---|---|
| Livre (24 sous) | 11½d. |
| Ecu (6 livres) | 4s. 8¼d. |
| Franc (1795) | 9½d. |

*Weights and Measures*
| | |
|---|---|
| Livre | 1 lb. 1 oz. |
| Quintal | 221 lbs. |
| Hectolitre | 22 gallons |
| Hectare | over 2 acres |

### GERMANY
*Currency*
| | |
|---|---|
| Thaler (Prussian) | 3s. |
| Florin or Gulden (Austrian) | 1s. 8d. |
| Mark (1871) | 1s. |

*Weights and Measures*
| | |
|---|---|
| Pfund (Zollverein) | 1 lb. 1 oz. |
| Scheffel (Prussian) | 12 gallons |
| Morgen (Prussian) | ⅔ acre |
| Meile (Hague) | 4⅗ miles |

### RUSSIA
| | |
|---|---|
| Rouble (100 copecks) (1897) | 2s. 1½d. |

*Weights and Measures*
| | |
|---|---|
| Pud | 36 lbs. |
| Verst | ⅔ mile |

# SELECT BIBLIOGRAPHY[1]

## General

Ashworth, W. *A Short History of the International Economy 1850–1950* (1952).

Birnie, Arthur. *An Economic History of Europe 1760–1930* (edn. of 1933).

Blanqui, J. A. *History of Political Economy in Europe* (1880).

Bogart, E. L. *Economic History of Europe 1700–1939* (1942).

Clapham, Sir John. *Economic Development of France and Germany* (edn. of 1936).

Clough and Cole, *Economic History of Europe* (revised edition, Boston, Mass., 1946).

Curtis, G. B. *The Industrial Development of Nations* (2 vols. New York, 1912).

East, W. G. *An Historical Geography of Europe* (edn. of 1935).

Heaton, Herbert. *Economic History of Europe* (revised edition, New York, 1948).

Hobson, J. A. *The Evolution of Modern Capitalism* (new edn. 1917).

Knight, Barnes and Flugel, *Economic History of Europe* (Boston, Mass., 1928).

Knowles, L. C. A. *Economic Development of the Nineteenth Century* (edn. of 1942).

Marshall, Alfred. *Industry and Trade* (1919).

Nussbaum, F. L. *A History of the Economic Institutions of Modern Europe* (New York, 1935): an abridgement of Werner Sombart, *Der moderne Kapitalismus* (3 vols., 1921–8).

Ogg and Sharp. *Economic Development of Modern Europe* (New, York, edn. of 1932).

Partsch, J. *Central Europe* (1903).

Usher, A. P. *A History of Mechanical Inventions* (revised edn. of 1954).

Usher, Bowden and Karpovich. *An Economic History of Europe* (1937).

Weber, Max. *General Economic History* (1927).

---

[1] Only books written in English or translated into English are listed in this bibliography.

247

## France

Bamford, P. W. "Entrepreneurship in Seventeenth and Eighteenth Century France . . ." (*Explorations in Entrepreneurial History*, Vol. IX., No. 4, April 1957).

Beatty, C. *Ferdinand de Lesseps* (1956).

Cahill, R. *Economic Conditions in France* (Dept. of Overseas Trade, 1924).

Cameron, R. E. "The Crédit Mobilier and the Economic Development of Europe" (*Journal of Political Economy*, Vol. LXI, No. 6, Dec. 1953).

Chaloner, W. H. "De Lesseps and the Suez Canal" (*History Today*, Oct. 1956).

Chapman, J.M. and Brian. *The Life and Times of Baron Haussmann: Paris in the Second Empire* (1957).

Clarendon, Lord. *Ten Years of Imperialism in France: Impressions of a Flaneur* (1862): appeared anonymously.

Clough, S. B. "Retardative Factors in French Economic Development" (*Journal of Economic History*, Vol. IV, 1946) (supplement).

Clough, S. B. *France, A History of National Economics 1789–1939* (1939).

Cole and Watts. *The Handicrafts of France in 1761–88* (Baker Library, Harvard Graduate School of Business Administration, 1952).

Dunham, A. L. *The Industrial Revolution in France 1815–48* (Exposition University Press, New York, 1955).

Dunham, A. L. *The Anglo-French Treaty of Commerce of 1860 . . .* (University of Michigan Press, 1930).

Du Pont de Nemours. *The Dangers of Inflation*, 1790 (translated by E. E. Lincoln: Baker Library, Boston, Mass., 1950).

Forrester, R. B. *The Cotton Industry in France* (1921).

Girault, A. *The Colonial Tariff Policy of France* (1916).

Haight, F. A. *A History of French Commercial Policies* (1941).

Goodwin, A. *The French Revolution* (edn. of 1959).

Henderson, W. O. "The Anglo-French Commercial Treaty of 1786" (*Economic History Review*, second series, Vol. X, No. 1, 1957).

Henderson, W. O. and Chaloner, W. H. "Aaron Manby, Builder of the first Iron Steamship" (*Transactions of the Newcomen Society*, Vol. xxix, 1953-5, pp. 77-91).

Henderson, W. O. and Chaloner, W. H. "The Manbys and the Industrial Revolution in France" (*Transactions of the Newcomen Society*, Vol. xxx, 1955-7, pp. 63-75).

Jordan, S. "Notes on the Resources of the Iron Manufacture in France" (*Journal of the Iron and Steel Institute*, 1878).

Landes, D. S. "French Business and the Businessman" (in *Modern France*, Princeton University Press, 1951).

Landes, D. S. "The Statistical Study of French Crises" (*Journal of Economic History*, 1950).

Lee, H. Austin. *Agricultural Education in France* (Diplomatic & Consular Reports, Miscellaneous Series, No. 505, Foreign Office, June 1899).

Lefranc, G. "The French Railroads" (*Journal of Business and Economic History*, Vol. II, 1929–30).

Leuillot, Paul. "The Industrial Revolution in France" (*Journal of Economic History*, June 1957).

Levine, L. *The Labor Movement in France* . . . (Columbia University Studies in History, Economics and Public Law, Vol. 46, No. 3, 1912).

McCloy, S. T. *French Inventions of the Eighteenth Century* (1952).

McCloy, S. T. *The Humanitarian Movement in Eighteenth Century France* (1957).

McKay, D. C. *The National Workshops. A Study in the French Revolution of 1848* (Harvard University Press, 1933).

Meredith, H. O. *Protection in France* (1904).

Michael, C. "Agricultural Survey of France" (*United States Department of Agriculture Bulletin*, Vol. 37, 1938).

Monkswell, Lord (R. Collier). *French Railways* (1911).

Peel, G. *Economic Policy of France* (1937).

Pinkney, D. H. "Money and Politics in the Rebuilding of Paris 1860–70" (*Journal of Economic History*, March 1957).

Pinkney, D. H. *Napoleon III and the Rebuilding of Paris* (1958).

Priestley, H. I. *France Overseas. A Study of Modern Imperialism* (American Historical Association, New York, 1938).

Redlich, Fritz. "Jacques Laffitte and the Beginnings of Investment Banking in France" (*Bulletin of the Business Historical Society*, December 1948).

Roberts, S. H. *History of French Colonial Policy* (1929).

Saunders, Edith. *The Age of Worth* (1954).

Schonfield, H. J. *Ferdinand de Lesseps* (1937).

Simpson, F. A. *The Rise of Louis Napoleon* (3rd edn., 1951).

Smith, G. B. *The Life and Enterprises of Ferdinand de Lesseps* (1893).

Steele, H. *Working Classes in France* (1904).

Vidal de la Blache, P. *The Personality of France* (1928).

Wilks, Patricia. "An Entrepreneur at the Court of Napoleon III" (*Explorations in Entrepreneurial History*, Vol. VII, No. 4, April 1955).

Young, Arthur. *Travels in France during the Years 1787, 1788, 1789* (edited by Betham-Edwards, 1915).

## Germany

Ashley, Annie. *The Social Policy of Bismarck* (preface by Gustav Schmoller) (1912).

Ashley, Sir William. *The Progress of the German Working Classes in the Last Quarter of a Century* (1904).

Auerbach, Felix. *The Zeiss Works* (second edition, 1904).

Banfield, T. C. *Industry of the Rhine* (Vol. I, 1846, Vol. II, 1848, bound together).

Berdrow, Wilhelm (ed.). *The Letters of Alfred Krupp, 1826–27* (1930).

Berdrow, Wilhelm. *The Krupps: 150 years Krupp History* (1937).

Bowen, G. H. "The Roles of Government and Private Enterprise in German Industrial Growth" (*Journal of Economic History*, Supplement X, 1950).

Bowring, Sir John. *Report on the Prussian Commercial Union* (Parliamentary Papers, 1840, Vol. XXI).

Brinkmann, Carl. "The Place of Germany in the Economic History of the Nineteenth Century" (*Economic History Review*, Vol. IV, April 1933).

Brinkmayer, H. *Hugo Stinnes* (New York, 1921).

Bruck, F. W. *Social & Economic History of Germany . . . 1888–1938* (1938).

Bruck, F. W. *The Road to Planned Economy. Capitalism and Socialism in Germany's Development* (1934).

Cameron, R. E. "Founding the Bank of Darmstadt" (*Explorations in Entrepreneurial History*, Vol. VIII, No. 3, February 1956).

Dawson, W. H. *Social Insurance in Germany 1883–1911* (1912).

Dawson, W. H. *The Evolution of Modern Germany* (edn. of 1919).

Dawson, W. H. *Protection in Germany* (1911).

Dehn, R. M. R. *The German Cotton Industry* (1913).

Dickinson, R. E. *The Regions of Germany* (1945).

Dickinson, R. E. *Germany* (1953).

Elkins, T. H. "An English Traveller in the Siegerland" (*Geographical Journal*, September 1956).

G. F. Ford, *Stein and the Era of Reform in Prussia* (1922).

Gastrell, —. *Development of Commercial, Industrial, Maritime and Traffic Interests in Germany, 1871 to 1898* (Diplomatic and Consular Reports, Miscellaneous Series, No. 490, Foreign Office, January 1899).

Hamerow, T. S. *Restoration, Revolution, Reaction, Economics and Politics in Germany 1815–71* (1958).

Hansen, M. L. "German Emigration in the Fifties" (*Journal of Economic and Business History*, August 1930).

Helfferich, Karl. *Germany's Economic Progress and National Wealth 1888–1913* (New York, 1914).

Henderson, W. O. *The Zollverein* (second edition 1959).

Henderson, W. O. *The State and the Industrial Revolution in Prussia 1740–1870* (1958).

Henderson, W. O. "The Rise of German Industry" (*Economic History Review*, April 1935).

Henderson, W. O. "Walther Rathenau, a Pioneer of the Planned Economy" (*Economic History Review*, second series, Vol. IV, No. 1, 1951).

Henderson, W. O. "The German Colonial Empire 1884–1918" (*History*, September 1935).

Henderson, W. O. "German Colonisation" (*German Life and Letters*, July 1937).

Herring, C. E. *German Iron and Steel Industry* (United States Department of Commerce, Trade Information Bureau, No. 96, May 1923).

Hirst, Margaret E. *Life of Friedrich List* (1909).

Hoffmann, R. J. S. *Great Britain and the German Trade Rivalry* (Philadelphia, 1935).

Hoffmann, W. G. "The Take-Off in Germany" (*Conference on the Economics of "Take-Off" into Sustained Growth*, International Economic Association meeting at Constance, September 2-11, 1960).

Howard, E. L. *Causes and Extent of Recent Industrial Progress in Germany* (1907).

Huldermann, B. *Albert Ballin* (1922).

Jostock, P. "The Long Term Growth of National Income in Germany" (*Income and Wealth*, Series V, 1955).

Klass, Gert von. *Krupps, The Story of an Industrial Empire* (1954).

Koch, P. *German Imperial Banking Laws* (1910).

Kuczynski, Jürgen. "A Short History of Labour Conditions under Industrial Capitalism", Vol. III, Part I, *Germany 1800 to the Present Day* (1945).

List, Friedrich. *The National System of Political Economy, 1841* (English translations by G. A. Matile, 1856, and by S. S. Lloyd, 1904 and 1922).

Long, D. C. "Efforts to secure an Austro-German Customs Union in the Nineteenth Century" (in A. E. Boak (ed.), *University of Michigan Historical Essays* (1937), ch. 3).

Lunn, H. S. *Municipal Lessons from Southern Germany* (1908).

Menne, Bernhard. *Krupp or the Lords of Essen* (translated by G. H. Smith, 1937).

Morgan, F. W. "The Pre-War Hinterlands of the German North Sea Ports" (*Transactions of the Institute of British Geography* 1948).

Morgan, F. W. "Pre-War Hinterlands of the German Baltic Ports" (*Geography*, December 1949).

Parker, W. N. "Entrepreneurial Opportunities and Response in the German Economy" (*Explorations in Entrepreneurial History*, Vol. VII, No. 1, October 1954).

Passant, E. J. *A Short History of Germany 1815–1945* (1959). See Ch. 1 (iv) and ch. 2 (iii) by W. O. Henderson.

Postinett, J. "The Basic-Bessemer Steelworks of the Mannesmann Tube Works" (*Iron and Coal Trades Review*, Vol. 121, 1930).

Pounds, N. J. G. *The Ruhr* (1952).

Price, A. H. *The Evolution of the Zollverein* (University of Michigan Press, 1949).

Redlich, F. "The Leaders of the German Steam-engine Industry during the first Hundred Years" (*Journal of Economic History*, Vol. IV, 1944).

Redlich, F. "Entrepreneurship in the initial Stages of Industrialisation with special Reference to Germany" (*Conference on Entrepreneurship and Economic Growth*. Harvard University, 1954).

Redlich, F. "Academic Education for Business: its Development and the Contribution of Ignaz Jastrow, 1856–1937 . . ." (*Business History Review*, Vol. XXXI (i) 1957).

Redlich, F. "The Beginnings and Development of German Business History" (supplement of *Bulletin of the Business Historical Society*, Sept. 1952).

Redlich, F. "A German Eighteenth-Century Ironworks during its first Hundred Years" (*Bulletin of the Business Historical Society*, June, September and December 1953).

Redlich, F. "An Eighteenth-Century German Guide for Investors" (*Bulletin of the Business Historical Society*, June 1952).

Redlich, F. "Recent Developments in German Economic History" (*Journal of Economic History*, Dec. 1958).

Riesser, J. *The German Great Banks* . . . (U.S. National Monetary Commission, Washington, 1911).

H. R. Rudin, *Germans in the Cameroons, 1884-1914* (1938).

Russell, Bertrand. *German Social Democracy* (1896).

Samuelson, James. *The German Working Man* (1869).

Sanders, W. S. *The Socialist Movement in Germany* (Fabian Tract, No. 169, 1913).

Schmoller, Gustav. *The Mercantile System and its Historical Significance illustrated chiefly from Prussian History*, 1884 (New York, 1931).

Schorske, Carl. *German Social Democracy 1905–1917* . . (1955).

Small, A. W. *The Cameralists* . . . (1909).

Stockder, A. H. *Regulating an Industry. The Rhenish-Westphalian Coal Syndicate 1893–1929* (Columbia University Press, 1932).

Stolper, Gustav. *German Economy 1870–1940* (1940).

Tirrell, S. R. *German Agrarian Politics after Bismarck's Fall* (New York, 1951).

Townsend, Mary Evelyn. *The Rise and Fall of Germany's Colonial Empire 1884–1918* (1930).

Veblen, Thorstein. *Imperial Germany and the Industrial Revolution* (1939).

Walker, F. *Monopolistic Combinations in the German Coal Industry* (American Economic Association, Vol. V, third series, 1904).

Wendel, H. C. M. *The Evolution of Industrial Freedom in Prussia 1845–9* (1921).

Whale, P. B. *Joint Stock Banking in Germany* (1930).

Williams, F. E. *"Made in Germany"* (1896).

Wright and Brooks. *Compulsory Insurance in Germany* (Fourth Special Report of the Commissioner of Labour, Washington, 1893).

### Russia

Aitken, H. G. J. *The State and Economic Growth* (1959), ch. 4.

Ames, Edward. "A Century of Russian Railroad Construction, 1837–1936" (*American Slavic and East European Review*, December 1947).

Antsuiferov, A. N. (and others). *Russian Agriculture during the War* (1930).

Baddeley, J. F. *The Russian Conquest of the Caucasus* (1908).

Baddeley, J. F. *Russia, Mongolia, China* (2 vols., 1919).

Baikalov, A. V. "A brief Outline of the Russian Co-operative Movement" (*Slavonic and East European Review*, Vol. I, 1922–3, pp. 130–43).

Baikalov, A. V. "Siberia since 1894" (*Slavonic and East European Review*, Vol. XI, 1932–3, pp. 328–40).

Barghoorn, F. L. "The Russian Radicals of the 1860s and the Problem of the Industrial Proletariat" (*Slavonic and East European Review*, Vol. XXI, 1942–3, pp. 57–69).

Baring, Maurice. *The Mainsprings of Russia* (1914).

Barrett, R. J. *Russia's New Era* (1908).

Baykov, Alexander. "The Economic Development of Russia" (*Economic History Review*, 1954, No. 2).

Cheshire, H. T. "The Radicals of the Sixties and their Leaders" (*Slavonic Review*, Vol. I, 1922–3, pp. 110–20).

Cheshire, H. T. "The Expansion of Imperial Russia to the Indian Border" (*Slavonic Review*, Vol. XIII, 1934–5, pp. 85–97).

Crawford, J. M. (ed.). *The Industries of Russia* (World's Columbia Exposition at Chicago) (St. Petersburg, 3 vols., 1893).

Crisp, Olga. "Russian Financial Policy and the Gold Standard at the end of the Nineteenth Century" (*Economic History Review*, second series, VI, No. 2, December 1953).

Crisp, Olga. "Some Problems of French Investment in Russian Joint Stock Companies, 1894–1914" (*Slavonic and East European Review*, XXXV, 1956–7).

Crisp, Olga. "The State Peasants under Nicholas I" (*American Slavic and East European Review*, June 1959).

Crisp, Olga. "French Investment in Russian Joint Stock Companies, 1894–1914" (*Business History*, II, No. 2, June 1960).

Dallin, D. *The Rise of Russia in Asia* (1949).

Drage, Geoffrey. *Russian Affairs* (1904).

Dubs, H. H. "Land Hunger and Nationalism in the Ukraine 1905–17" (*Journal of Economic History*, May 1942).

Faas, V. V. *Russia's Export Trade in Timber . . .* (1919).

Fisher, R. H. *The Russian Fur Trade 1500–1700* (1943).

Gay, J. E. "Anglo-Russian Economic Relations" (*Economic Journal*, June 1917).

Gerschenkron, A. "The Rate of Industrial Growth in Russia since 1885" (*Journal of Economic History*, Supplement, VII, 1947).

Hare, R. *Pioneers of Russian Social Thought* (1951).

Hare, R. *Portraits of Russian Personalities between Reform and Revolution* (1959).

Kachorovsky, K. "The Russian Land Commune in History and Today" (*Slavonic and East European Review*, Vol. VII, 1928–9, pp. 565–76).

Kayden, E. M. (and others). *The Co-operative Movement in Russia during the War* (1929).

Keep, J. L. H. "Russian Social-Democracy and the First State Duma" (*American Slavic and East European Review*, 1955–6).

Kerensky, A. "Why the Russian Monarchy fell" (*Slavonic and East European Review*, 1929–30).

Kerner, R. J. *The Urge to the Sea: the Course of Russian History* (1942).

Keynes, J. M. "Russia" (*Manchester Guardian Commercial:* "Reconstruction of Europe", No. 4, July 6, 1922).

King. V. "The Liberal Movement in Russia, 1904–5" (*American Slavic and East European Review*, 1935–6).

Kirchner, Walther. "Samuel Benthan and Siberia" (*Slavonic and East European Review*, XXXVI, 1957–8).

Kontaissof. "The Ural Metal Industry in the Eighteenth Century" (*Economic History Review*, second series, IV, 1951).

Laue, T. H. von. "The Industrialisation of Russia in the Writings of Sergei Witte" (*American Slavic and East European Review*, Vol. X, 1951, pp. 177–90).

Laue, T. H. von. "The High Cost and the Gamble of the Witte System. A chapter in the industrialisation of Russia" (*Journal of Economic History*, 1953).

Laue, T. H. von. "A Secret Memorandum of Sergei Witte on the Industrialisation of Imperial Russia" (*Journal of Modern History*, 1954).

Lenin, N. *The Development of Capitalism in Russia*, 1899 (English translation, Moscow, 1956).

Lewery, L. J. *Foreign Capital Investments in Russian Industries and Commerce* (United States Bureau of Foreign and Domestic Commerce, Miscellaneous Series, No. 124. Washington, 1923).

Litoshenko, L. "Landed Property in Russia" (*Russian Review*, 1913).

Lobanov-Rostovsky, A. *Russia and Asia* (1933).

Lobanov-Rostovsky, A. "Russian Imperialism in Asia" (*Slavonic and East European Review*, Vol. VIII, 1929–30, pp. 28–47).

Long, R. E. C. "M. Witte: Atlas of the Autocracy" (*Fortnightly Review*, January 1903).

Lumley, —. *Report on the Trade and Manufacture of Cotton in Russia* (*Parliamentary Papers*, 1865, LIV, 438).

Lyashchenko, P. J. *History of the National Economy of Russia* (1949).

Maklakov, Basil. "The Peasant Question and the Russian Revolution" (*Slavonic Review*, Vol. II, 1923–4, pp. 225–48).

Mamanov and Zdiarsky. *Guide to the Great Siberian Railway* (Russian Ministry of Transport, 1900; English translation).

Mavor, J. *An Economic History of Russia* (second edition, 2 vols., 1925).

Miller, Margaret S. *The Economic Development of Russia 1905–14* (1926).

Miller, Margaret S. "Co-operation in Russia" (*Economica*, October 1921).

Miller, Margaret S. "The Trade Balance of Russia" (*Slavonic Review*, Vol. I, 1922–3, pp. 401–18).

Minsky, D. S. *Russia: a Social History* (edited by Seligman) (1931).

Mitchell, T. Report on the present State of Trade between Great Britain and Russia (*Parliamentary Papers*, 1866. LXXII, 594).

Odell, R. M. *Cotton Goods in Russia* (United States Bureau of Manufactures, Special Agents Series, No. 51, Washington, 1912).

Owen, L. A. *The Russian Peasant Movement*, 1906–17 (1937).

Pavlovsky, G. *Agricultural Russia on the Eve of the Revolution* (1930).

Putnam, P. (ed.). *Seven Britons in Imperial Russia 1698–1912* (Princeton Studies in History, Vol. VII, 1912).

Raeff, Marc. "Russia after the Emancipation" (*Slavonic and East European Review*, Vol. XXIX, 1950–1, pp. 470–85).

Raffalovich, A. *Russia. Its Trade and Commerce* 1918).

Reading, D. K. *The Anglo-Russian Commercial Treaty of 1734* (1938).

Rimlinger, Gaston V. "Autocracy and the Factory Order in Early Russian Industrialisation" (*Journal of Economic History*, March 1960).

Robinson, Eric. "Birmingham Capitalists and Russian Workers" (*History Today*, VI, 1956).

Robinson, G. T. *Rural Russia under the Old Régime* (1932 and 1949).

Rodichev, F. "The Liberal Movement in Russia, 1885–1917" (*Slavonic Review*, Vol. II, 1923–4, pp. 1–13 and 249–62).

Rosorsky, Henry. "The Serf Entrepreneur in Russia" (*Explorations in Entrepreneurial History*, VI, No. 4, 1953–4).

Rubinow, I. M. *Russia's Wheat Surplus* (United States Department of Agriculture, Bureau of Statistics. Bulletin No. 42, Washington, 1906).

Shuyler, E. *Turkistan* (1876).

Stepniak, S. *The Russian Peasantry* (2 vols., 1883).

Stone, N. "Capitalism on Trial in Russia" (*Political Science Quarterly*, March 1898).

Storch, H. F. von. *The Picture of St. Petersburg* (1801).

Tompkins, S. R. "Witte as Minister of Finance, 1892–1903" (*Slavonic and East European Review*, Vol. XI, 1932–3, pp. 590–606).

Treadgold, D. W. *The Great Siberian Migration* (1958).

Treadgold, D. W. "Was Stolypin in Favour of Kulaks?" (*American Slavic and East European Review*, Vol. XIV, 1955, pp. 1–14).

Tschuprow, A. L. "The Break-up of the Village Community in Russia" (*Economic Journal*, June 1912).

Turin, S. R. *A History of the Russian Labour Movement with Special Reference to Trade Unionism* (1935).

Volin, L. "The Russian Peasant and Serfdom" (*Agricultural History*, 1943).

Wallace, Sir Robert Mackenzie. *Russia* (new edition, 2 vols., 1905).

Wallace, Sir Robert Mackenzie. Introduction to: "*The Times*" *Book of Russia: Finance, Commerce, Industry* (1916).

Walkin, J. "The Attitude of the Czarist Government towards the Labour Problem" (*American Slavic and East European Review*, XIII, 1954, pp. 163–84).

Whitman, John. "Turkestan Cotton in Imperial Russia" (*American Slavic and East European Review*, April 1956).

Williams, David. "Welsh Settlers in Russia" (*The National Library Of Wales Journal*, III, 1943–4, pp. 55–8).

Witte, S. *The Memoirs of Count Witte* (1921).

Zaitsev, Cyril. "The Russian Agrarian Revolution" (*Slavonic and East European Review*, Vol. IX, 1930–1, pp. 547–66).

Zaitsev, Cyril. "Economic Aspects of the Agrarian Question in Russia before and after the Bolshevik Revolution" (*Journal of Business History*, August 1931).

## Special Topics

Ashley, Percy. *Modern Tariff History* (1904).

Benham, F. *The Iron and Steel Industry of Germany, France, Belgium, Luxemburg and the Saar* (London and Cambridge Economic Service, No. 39, 1934).

Brooke, E. *Factory Laws of European Countries* (1898).

Chamberlain, Joseph. *Trade of the British Empire and Foreign Countries. Despatch from Mr. Chamberlain to the Governors of Colonies . . . and the Replies thereto* (C.8449 of 1897).

Clark, Colin. *The Conditions of Economic Progress.* (1951).

Coleman, D. C. "Industrial Growth and Industrial Revolution" (*Economica*, New Series, Vol. XXIII (1956)).

Corti, Count. *The Rise of the House of Rothschild* (1928).

Corti, Count. *The Reign of the House of Rothschild* (1928).

Day, Clive. *A History of Commerce* (1907).

Dingley, F. L. *European Emigration* (1890).

Dunham, A. L. *The Pioneer Period of European Railroads* (Baker Library, Harvard Graduate School of Business Administration, 1946).

Dupriez and Hague (eds.). *Economic Progress* (Louvain, 1955).

Fay, C. R. *Co-operation at Home and Abroad* (2nd edn., 1920).

Feis, H. *Europe, the World's Banker 1870–1914* (1930).

Forbes, R. J. *Man the Maker* (1958).

Gerschenkron, A. "Social Attitudes, Entrepreneurship and Economic Development" (*Explorations in Entrepreneurial History*, Vol. VI, No. 1, 1953–4).

Hansen, M. *The Atlantic Migration* (edn. of 1945).

Heckscher, E. F. *The Continental System* (1922).

Henderson, W. O. *Britain and Industrial Europe 1750–1870* (1954).

Henderson, W. O. "The Cotton Famine on the Continent" (*Economic History Review*, April 1933).

Henderson, W. O. "The Genesis of the Industrial Revolution in France and Germany" (*Kyklos*, fase. 2, 1956).

Henderson, W. O. "A Nineteenth Century Approach to a West European Common Market" (*Kyklos*, fasc. 4, 1957).

Henderson and Chaloner. "Some Aspects of the early History of Automation" (*Research*, September 1957).

Hexner, E. *The International Steel Cartel* (1943).

Hobson, C. K. *The Export of Capital* (1914).

Hoffmann, W. G. *The Growth of Industrial Economies* (translated by W. O. Henderson and W. H. Chaloner, 1958).

Jagtiani, H. M. *The Role of the State in the Provision of Railways* (1924).

Jenks, L. H. *The Migration of British Capital to 1875* (1927).

Joll, J. *The Second International 1889–1914* (1955).

Kuczynski, J. *Labour Conditions in Western Europe 1820–1935* (1937).

Kuczynski, J. *A Short History of Labour Conditions under Industrial Capitalism* (4 vols., 1944–6).

Landes, D. S. "Social Attitudes, Entrepreneurship and Economic Development: a Comment" (*Explorations in Entrepreneurial History*, Vol. VI, No. 4, 1953–4).

Lardner, Dionysius. *Railway Economy . . .* (1850).

Lewis, W. A. *The Theory of Economic Growth* (1955).

Lewis, W. A. "Economic Development with Unlimited Supplies of Labour" (*Manchester School*, May 1954).

Lewis, W. A. *Economic Survey 1919–39* (1949).

Liefmann, R. *Cartels, Concerns and Trusts* (1932).

Lindley, W. H. *Report on the Waterways of France, Belgium, Germany and Holland* (Cd. 4841 of 1909).

Luxemburg, Rosa. *The Accumulation of Capital*, 1913 (English translation 1951).

McConagha, W. A. *Development of the Labour Movement in Great Britain, France and Germany* (1942).

Macgregor, John. *Commercial Statistics* (5 vcls., 1847–50).

BIBLIOGRAPHY

Mackenzie, K. *The Banking Systems of Great Britain, France, Germany and the United States of America* (1945).

Matschoss, Conrad. *Great Engineers* (1938).

Mulhall, M. G. *The Progress of the World* (2nd edn. 1880).

Newbold, J. T. W. "The Beginnings of the World Crisis 1873–96" (*Economic History*, January 1932).

Oddy, J. J. *European Commerce* (1805).

Palgrave, Sir Robert. *Bank Rate and Money Market in England, France, Germany, Holland, Belgium, 1844–90* (1903).

Pim, Sir Alan. *The Financial and Economic History of the African Tropical Territories* (1940).

Pollard, S. "Investment, Consumption and the Industrial Revolution" (*Economic History Review*, 2nd series, Vol. XI, No. 2, 1958).

Pounds and Parker. *Coal and Steel in Western Europe* (1957).

Reeves, John. *The Rothschilds* (1887).

Robinson, Eric. "The International Exchange of Men and Machines" (*Business History*, Vol. I, No. 1, December 1958).

Roscher, Wilhelm. *Principles of Political Economy* (two volumes, 1878–82).

Rosenburg, H. "Political and Social Consequences of the Depression of 1873–96 in Central Europe" (*Economic History Review*, 1943).

Rostow, W. W. "The Take-Off into Self-sustained Growth" (*Economic Journal*, Vol. LXVI, March 1956).

Rostow, W. W. "The Stages of Economic Growth" (*Economic History Review*, 2nd Series, Vol. XII, No. 1, August 1959).

Rostow, W. W. *The Process of Economic Growth* (New York, 1952).

Sargent, A. J. *Seaports and Hinterlands* (1938).

Schulze-Gaevernits, G von. *The Cotton Trade in England and on the Continent* (1895).

Sombart, Werner. *Socialism and the Social Movement* (1909).

Sombart, Werner. *The Jews and Modern Capitalism* (1913).

Studenski, P. *The Income of Nations . . .* (New York, 1958).

Symons, J. C. *Arts and Artisans at Home and Abroad* (1839).

Ure, Andrew. *Dictionary of Arts, Manufactures and Mines* (2nd edn., 1840).

Weber, A. *Growth of Cities in the Nineteenth Century* (New York. 1899).

# MAPS

ACKNOWLEDGEMENTS

(I) Industrial Regions of France, Belgium and North West Germany [From: W. O. Henderson, *Britain and Industrial Europe 1750–1870* (Liverpool University Press, 1954)].

(III) The Ruhr in the Middle of the Nineteenth Century [From: W. O. Henderson, *Britain and Industrial Europe 1750–1870* (Liverpool University Press, 1954)].

(V) Zollverein and Tax Union 1834 [From: W. O. Henderson, *The Zollverein* (second edition, F. Cass)].

(VII) Bruck's proposed Austro-German Customs Union 1849 [From: W. O. Henderson, *The Zollverein* (second edition, F. Cass)].

(VIII) The new Zollverein 1867 [From: W. O. Henderson, *The Zollverein* (second edition, F. Cass)].

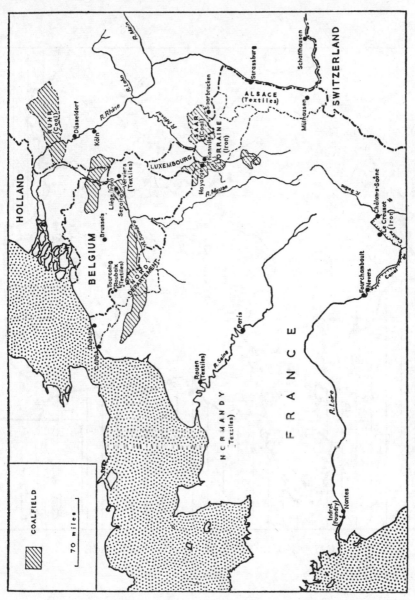

I. INDUSTRIAL REGIONS OF FRANCE, BELGIUM and N.W. GERMANY
IN THE MIDDLE OF THE NINETEENTH CENTURY

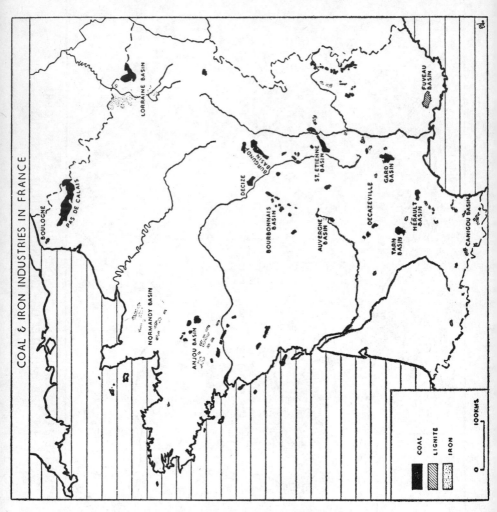

COAL & IRON INDUSTRIES IN FRANCE

II. COAL AND IRON INDUSTRIES IN FRANCE

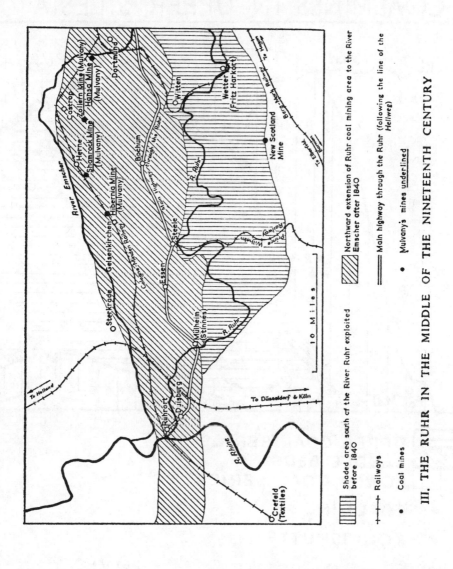

III. THE RUHR IN THE MIDDLE OF THE NINETEENTH CENTURY

Legend:
- Shaded area south of the River Ruhr exploited before 1840
- Railways
- Coal mines
- Northward extension of Ruhr coal mining area to the River Emscher after 1840
- Main highway through the Ruhr (following the line of the Hellweg)
- Mulvany's mines underlined

Map labels:
To Holland, To Düsseldorf & Köln, R. Rhine, Crefeld (Textiles), Ruhrort, Duisburg, Mülheim (Stinnes), R. Ruhr, Essen, Steele, Prince Wilhelm Railway, Cologne-Minden Railway, Bahn-nach Railway, Steinkröge, Gelsenkirchen, Hibernia Mine (Mulvany), Herne, Shamrock Mine (Mulvany), Zollern Mine (Mulvany), Hansa Mine (Mulvany), Castrop, Dortmund, River Emscher, Bochum, Main Highway through the Ruhr, R. Ruhr, Witten, Wetter (Fritz Harkort), New Scotland Mine, Bergisch-Märk Railway, To Hagen

10 Miles

COALMINES IN UPPER SILESIA

Klodnitz Canal
Kosel
Gleiwitz
Beuthen
RUSSIA
1914
Zabre
K
Kattowitz
Myslowitz
Nikolai
R. Oder
Rybnik
R. Vistula
AUSTRIA
1914
Mährisch-Ostrau

UPPER COAL SERIES
SADDLE BEDS
LOWER COAL SERIES

• COALMINE
K KÖNIGSHÜTTE

O               20 MLS.

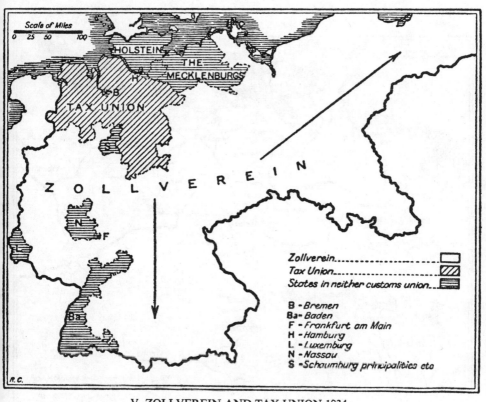

V. ZOLLVEREIN AND TAX UNION 1834

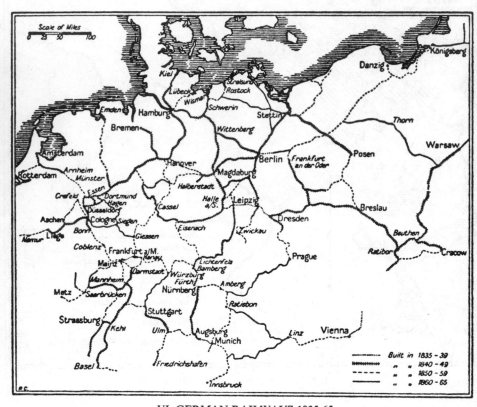

Scale of Miles
0   25   50        100

Königsberg
Danzig
Kiel
Lübeck
Wismar
Stralsund
Rostock
Schwerin
Thorn
Emden
Hamburg
Bremen
Wittenberg
Stettin
Warsaw
Amsterdam
Hanover
Berlin
Frankfurt
an der Oder
Posen
Rotterdam
Arnheim
Münster
Magdaburg
Crefeld
Essen
Dortmund
Hagen
Halberstadt
Cassel
Halle
a./S.
Leipzig
Breslau
Düsseldorf
Aachen
Cologne
Siegen
Dresden
Bonn
Eisenach
Zwickau
Beuthen
Namur
Liège
Coblenz
Giessen
Ratibor
Cracow
Frankfurt a/M.
Prague
Hanau
Mainz
Lichtenfels
Bamberg
Darmstadt
Würzburg
Fürth
Amberg
Mannheim
Metz
Saarbrücken
Nürnberg
Strassburg
Kehl
Stuttgart
Ratisbon
Ulm
Augsburg
Linz
Vienna
Munich
Basel
Friedrichshafen
Innsbruck

|   |   |
|---|---|
| –––––––– | Built in 1835 – 39 |
| ▬▬▬▬▬▬ | „ „ 1840 – 49 |
| – – – – – | „ „ 1850 – 59 |
| ———— | „ „ 1860 – 65 |

R.C.

## VI. GERMAN RAILWAYS 1835-65

Miles
0 50 100 150

Unattached

TAX UNION

ZOLLVEREIN

HAPSBURG EMPIRE

←Austro-Hungarian customs frontier abolished 1850

R.C.

VII. BRUCK'S PROPOSED AUSTRO-GERMAN CUSTOMS UNION 1849

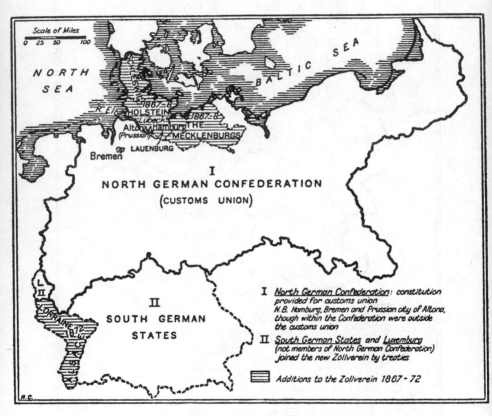

VIII. THE NEW ZOLLVEREIN 1867

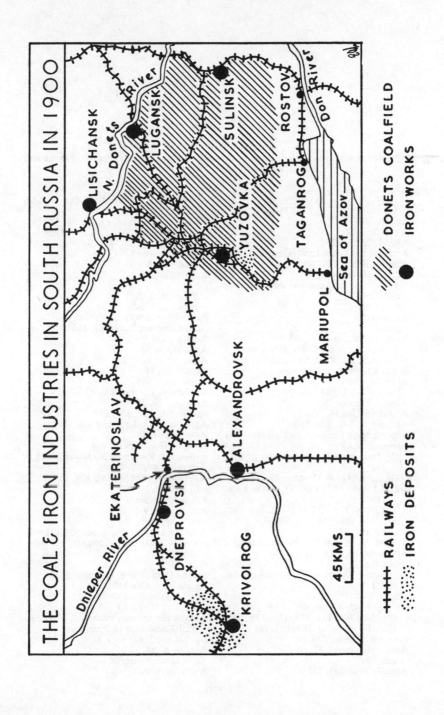

## THE COAL & IRON INDUSTRIES IN SOUTH RUSSIA IN 1900

LISICHANSK

N. Donets River

LUGANSK

SULINSK

ROSTOV

Don River

YUZOVKA

TAGANROG

Sea of Azov

MARIUPOL

ALEXANDROVSK

EKATERINOSLAV

Dnieper River

DNEPROVSK

KRIVOI ROG

45 KMS

++++ RAILWAYS

⋮⋮⋮ IRON DEPOSITS

▨ DONETS COALFIELD

● IRONWORKS

# INDEX

Names mentioned very frequently in the text, such as Germany, Prussia, France and Russia, have not been included in the index.

# INDEX

Danzig, 90
Darmstadt, 16
Dauphiné, 105
Davidov (Factory Inspector), 236
De Bourrienne (1769–1834), 82, 85
Decazeville ironworks, 95, 96, 100, 117, 118, 158, 169
Decemberist exiles, 243
*Defiance*, 22
Delbrück, Rudolph (1817–1903), 26, 34
Delessert, 85
Demidov, Nikita, 214
Denain, 118, 158, 159
Denmark, 14
Department of Highways and Bridges (French), 97, 98, 111, 114, 130, 140
Departments (French), 76, 77
Dervishes, 190
Deryalin, 217
Desaguliers, 217
*Deutsche Bank*, 62, 63, 64
Deutsch-Luxemburg Company, 63, 67
*Devoir mutuel* (Lyons), 124
De Wendel. See Wendel
Dhuis, River, 144
Dieppe, 105
Diesbach, 8
Diesel, R. (1858–1913), 65
Diet, Federal (German), 16
Dietrich (of Niederbronn), 159
Differdange (Luxemburg), 67
Dill, River, 35, 67
Direct Action, 188
Directory, 78, 83
Discount Company (Berlin), 30, 62, 63, 64, 148
Dixon, Job, 98
Dneprovsky ironworks, 216, 225
Dobson and Barlow (of Manchester), 163
Dollfus family (Mulhouse), 87, 102
Don, River, 222
Donetz coalfield, 203, 215, 216, 218, 220, 221, 224
Donetz Coal Trust (*Produgol*), 203, 218
Dortmund (Ruhr), 65
Douai, 104
Doubs, 97, 116
Douglas, William (of Paris), 88, 103
Dowlais, 216
Drage, Geoffrey, 222
Dreyfus, A. (1859–1935), 187
Droitaumant, 180
Dual Control in Egypt, 190
Dubois, 122
Du Chaillou. See Chaillou
Duclerc, 132, 133
Dufaud, Georges, 96
Duisburg (Ruhr), 35, 65
Duma, Russian, 226

Dumas, A. (the elder) (1802–70), 191
Dunham, A. L., 97, 103, 106
Dupin, F. P. C., 102, 116
Dupouilly (of Paris), 103
Durham, 35
Düsseldorf, 20
Dutch East Indies, 201
Dyer family (of Gemaches), 101
Dyes, 87
Dynamo, 65, 72
Dzhugaskvili. See Stalin

# E

East Africa, German, 23, 52, 53
East Africa Bank (German), 64
*École Centrale* (Paris), 128, 129, 130
Economic Commission (Frankfurt 1848), 25
Eden Commercial Treaty (1786), 77, 83, 101
Edison. See German Edison Electric Company
Edwards, Humphrey, 98
Egypt, 135, 136, 149, 150, 151, 152, 161
Eifel, 35, 36
Eisenach programme (of German Socialists), 43
Ekaterinburg, 214, 224, 225
Ekaterinoslav, 224
Elbe, River, 15, 18, 21, 36, 83
Elberfeld-Barmen, 20, 23, 24, 32, 33, 41, 69
Elbeuf, 98, 102, 181
Elections, German, 50, 57
Electrical Industry, 63, 64, 71, 182, 183
El Guisr (Le Seuil), 151
El Hadj Omar, 192
Emancipation of Serfs, 24, 76, 208, 231, 232, 234
Emancipation of Slaves, 79, 127, 191
Emba, River, 244
Embargo Act (U.S.A.), 84
Emden, 66, 83
Emigration, 43, 44
Employers Associations, 35, 49, 60, 159
Emscher, River, 34
Enclaves, 16
Enfantin, B. P. (1794–1864), 111, 137, 150
Engels, Friedrich (1820–96), 39, 40, 42
Engineering, 100, 101
Engineers Mutual Aid Society (Moscow), 238
England. See Britain
Epinac, 116
Equatorial Africa, 198
Erin colliery (Castrop), 35
Erzgebirge, 32, 35

275